SOCIOMETRY, EXPERIMENTAL METHOD AND THE SCIENCE OF SOCIETY

AN APPROACH TO A NEW POLITICAL ORIENTATION

By

J. L. MORENO

Foreword by

GARDNER MURPHY

BEACON HOUSE INC.
Beacon, N. Y.

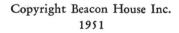

FOREWORD

By Gardner Murphy

Chairman, Department of Psychology
College of the City of New York

It is entirely natural and human, I think, that the term "sociometry" should be used both to designate a technical quantitative method and to define a broad area of research and conceptualization. Final and categorical definitions are always broken by the sheer vital growth which underlies them, as a hardy plant forces open my wooden shutters in the spring. I have no quarrel with the present terminology of Moreno's system.

I say "system" because the careful reader of *Who Shall Survive* and of *Sociometry* will note the intimate relation between three systematic endeavors: spontaneity testing, spontaneity training, and sociometry, and will notice the relations of all three to the basic theory of spontaneity, the conception of the ego, and the technical uses of the psychodrama. The vitality of the system lies largely in the vitality of the individual leader; things are held in cohesion by his personality. The methods and even the problems will, in time, drift apart and undergo reclassification, as is always the case in any type of endeavor, scientific or artistic.

There is not, for me, the slightest question that sociometry —the term now being used in the widest possible sense to include all of Dr. Moreno's work—is one of the great vitalizing forces in contemporary social science. At a period when many scholars were tired of old ideas and quite frankly more interested in technical polishing of their instruments, the Moreno approach bludgeoned its way into even the drowsiest library and classroom, and compelled attention. There was no doubt whatever that the practical utilization of this group of methods made a vast human difference in the specific settings, such as Hudson, in which it was used, and that it deeply inspired those who were seeking to comprehend the basis of human compatibilities and incompatibilities, as well as those who sought for the emotional basis of education, the core which makes the individual wish to learn, to grow, and to find himself.

It would be ridiculous to attempt a tabloid summary of all that Dr. Moreno has done. It is sufficient to point out that schools, hospitals, welfare and penal institutions, old settled communities and new resettlement groups, have all offered useful fields for the application of the sociometric technique, and that behind it all, recognition has constantly grown that therapy ultimately depends on breaking the shell of hardened habits, finding within each individual what is really capable of growth. The familiar conceptions of conditioning and reconditioning, or of reward and punishment, have been in many places replaced by a conception of finding, as one finds in a tree, which of the tissue systems are capable of growth, and making the most of them. I shall never forget how, on returning from Hudson after a visit, W. H. Kilpatrick said to me, "If Moreno is as much as half right, then Thorndike is more than half wrong." It was one of those perfect phrases, so complete in its connotations as well as denotations, that it is the best I can do by way of summarizing an outlook—which is not, of course, exclusively the property of Moreno, but of which he has been one of the most eloquent advocates.

CONTENTS

PART III

POLITICAL SOCIOMETRY

PART IV

MILITARY SOCIOMETRY

PART V

SOCIOMETRY AND MICROSOCIOLOGY

I.

SOCIOMETRY AND THE EXPERIMENTAL METHOD

PROLOGUE TO SOCIOMETRY
(1949)

The contribution which sociometry makes consists of ideas. It is not a sum of several techniques here or there. Its ideas are the fountainhead from which theoretical frameworks, concepts and methods spring. Probably the most important influence which sociometry exercises upon the social sciences is the urgency and the violence with which it pushes the scholars from the writing desk into actual situations, urging them to move into real communities and to deal there with real people; urging them to move in personally and directly, with a warm and courageous heart, implemented with a few hypotheses and instruments, instead of using go-betweens as translators and informants; urging them to begin with their science now and here, action research, not writing for the milennium of the library shelves.

My premise before starting to build the theoretical framework of sociometry was to doubt the value of and discard all existing social concepts, not to accept any sociological hypothesis as certain, to start from scratch, to start as if nothing would be known about human and social relations. It was a radical pushing out, from my consciousness at least, all knowledge gained from books and even from my own observations. I insisted upon this departure not because I did not assume that other scholars before me had excellent ideas, but because their observations were in most cases authoritative instead of experimental. The naiveté therefore, with which I went after my objectives was not that of a man who is ignorant of what other scholars have done before him, but that of one who *tries* to be ignorant in order to free himself from clichés and biases, in hope that by warming up to the role of the naive he might be inspired to ask a novel question.

I tried to erase from my memory and particularly from my operations terms and concepts as individual, group, mass, society, culture, We, community, state, government, class, caste, communion and many others for which there were dozens of good and bad definitions, but which appeared to block my way of making the simplest possible start. I could not help, of course, using these terms frequently in my writings, but I always used them with the overt suspicion that they did not represent social reality and will have to be replaced by the truly reality-bearing social concepts.

5

THREE POINTS OF REFERENCE FOR SOCIOMETRIC RESEARCH
(1923-1950)

The experimental method in physics was furthered in the first half of the seventeenth century, under the leadership of Galileo, Bacon and Newton. The experimental method in the social sciences was handicapped as long as it tried to follow the physical model; it really got under way in the first half of the twentieth century under the leadership of sociometry, accompanied by overt and covert battles against nominalistic trends of some of the current sociological and psychological schools in the late twenties and early thirties; Gestalt and psychoanalysis are illustrations to this point—they too, however realistically they behaved within their own territory, were nominalistic and symbolistic as soon as they entered into the field of human relations with their concepts. The influence of sociometry has changed the situation for the better in the last twenty years.

Historically the turning point was from the observational methods of Walther Moede's "Experimentelle Massen Psychologie" (1920) to the action methods of my book "Das Stegreiftheater" (1923). It added action, movement and gestures to verbalization and thus started the change from Freud's observational and interpretative psychoanalysis of children and adults into the modern play techniques and play therapy culminating in psychodrama and the therapeutic theater. The turning point on the sociological plane came from the adaptation of the experimental method to the human, social situation. The productivity of the new approach is seen in the large number of experiments which sociometry has inspired and developed, experiments in spontaneity research and audience participation, experiments with spontaneous group formation and group dynamics, experiments with role testing and role playing, experiments with authoritarian, sociometric and laissez faire groupings.

Sociometry has three references: socius-companion, metrum-measurement, and drama-action. It resulted in three areas of research: group research, metric research and action research. These three areas can be traced in the terms and definitions of sociometry and its allied concepts. It emphasized the link between group and action research and recognized two types of the metric, the quantitative and the "locometric," see "Theometry of Spaces" (1923, opus cited, p. 3). I coined the term sociometry and used it first in a letter to the Department of Interior of the late Austro-Hungarian monarchy (1915). It was introduced into American literature in my paper "Application of the Group Method to the Classification of Prisoners" (1932, reprinted in "Group Psychotherapy", Beacon House, 1945, p. 39).

Microsociology actually started with the introduction of my *theory* of "social microscopy" (see chapter bearing this title in "Who Shall Survive?", 1934, and "Group Method and Group Psychotherapy", p. 101, 1931); combined with sociometric techniques it established the theoretical-practical foundations of microsociology. Without them the later coining of the term microsociology (independently by Georges Gurvitch and J. L. Moreno) and their discussions about it may well have remained inconclusive.

Definitions of Socionomy and Sociometry

Socionomy explores and treats the *laws* of social development and social relations. It is within the system of socionomy that the yet metaphorical We, the mass, the community, the communion, as well as the class, state, church, and many other collectives and cooperatives have their place. It is up to sociometric research to give these approximations of truth an exact and dynamic meaning.

Sociometry means measurement of social relations, in its broadest sense, *all* measurement of *all* social relations. Because of the dialectic character of human relations all sociometric terms and instruments have a dialectic character; dialectic means here that in the course of advancing the cause of sociometric consciousness a reconciliation of opposites and of numerous social dimensions, a flexibility of position and definition, may be required. For illustration, as long as vital statistics and the current public opinion polls are the only kind of sociometry acceptable to the sociometric consciousness of a population, they are all that sociometry can be. (It is most fortunate that social science technicians grossly underrate the social spontaneity of people when they deal directly with their own, immediate projects, and their readiness for sociometric procedure.) But as soon as finer instruments are acceptable to a population they can be applied towards the improvement and measurement of interpersonal and intergroup relations; then the older methods become less desirable, and also reactionary, unscientific and unsociometric. As long as a population has a low sociometric consciousness distinctions between psychological and social properties of populations have no value. Indeed, from the point of view of action methods over-emphasis upon logical purity of definitions may be outright harmful and over-developed logical systems may produce a false sense of security and of scientific well-being which discourages and delays action practice.

1931, "Application of the Group Method to Classification", (p. 102): Sociometry deals "with the inner structure of social groups which can be compared with the nuclear nature of the atom or the physiological structure of the cell." It studies "the complicated forms emerging from attractions and repulsions between the different persons of specific groups." It is chiefly concerned with the social forms emerging and not only with the various processes leading up to them, as "relationships" and "interactions" between persons and groups; however, no one could ever arrive to an accurate picture of social wholes except by the methods of sociometry.

1933, "Psychological Organization of Groups in the Community", Year Book of Mental Deficiency, Boston, (p. 1): "The mathematical study of psychological properties of populations, the experimental technique of and the results obtained by the application of quantitative and qualitative methods is called *sociometry*."

1936, "Plan for the Re-Grouping of Communities", Sociometric Review, February (p. 59): "Sociometry offers all the advantages of a pioneering enterprise of self reliance and free development, combined with all the advantages of an organized movement."

1937, "Sociometry In Relation to Other Social Sciences", SOCIOMETRY, Volume I, No. 1-2, (p. 209-210): "The participant observer of the social laboratory, counterpart of the scientific observer in the physical laboratory, undergoes a profound change. . . . The observed persons become open promoters of the project; the project becomes a cooperative effort. They become participants in and observers of the problems of others as well as their own."

1942, "Sociometry in Action", SOCIOMETRY, Volume V, No. 3, (p. 299, p. 301): "Genuine sociometry is always a science of action." "A sociometric test is first of all an action and behaviour test" of social groups.

1947, "Contributions of Sociometry to Research Methodology in Sociology", American Sociological Review, Volume XII, No. 3, (p. 288): "Sociometry became then, . . . the sociology of the people, by the people and for the people."

Definitions of Tele, Social Atom, Emotional Expansiveness and Network

1934, "Who Shall Survive?", (p. 159): "The attractions and repulsions which we find, therefore, oscillating from one individual to the other, however varying the derivatives, as fear, anger, or sympathy, it may be assumed have a socio-physiological correlate."

"The innumerable varieties of attractions and repulsions between individuals need a common denominator. A feeling is directed from one individual towards another. It has to be projected into distance. Just as we use the words tele-perceptor, telepathy, telencephalon, telephone, etc., to express action at distance, so to express the simplest unit of feeling transmitted from one individual towards another we use the term *tele*." Tele has two portions, a projective (outgoing) and a "retrojective" (returning) portion.

1945, "Two Sociometries, Human and Subhuman", SOCIOMETRY, Volume VIII, No. 1 (p. 75): "I pose the following hypothesis: Human and non-human social structures formed by actual individuals have a characteristic type of organization which differs significantly from structures which are formed by "chance" or by imaginary individuals. This has been proven for the human group by experiments, statistical and mathematical analysis. There must be a factor, 'tele,' operating between individuals, (for instance, in the exploration of appropriate mates) which draws them to form more positive or negative relations, pair relations, triangles, chains, quadrangles, polygons, etc., than on chance. A parallel process should be demonstrable for non-human groups as well. It is the inter-action of the individuals which gives the groups its social reality, whatever the hereditary forces are which direct individual maturation, and the environmental forces which surround them. Their influence is, of course, not denied, but they cannot operate but via the inter-individual channels. By this measure it is possible to determine the degree of social reality of the organization of groups. Certain social configurations have a structure which may place them nearer to the chance level, other social configurations may have a structure which places them nearer the optimum of cohesion. In accordance with this hypothesis, a group of primates or a group of human infants should rank lower on the scale than, for example, a group of human adults. There may be evidence available that such a factor as tele might operate more in certain species which show a comparatively great flexibility of inter-individual relations, but less in other species which tend towards rigid and hereditary social orders. There may be some usefulness in concepts as tele, social atom and psycho-social network as primitive means of communication particularly among higher mammalian and primate societies."

1948, "Discussion of Group Psychotherapy, An Appraisal", by J. L. Moreno, Failures in Psychiatric Treatment, Edited by Paul Hoch (p. 129): "Tele is assumed to be responsible for the cohesion within groups."

1934, "Who Shall Survive?" (p. 141): "The smallest living social unit, itself not further divisible, is the social atom." (p. 162) "The smallest living unit of social matter which we can comprehend is the social atom."

1934, "Who Shall Survive?" (p. 136): Emotional expansiveness is a tele phenomenon. "One individual (housemother) is able to attract the attention of more individuals (children) than another (housemother) and some individuals (housemothers) fatigue more rapidly. After a few tests we can rank the individuals (housemothers) roughly according to their emotional expansiveness."

1934, "Who Shall Survive?" (p. 256): "There are more or less permanent structures which bind individuals and social atoms together into large networks."

"LOCOMETRY", THE SCIENCE OF SPACES AND OF SITES

(1923)

By means of geometry of spaces the locus of geometric configurations is determined. By means of locometry the locus nascendi of ideas and of things (animate or inanimate), and their movement from locus to locus is determined. The locus of a flower, for instance, is in the bed where it grows into a flower, and not its place in a woman's hair. The locus of a painting is its specific, original surroundings. If the painting is removed in space from its original surroundings, it becomes just another "thing"—a secondary, exchangeable value.

The locus of a word is the tongue of the one who utters it, or the lines in which the pen first forms it. This word, repeated, becomes but another and more ugly sound; the handwriting, multiplied in print, becomes but an intellectual commodity. Again, the uniqueness is obliterated.

From the point of view of usefulness and practicability only, there is no difference between the original painting and the copies of it. The words spoken by a man and their printed reduplications communicate the same content to the outsider. The existence of many copies identical with the original creates the deceptive impression that there are many originals, or that the original and the copies have the same meaning. It may even give the impression that there is no true original—only derivatives, all copies of a book being alike.

It is important to reflect upon the inner process of transformation which takes place in the course of the removal of a creative expression from its locus nascendi to new places or media. One "thing" changes into another "thing"—although, due to the lag of language, the same word may be used for many different objects or events; but far more, due to our distorted perceptions of the dead thing, the dead thing may be considered alive, the alive thing may be considered dead. Thus, the "David" of Michael Angelo in its locus nascendi is the true "David" of Michael Angelo. Placed in a museum it is no longer truly itself: it is lending itself to the composition of another "thing", the museum. Now it is one of the "things" which go to make up a museum. Similarly, the lily in the hand of a woman is no longer purely a lily but a decorative extension of her hand, her body. The primary situation of a thing is in the place which gave it birth.

Every thing, form, or idea has a place, a locus, which is most adequate and appropriate for it, in which it has the most ideal, the most perfect expression of its meaning. Go to the locus nascendi of an event and you will breathe in some of its original atmosphere. One can construct the true locus of the theatre, the letter, the book. The true locus of the theatre is the theatre for spontaneity. A letter has its ideal locus in the hand of the person to whom it is written; in the hands of an unwanted person, a stranger, to whom the letter is not directed the expressed contents and the unexpressed implications are meaningless, the letter is as in exile, out of locus.

Locometry has a dialectic character, corresponding to the dialectic character of moving things and events. The living lamb and the dead lamb carry the same name although their locus and their structure have changed. Lamb chops still carry the connotational illusion of the same thing, although it is now a cooked thing, part of a tasty mixture of various ingredients and represents a phase in the circulation of nourishment. The things are only in the locometric moment; although extinct, their past images and semblances, their influences and their names are still cluttering their graves. There is no preservation and reproduction of the same thing, there are only transitory positions within a single universe from one locus to another. The place of transformation found through locometric investigation announces the end of a thing and the simultaneous beginning of a second thing.

The "Locogram" (1949)

The locometric approach has all the advantages but none of the disadvantages of the so-called field theory. The term "field" has been borrowed from physics with the connotation that the social field resembles an electro-magnetic field. Whenever social concepts borrow terms from biology or physics they carry the risk of magic thinking; they usually require strict operational redefinitions growing out of the materials for which they stand. Locometry, on the other hand, is a *neutral* term; it is related to none of these sciences, physics, biology or sociology. It is free of metaphoric heritage and obligations. Locometry comes from the Latin and Greek—locus meaning place, locality, and metry from the word metron, meaning measurement.

The new experimental methods in the social sciences and the new graphic methods aiming to portray social dynamics—the sociogram, the space-time diagram and the inter-action diagram have grown out of my interpersonal theory, the psychodrama in situ and the "Bewegungsdiagram" (the "locogram"). See "Das Stegreiftheater", pp. 56, 88. The latter were the fountainhead of numerous ideas of social experimentation, a productivity which is not yet exhausted.

Productivity of a theory is the best argument in its favor. The locometric-sociometric and psychodramatic theories have proven their worth. The field theory, on the other hand, after having tried its hand in embryology and animal psychology, was unproductive in the social sciences, or at least it arrived too late in the arena of social research. All the modern problem formulations, experimental projects and discoveries were already made or at least initiated by sociometry. A careful reader of the sociometric and socio-psychological literature of the last twenty years will find that field theory ran second, with sociometry leading the race. Therefore, it was forced to imitate, supplement or continue the work which was already on the way, without contributing, to my knowledge, any new idea which could be credited to field theory. Field theory, being advocated largely by academicians, should arouse the suspicion that it is promoting the return of a latent nominalism from which sociometry has tried to save the drowning sociology of our century.

NOTES ON SOCIOMETRY, GESTALT THEORY, AND PSYCHOANALYSIS (1933)

Psychoanalysis and Gestalt doctrine naturally coincide in sociometry because it is a synthesis of the two. The study of the characteristic patterns of group organization and their relation to evolutionary (temporal) and geographical aspects may appeal to the Gestalt students as corresponding to his studies in the sensory fields. But sociometry accomplishes a thing which the Gestalt theory does not approach: it studies expression and organization in relation to the act or acts which produces them. It never considers Gestalt separated from the creator and the creative act.

The most general critique of sociometric procedure one can imagine is that it is an invention fashioned to fit certain social phenomena. The data may be therefore to a large extent determined by the frame of the procedure used in fact-finding. To this frame of testing, the tested individuals submit themselves for various reasons. As the individuals submit themselves freely to the procedures, the tester knows, a priori, the theoretical distribution and possibilities of relationships. The materials to be correlated are the responses of the individuals within the frame of the procedure which has been invented. The single elements of which the configurations can consist are as theoretical possibilities familiar in advance. The resulting configurations can be treated statistically and rationally because there is already knowledge of the single elements of which they are composed.

These sociometric configurations are not what is usually called a Gestalt. They have characteristics which might be attributable to Gestalt. One part of the structure is interdependent with another part; a change in position of one individual may effect the whole structure. But *it is known with analytical exactitude how the whole configuration is built up by its single elements. It has some characteristics of a Gestalt but not the crucial one that the atomic elements have no reality in themselves except as part of a whole. The atomic elements of a sociogram are determinable analytically.*

The sociometrist, as a student of group dynamics and of social configurations is therefore in a different situation from the Gestalt theorist. He does not approach something given, a Gestalt; he is himself the framer of a Gestalt and therefore a *Gestalter,* the inventor of the framework. And it is within these frameworks that he approaches the social phenomena he studies and not outside of them. The creator of a Gestalt may know the single elements which he manipulated in the original framework and he alone may understand why the configurations resulting look as they do. A later observer who did not know the original creation might have reasons to develop a Gestalt theory, but the originators of a frame are in a different position. For the original maker and inventor of music, for instance, if we may visualize such a supreme mind, the melody may not be a Gestalt. He would know about the units which go into its formation. The units of which we would know, however, may be totally different from the parts, the single tones, into which *we* divide melody. Sociometric structures like musical notations, are languages, symbolic references, not the process itself. They are analogous to the frames of time and space in the sense of Kant. The conceptual mind uses them to align the phenomena.

On the other hand, sociometry studies individuals just when they enter *spontaneously* into interrelationships which lead to the forming of groups, *sub species momenti.* And as we study these spontaneous reactions in the initial stage of group formation and the organized attitudes developed in the course of such organization, we may coincide with the psychoanalyst. We are *present* during the "trauma" of birth and attempt to foretell the future: the psychoanalyst faces the ashes, the derivatives. It is as if psychoanalysis is reversed. Our procedure is "sociocreative". We begin with the act, the initial attitude one person shows for the other, and follow up to what fate these interrelations lead, what kind of organization they develop. The psychoanalyst approaches a late developed stage and runs back the historical line to reconstruct the "trauma". It should be expected, therefore, that sociometric findings may corroborate many psychoanalytic concepts. However, sociometry, due to its methodology, promises two things which psychoanalysts never could accomplish: (a) a more precise presentation of the facts, as our procedure moves from the act to the symbol instead of from the symbol to the act: and (b) the actual organization of groups and masses. For instance, the psychoanalytic concept that a pregenital period of development is followed by a period of latency and the recurrence of a heterosexual attitude, etc. appears to correspond to our findings. But the psychoanalyst covers only the attitude of the individual. Yet it is the effect which these attitudes have upon group organization in different age levels and the countereffect group organization has upon these attitudes which can be disclosed through sociometric approach only. And this seems to be the salient point.

The psychoanalytical approach of the Oedipus drama is correct as long as it considers the Oedipus complex as an individual reaction of Oedipus mirroring all other persons around him. But to represent the real, whole Oedipus drama, an interrelation analysis is necessary. An individual analysis of each of the three persons, Oedipus, his father Laius and his mother Jocaste, has to be made. We will find, then, just as Oedipus may have in his complex hate towards his father and love towards his mother, that his father has towards him and Jocaste a complex which we may call here briefly "Laius" complex and that his mother Jocaste has toward him and towards Laius a complex which we may call "Jocaste" complex. Then you will find complexes which Laius has in relation to Jocaste and complexes which Jocaste has in relation to Laius. The interlocking of these three persons, the frictions between them, the clashes between their complexes will produce the actual psycho-social process of their interrelations which is different from the manner in which the dramatic process reflects in Oedipus alone, or how it is reflected within his father or mother singly, each part from the other. In other words, we get a multiplicity of interrelationships which are, so to speak, ambicentric, and through this kind of study we get an insight from within as to how the total family group is organized.

SOCIOMETRY IN RELATION TO OTHER SOCIAL SCIENCES

(1937)

STUDYING THE STRUCTURE OF HUMAN SOCIETY

Religious, economic, technological, and political systems have been constructed to date with the tacit assumption that they can be adequate and applicable to human society without an accurate and detailed knowledge of its structure. The repeated failure of so many plausible and humane remedies and doctrines has led to the conviction that the close study of social structure is the only means through which we may treat the ills of society. Sociometry, a relatively new science developed gradually since the World War of 1914-18, aims to determine objectively the basic structures of human societies.

From the point of view of a *medical* sociology, it is essential to know the actual structure of human society at a given moment. The difficulties in the way of attaining such knowledge are enormous and discouraging. These difficulties may be considered essentially in three categories: the large number of people, the need for obtaining valid participation, the need for arranging for continued and repeated studies. These difficulties may be considered in a more detailed fashion together with the steps thus far taken toward overcoming them in the development of sociometric techniques.

First, human society consists of approximately two billion individuals. The number of interrelations among these individuals, each interrelation influencing the total world situation in some manner, however slight, must amount to a figure of astronomical magnitude. Recognizing this fact, the field work of sociometry was started with small sections of human society, spontaneous groupings of people, groups of individuals at different age levels, groups of one sex, groups of both sexes, institutional and industrial communities. To date, various groups and communities, the total populations of which are more than 10,000 persons, have been sociometrically tested. A considerable amount of sociometric knowledge has been accumulated. We should not forget, though, however much we may learn in the course of time, however accurate our sociometric knowledge of certain sections of human society may become, that no "automatic" conclusions can be carried over from one section to another and no "automatic" conclusions can be drawn about the same group from one time to another. Each part of human society must always be considered in its concreteness.

16

Second, as we have to consider every individual in his concreteness and not as a symbol, and every relationship he may bear to each other person or persons in its concreteness and not as a symbol, we can not gain a full knowledge unless every individual participates *spontaneously* in uncovering these relationships to the best of his ability. The problem is how to elicit from every man his maximum spontaneous participation. This participation would produce as a counterpart of the physical geography of the world, a psychological geography of human society. Sociometry has endeavored to gain such participation by applying as a fundamental part of the procedure an important aspect of the actual social situation confronting the people of the community at the moment. This was made possible by broadening and changing the status of the participant observer and researcher so as to make him an auxiliary ego of that individual and all other individuals of the community; that is, one who identifies himself as far as possible with each individual's aims and tries to aid him in their realization. This step was taken after a careful consideration of the spontaneous factor in social situations. General definitions of physical and mental needs do not suffice. There is such a uniqueness about each actual momentary position of an individual in the community that a knowledge of the structure surrounding and pressing upon him at that moment is necessary before drawing conclusions.

Third, as we have to know the actual structure of a human society not only at one given moment but in all its future developments, we must look forward to the maximum spontaneous participation of every individual in all future time. The problem is how to motivate men so that they all will give repeatedly and regularly, not only at one time or another, their maximum spontaneous participation. This difficulty can be overcome through fitting the procedure to the administration of the community. If the spontaneous strivings in regard to association with other persons or in regard to objects and values are aided officially and permanently by respective community agencies, the procedure can become repeatable at any time, and the insight into the structure of the community as it develops in time and space can become constantly available.

In undertaking the study of the structure of human society, the first step has been to define and develop sociometric procedures which would surmount the difficulties described above. Sociometric procedures try to lay bare the fundamental structures within a society by disclosing the affinities, attractions and repulsions, operating between persons and persons and between persons and objects.

Types of Sociometric Procedures

Every type of procedure enumerated below can be applied to any group, whatever the developmental level of the individuals in it. If the procedure applied is, in degree of articulation, below the level of that which a certain social structure demands, the results will reflect but an incomplete, "infra-structure" of that community. An adequate sociometric procedure should be neither more nor less differentiated than the assumed social structure which it is trying to measure.

One type of procedure is to disclose the social structure between individuals by merely recording their movements and positions in space in regard to one another. This procedure of charting gross movements was applied to a group of babies. At their level of development no more differentiated technique could have been applied fruitfully. This procedure discloses the structure developing between a number of babies, between the babies and their attendants, and between the babies and the objects around them in a given physical space, a room. At the earliest developmental level, physical and social structure of space overlap and are congruous. At a certain point of development the structure of the interrelationships begins to differentiate itself more and more from the physical structure of the group, and from this moment onward social space in its embryonic form begins to differentiate itself from physical space. The sociogram is here a diagram of positions and movements. A more highly developed structure appears when the children begin to walk. They can now move towards a person whom they like or away from a person whom they dislike, towards an object which they want, or away from an object which they wish to avoid. The factor of nonverbal, spontaneous participation begins to influence the structure more definitely.

Another development of the procedure is used in groups of young children who (before or after walking) are able to make intelligent use of simple verbal symbols. The factor of simple "participation" of the subject becomes more complex. He can choose or reject an object or person without moving bodily. A still further development of the procedure sets in when children are influenced in their making of associations by the physical or social characteristics of other people: sex, race, social status, etc. This factor of differential association signifies a new trend in the development of structure. Up to this point only *individuals* stood out and had a position in it. From here on associations of individuals stand out and have a position in it as a group. This differentiating factor is called a criterion of the group. As societies of individuals develop, the number of criteria around which associations are or may be formed increases rapidly. The more numerous and the more complex the criteria, the more complex also becomes the social structure of the community.

These few samples may make clear that sociometric procedure is not a rigid set of rules but that it has to be modified and adapted to any group situation as it arises. Sociometric procedure has to be shaped in accord with the momentary potentialities of the subjects, so as to arouse them to a maximum of spontaneous participation and to a maximum of expression. If the sociometric procedure is not attuned to the momentary structure of a given community, we may gain only a limited or distorted knowledge of it.

The participant observer of the social laboratory, counterpart of the scientific observer in the physical or biological laboratory, undergoes a profound change. The observing of movements and voluntary association of individuals has value as a supplement if the basic structure is known. But how can an observer learn something about the basic structure of a community of one thousand people if the observer tries to become an intimate associate of each individual simultaneously, in each role which he enacts in the community? He can not observe them like heavenly bodies and make charts of their movements and reactions. The essence of their situations will be missed if he acts in the role of a scientific spy. The procedure has to be open and apparent. The inhabitants of the community have to become participants in the project in some degree. The degree of participation is at its possible minimum when the individuals composing the group are willing *only to answer questions about one another*. Any study which tries to disclose with less than maximum possible participation of the individuals in the group the *feelings which they have in regard to one another* is *near*-sociometric. Near-sociometric procedures of the research or the diagnostic type are of much value in the present stage of sociometry. They can be applied on a large scale, and within certain limits without unpleasantness to the participants. The information gained in near-sociometric studies is based, however, on an inadequate motivation of the participants, they do not fully reveal their feelings. In near-sociometric situations the participants are rarely spontaneous. They do not warm up quickly. An individual, if he is asked, "Who are your friends in town?" may leave one or two persons out, the most important persons in his social atom, persons with whom he entertains a secret friendship of some sort which he does not want known.

The observational method of group research, the study of group formation from the *outside* is not abandoned by the sociometrist. This becomes, however, a part of a more inclusive technique, the sociometric procedure. In fact, the sociometric procedure is operational and observational at the same time. A well-trained sociometrist will continuously collect other observational and experimental data which may be essential as a supplement to his knowledge of the *inside* social structure of a group at a particular time. Observational and statistical studies may grow out of sociometric procedures which supplement and deepen structural analysis.

The transition from near-sociometric to basic sociometric procedures depends upon the methods of creating the motivation to more adequate participation. If the participant observer succeeds in becoming less and less an observer and more and more of an aid and helper to every individual of the group in regard to their needs and interests, the observer undergoes a transformation, a transformation from observer to auxiliary ego. The observed persons, instead of revealing something, more or less unwillingly, about themselves and one another, become open promoters of the project; *the project becomes a cooperative effort.* They become participants in and observers of the problems of others as well as their own; they become key contributors to the sociometric research. They know that the more explicit and accurate they are in expressing whom they want, whether as associates in a play, as table mates in a dining room, as neighbors in their community, or as co-workers in a factory, the better are their chances to attain the position in their group which is as near as possible to their anticipations and desires.

The first decisive step in the development of sociometry was the disclosure of the actual organization of a group. The second decisive step was the inclusion of subjective measures in determining this organization. The third decisive step was a method which gives to subjective terms the highest possible degree of objectivity, through the function of the auxiliary ego. The fourth decisive step was the consideration of the criterion (a need, a value, an aim, etc.) around which a particular structure develops. The true organization of a group can be disclosed if the test is constructed in accord with the criterion around which it is built. For instance, if we want to determine the structure of a work group, the criterion is their relationship as workers in the factory, and not the reply to a question regarding with whom they would like to go out for luncheon. We differentiate therefore between an essential and an auxiliary criterion. Complex groups are often built around several essential criteria. If a test is near-sociometric or inadequately constructed, then it discloses, instead of the actual organization of the group, a distorted form of it, a less differentiated form of it, an *infra*-level of its structure.

Within sociometric work several approaches can be distinguished: (1) the research procedure, aiming to study the organization of groups; (2) the diagnostic procedure, aiming to classify the positions of individuals in groups and the position of groups in the community; (3) therapeutic and political procedures, aiming to aid individuals or groups to better adjustment; and finally, (4) the complete sociometric procedure, in which all these steps are synthetically united and transformed into a single operation, one procedure depending upon the other. This last procedure is also the most *scientific* of all. It is not more scientific because it is more practical; rather, it is more practical because it is more scientifically accurate.

PRESENTATION AND EXPLORATION OF SOCIOMETRIC DATA

The responses received in the course of sociometric procedure from each individual, however spontaneous and essential they may appear, are materials only and not yet sociometric facts in themselves. We have first to visualize and represent how these responses hang together. The astronomer has his universe of stars and of the other heavenly bodies visibly spread throughout space. Their geography is given. The sociometrist is in the paradoxical situation that he has to construct and map his universe before he can explore it. A process of charting has been devised, the sociogram, which is, as it should be, more than merely a method of presentation. It is first of all a method of exploration. It makes possible the exploration of sociometric facts. The proper placement of every individual and of all interrelations of individuals can be shown on a sociogram. It is at present the only available scheme which makes structural analysis of a community possible.

As the pattern of the social universe is not visible to us, it is made visible through charting. Therefore the sociometric chart is the more useful the more accurately and realistically it portrays the relations discovered. As every detail is important the most accurate presentation is the most appropriate. The problem is not only to present knowledge in the simplest and shortest manner, but to present the relations so that they can be studied.

Numerous types of sociogram have been devised. They have in common that they portray the pattern of the social structure as a whole and the position of every individual within it. One type shows the social configurations as they grow in time and as they spread in space. Other types of sociograms present the momentary and transitory picture of a group. As the technique of charting is a method of exploration, the sociograms

are so devised that one can pick from the *primary* map of a community
small parts, redraw them, and study them so to speak under the microscope.
Another type of derivative or secondary sociogram results if we pick from
the map of a community large structures because of their functional
significance, for instance, psychological networks. The mapping of networks indicates that on the basis of primary sociograms we may devise
forms of charting which enable us to explore large geographical areas.

Concept and Discoveries

Sociometry started practically as soon as we were in the position to
study social structure as a whole and in its parts at the same time. This
was impossible as long as the problem of the individual was still a main
concern, as with an individual's relation and adjustment to the group.
Once the full social structure could be seen as a totality it could be
studied in its minute detail. We thus became able to describe sociometric
facts (descriptive sociometry) and to consider the function of specific
structures, the effect of some parts upon others (dynamic sociometry).

Viewing the social structure of a certain community as a whole, related
to a certain locality, with a certain physical geography, a township filled
with homes, schools, workshops, the interrelations between their inhabitants
in these situations, we arrive at the concept of the psychological geography
of a community. Viewing the detailed structure of a community we see
the concrete position of every individual in it, also, a nucleus of relations
around every individual which is "thicker" around some individuals, "thinner" around others. This nucleus of relations is the smallest *social* structure
in a community, a *social atom*. From the point of view of a descriptive
sociometry, the social atom is a fact, not a concept, just as in anatomy
the blood vessel system, for instance, is first of a descriptive fact. It
attained conceptual significance as soon as the study of the development
of social atoms suggested that they have an important function in the
formation of human society.

Whereas certain parts of these social atoms seem to remain buried
between the individuals participating, certain parts link themselves with
parts of other social atoms and these with parts of other social atoms
again, forming complex chains of interrelations which are called, in terms
of descriptive sociometry, psychological networks. The older and wider
the network spreads the less significant seems to be the individual contribution toward it. From the point of view of dynamic sociometry these networks have the function of shaping social tradition and public opinion.

It is different and more difficult, however, to describe the process which attracts individuals to one another or which repels them, that flow of feeling of which the social atom and the networks are apparently composed. This process may be conceived as *tele*. We are used to the notion that feelings emerge within the individual organism and that they become attached more strongly or more weakly to persons or things in the immediate environment. We have been in the habit of thinking not only that these totalities of feelings spring up from the individual organism exclusively, from one of its parts or from the organism as a whole, but that these physical and mental states after having emerged reside forever within this organism. The feeling relation to a person or an object has been called attachment or fixation but these attachments or fixations were considered purely as individual projections. This was in accord with the materialistic concept of the individual organism, with its unity, and, we can perhaps say, with its microcosmic independence.

The hypothesis that feelings, emotions or ideas can "leave" or "enter" the organism appeared inconsistent with this concept. The claims of parapsychology were easily discarded as unfounded by scientific evidence. The claims of collectivistic unity of a people appeared romantic and mystical. This resistance against any attempt to break the sacred unity of the individual has one of its roots in the idea that feelings, emotions, ideas must reside in some structure within which they can emerge or vanish, and within which they can function or disappear. These feelings, emotions and ideas "leave" the organism; where then can they reside?

When we found that social atoms and networks have a persistent structure and that they develop in a certain order we had extra individual structures—and probably there are many more to be discovered—in which this flow can reside. But another difficulty stepped in. As long as we (as auxiliary ego) drew from every individual the responses and materials needed, we were inclined—because of our nearness to the individual—to conceive the tele as flowing out of him towards other individuals and objects. This is certainly correct on the individual-psychological level, in the preparatory phase of sociometric exploration. But as soon as we transferred these responses to the sociometric level and studied them not singly but in their interrelations, important methodological reasons suggested that we conceive this flowing feeling, the tele, as an inter-personal or more accurately and more broadly speaking, as a *sociometric structure*. Projected feelings do not make sense sociometrically. They require the complementation of "retrojected" feelings, at least, potentially. One part does not exist without the other. It is a continuum. We must assume at present, until further knowledge forces us to modify and refine this concept, that some real process in one person's life situation is sensitive and corresponds to some real process in another person's life situation and that there are numerous degrees, positive and negative, of these inter-personal sensitivities. The tele between any two individuals may be potential. It may never become active unless these individuals are brought into proximity or unless their feelings and ideas meet at a distance through some channel, for instance, the networks. These distance or tele effects have been found to be complex sociometric structures produced by a long chain of individuals each with a different degree of sensitivity for the same tele, ranging from total indifference to a maximum response.

A social atom is thus composed of numerous tele structures; social atoms are again parts of still a larger pattern, the psychological networks which bind or separate large groups of individuals due to their tele relationships. Psychological networks are parts of a still larger unit, the psychological geography of a community. A community is again part of the largest configuration, the psychological totality of human society itself.

THE STRATEGIC ROLE OF SOCIOMETRY AMONG THE SOCIAL SCIENCES

A full appreciation of the significance of sociometry for the social sciences cannot be gained unless we analyze some of the most characteristic developments in recent years. The one development is along Marxist lines as elaborated especially by George Lucacs and Karl Mannheim. The social philosophy of these students is full of near-sociometric divinations. They stress the existence of social classes, the dependence of ideology upon social structure. They refer to the position of individuals in their group, and to the social dynamics resulting from the changing of the position of groups in a community. But the discussion is carried on at a dialectical and symbolical level, giving the reader the impression that the writers had an intimate and authoritative knowledge of the social and psychological structures they are describing. They present social and psychological processes which are supposed to go on in large populations. But their own literature. These large generalizations encourage *pseudo*-totalistic assimilated from social and psychological reading shines through their own literature. These large generalizations encourage *pseudo*-totalistic views of the social universe. The basic social and psychological structure of the group remains a *mythological* product of their own mind, a mythology which is just as much a barrier to the progress from an old to a new social order as the fetish of merchandise was before Marx's analysis of it. The dialectial and political totalists have reached a dead-end. A true advance in political theory can not crystalize until more concrete sociometric knowledge of the basic structure of groups is secured.

The economic situation of a group and the dynamic influence it has upon the social and psychological structure of that group cannot be fully understood unless we also know the social and psychological situation of this group and unless we study the dynamic influence they have upon its economic situation. Indeed from the sociometric point of view the economic criterion is only *one* criterion around which social structure develops. Sociometric method is a *synthetic* procedure which through the very fact of being in operation releases all the factual relationships whether they have an economic, sociological, psychological or biological derivation. It is carried out as one operation. But it has several results: it secures knowledge of the actual social structure in regard to every criterion dynamically related to it, the possibility of classifying the psychological, social and economic status of the population producing this structure, and early recognition of psychological, social and economic changes in the status of this population. Knowledge of social structure provides the concrete basis for rational social action. This should not be surprising, even to staunch believers in the old dialectic methods. As long as it appeared certain that all that counts is the knowledge of economics structure, all other structural formations within society could be considered in a general manner intimating at random how the economic motive determines them. An economic analysis of every actual group was all that seemed necessary. Since the more inclusive sociometric technique of social analysis has developed which attacks the basic social structure itself, the possibility of a new line of development appears on the horizon. From the sociometric angle the totalism of the new-Marxists appears as flat and unrealistic as the totalism of Hegel appeared to Marx. Compared with the *elan* of the totalistic schools of thought, sociometric effort may seem narrow. Instead of analyzing social classes composed of millions of people, we are making painstaking analyses of small groups of persons. It is a retreat from the social universe to its atomic structure. In the course of time, through the cooperative efforts of many workers, a total view of human society will result again, but it will be better founded. This may be a deep fall after so much dialectic conceit, but it is a strategic retreat, a retreat to greater objectivity.

A different sort of symbolism comes from other lines of development which deal largely with psychological theory. An illustration of this trend is a recent phase of the Gestalt school. Thus J. F. Brown and Kurt Lewin schematized social structures and social barriers which no one has empirically studied. A conceptual scheme may become just as harmful to the growth of a young and groping experimental science as a political scheme. There are many links in the chain of interrelations which can not be divined. They have to be explored concretely in the actual group. It is not the result of a study which concerns us here, for instance whether it approximates the probable factual relations or not, but the contrast between empirical and symbolical methods of procedure. We have learned in the course of sociometric work how unreliable our best divinations were in regard to social structure. Therefore we prefer to let our concepts emerge and grow with the growth of the experiment and not to take them from any *aprioristic* or any non-sociometric source.

Degree of Sociometric Consciousness

The best test of the damage done by any sort of symbolical concept of social structure is to come face to face with the crucial experiment itself, a worker entering a group, however small or large, with the purpose of applying to it sociometric procedures. The introduction of sociometric procedure, even to a very small community, is an extremely delicate psychological problem. The psychological problem is the more intricate, the more complex and the more differentiated the community is. On first thought one would be inclined to minimize the difficulties involved. Sociometric procedures should be greeted favorably as they aid in bringing to recognition and into realization the basic structure of a group. But such is not always the case. They are met with resistance by some and even with hostility by others. Therefore a group should be carefully prepared for the test before submitting to it.

Sociometric techniques have to be fashioned in accord with the readiness of a certain population for sociometric grouping, in accord with their maturity and their disposition towards the test which may vary at different times. This psychological status of individuals may be called their degree of *sociometric consciousness*. The resistance against sociometric procedures is often due to psychological and educational limitations. It is important for the field worker to consider the difficulties one by one and to try to meet them.

The first difficulty which one ordinarily meets is ignorance of what sociometric procedure is. A full and lucid presentation, first perhaps to small and intimate groups, and then in a town meeting if necessary, is extremely helpful. It will bring misunderstandings in regard to it to open discussion. One reaction usually found is the appreciation of some that many social and psychological processes exist in their group which have escaped democratic integration. Another reaction is one of fear and resistance not as much against the procedure as against its consequences for them. These and other reactions determine the degree of sociometric consciousness of a group. They determine also the amount and character of preparation the group members need before the procedure is put into operation.

In the course of its operation we can learn from the spontaneous responses of the individuals concerned something about the causes underlying their fears and resistance. In one of the communities tested some individuals made their choice and gave their reasons without hesitancy; others hesitated long before choosing; one or two refused to participate at all. After the findings of the test were applied to the group a frequently chosen individual was much displeased. He had not received that man as neighbor with whom he had exchanged a mutual first choice. It took him weeks to overcome his anger. One day he said smilingly that he liked the neighbor he had now and he would not change him for his original first choice even if he could. There was another individual who did not care to make any choice. When the chart of the community was laid out it was found that in turn none of the other individuals wanted him. He was isolated. It was as if he guessed that his position in the group was that of an isolate; therefore he did not like to know too much about it. He did not have the position in the group he would like to have and so perhaps he thought it better to keep it veiled.

Other individuals also showed fear of the revelations the sociometric procedure might bring. The fear is stronger with some people, and weaker with others. One may be most anxious to arrange one's relationships in accord with actual desires; another may be afraid of the consequences. For instance, one of the persons remarked that it made him feel uncomfortable to say whom he liked for a co-worker. "You can not choose all and I do not want to offend anybody." Another person said, "If I don't have as a neighbor the person I like, i.e. if he lives farther away, we may stay friends longer. It is better not to see a friend too often." These and other remarks reveal a fundamental phenomenon, a form of inter-personal resistance, a resistance against expressing the preferential feelings which one has for others. This resistance seems at first sight paradoxical as it crops up in face of an actual opportunity to have a fundamental need satisfied. An explanation of this resistance of the individual versus the group is possible. It is, on the one hand, the individual's fear of knowing what position he has in the group. To become and to be made fully conscious of one's position may be painful and unpleasant. Another source of this resistance is the fear that it may become manifest to others whom one likes and whom one dislikes, and what position in the group one actually wants and needs. The resistance is produced by the extra-personal situation of an individual, by the position he has in the group. He feels that the position he has in the group is not the result of his individual make-up only but chiefly the result of how the individuals with whom he is associated feel towards him. He may even feel dimly that there are beyond his social atom invisible tele-structures which influence his position. The fear against expressing the preferential feelings which one person has for others is actually a fear of the feelings which the others have for him. The objective process underlying this fear has been discovered by us in the course of quantitative analysis of group organization. The individual dreads the powerful currents of emotions which "society" may turn against him—it is fear of the psychological networks. It is dread of these powerful structures whose influence is unlimited and uncontrollable. It is fear that they may destroy him if he does not keep still.

The sociometrist has the task of gradually breaking down the misunderstandings and fears existing or developing in the group he is facing. The members of the group will be eager to weigh the advantages which sociometric procedure is able to bring to them—a better balanced organization of their community and a better balanced situation of each individual within it. The sociometrist has to exert his skill to gain their full collaboration, for at least two reasons: the more spontaneous their collaboration, the more valuable will be the fruits of his research, and the more helpful will the results become to them.

SOCIOMETRY AND THE EXPERIMENTAL METHOD*

SOCIOMETRY AND THE EXPERIMENTAL METHOD IN SCIENCE

The experimental method in science, widely respected by scientists as their canon, has been given its authoritative formulation by John Stuart Mill (9). Mill's *System of Logic* was published about a century ago (1843). An intimate connection exists between Mill's work and the work of Auguste Comte. Mill admits that his own system of logic owes many valuable thoughts to Comte (5, 8). (Under the influence of Comte, Mill replaced among other things the à priori method in science by the à posteriori method.) My critique of Mill's canon of experimental method is therefore also directed toward Comte.

The model of how the findings of the social sciences should be validated were taken by Mill from the physical sciences. He came to the exasperating conclusion (9) that the experimental method cannot be applied to the social sciences, their subject matter being too complex. The question raised here is whether he did not start with a false premise, whether the model he held authoritatively before the social sciences was not the wrong one. In the generation when the two theorists, Comte and Mill, constructed their universal systems of experimental method Karl Marx was busy building his own. His system had a different slant. He was a theorist and a thinker of practice. He, their antagonist, pushed in the "Theses on Feurerbach" (1845) and in the "Communist Manifesto" (1848) into an opposite direction. One who is versed in sociometric methods could venture to say that he was unconsciously following a model of experimental method more indigenous to the social sciences, a model of social actors in a world of action. But there is no trace to be found of the Marxistic kind of logic in the system of logic of Mill. It should not be implied here that Marx was interested in experimental method per se. He was not interested in the type of precision and validation for which the experimental method stands. But he was interested in significant methods which work in practice and are borne out by "experiments of nature".

---

*A part of this paper was published by the University of Pittsburgh Press, Pittsburgh, Pennsylvania, under the title "Experimental Sociometry and the Experimental Method in Science", in *Current Trends in Social Psychology,* 1948, and appeared in French in the *Cahiers Internationaux de Sociologie* 1949, published by the Presses Universitaires de France, Paris, under the title "Methode Experimentale, Sociometrie et Marxisme".

The experimental method should therefore discern two parts, a *material* part and a *logical* part. Mill's canon deals exclusively with the logical part, or as he calls them, the *methods of experimental inquiry*. They were designed to be methods of discovering causal connections and methods of conclusive proof. He differentiated between the method of agreement, the method of difference, the joint method of agreement and difference, the method of concomitant variation and the method of residues. It is due to the apparently invincible pathos of the logical exposé of the experimental methods that they have become sacred to all worshipers of science. They rest on the dogma of the uniformity of nature or, in Mill's own words, "There are such things in nature as parallel cases, that what happens once, will, under a sufficient degree of similarity of circumstances, happen again." The uniformity of nature, he says, is the "ultimate major premise of all inductions."

There is reasonable doubt as to the absoluteness of general laws (17). The belief in general and uniform laws is the *credo* of "scientism." In the last analysis there are "lovers" of the idea of science, just as others are lovers of the idea of God. Whether true or false, without such a credo, science (at least as it is generally understood) would become meaningless. The construction of a higher domain of inquiry, of a "superscience" which may be neither metaphysics nor religion, is a postulate of our critical faculties. Such an inquiry would have the task to explore the logical limits of science and should not reduce its authority; for the chief attribute of science should be that it is always ready to study itself and to disagree with itself.

REVISED FOUNDATIONS OF THE EXPERIMENTAL METHOD; THE MATERIAL
AND THE LOGICAL PART

The hypothesis that nature is uniform, that the universe is ruled by general laws and that the same cause under the same circumstances will be accompanied by the same effect is not the subject of this paper. Its subject is a critique of the experimental methods because of the negligence of the *material* aspects of the situations to which they are applied. Whereas the logical aspects of experimentation have been stressed abundantly, from Francis Bacon (1) to Mill and up to our own time, the material part has been so sadly neglected that the development of the social sciences has been seriously crippled and with it the possibility of providing the total of human society with more rigorous and adequate instruments of social change than are available. It has become, therefore, an important task of the sociological thought of our own century to correct the most flagrant error of methodical insight which has made social research trivial and confusing while deteriorating its outlook.

The *experimental situation* in its broadest meaning consists of three phases: (*a*) the material part, that is, the matter for whose study an experiment is designed; (*b*) the logical part, that is, the methods constructed in order to test the validity of a hypothesis or of a universal law; and (*c*) the relationship between the material of the experiment and the logico-experimental part of the procedure. In the physical sciences and, to a degree, in the biological sciences the material target of the experimental method does not matter so much as in the social sciences. There are, of course, vast differences to be found in material structure: the difference between a star, a planet, a stone, and a plant; or the difference between a solid, a liquid, and a gas; the difference between an algae, a leaf of grass, and a tree; or the difference between a fish, a butterfly, and a rat. But however vast the difference in material structure between these phenomena of nature, by and large the same experimental method can be applied and adjusted to them. Because of the value which the experimental method has shown in these areas the conclusion has been drawn by many writers that it can be applied to the social sciences. But their optimism is unjustified. Mill's skepticism was correct in principle; but he did not realize that it was the experimental method which was at fault, and not the inaccessibility and fleeting inconsistency of social phenomena.

SOCIOMETRY: TERM, DEFINITION, AND MEANING

The chief methodological task of sociometry has been the revision of the experimental method so that it can be applied effectively to social phenomena. Sociometry has been defined as "the mathematical study of psychological properties of populations; the experimental technique of and the results obtained by application of quantitative methods"; also as "the inquiry into the evolution and organization of groups and the position of individuals within them" (12). As the "science of group organization" (11) "it attacks the problem not from the outer structure of the group, the group surface, but from the inner structure." The definition of sociometry was thus in accordance with its etymology, from the Latin, but the emphasis was laid not only on the second half of the term, i.e., on "metrum" meaning measure, but also on the first half of the term (i.e., on "socius" meaning companion). Both principles had been neglected, but the "socius" aspect had been omitted from the deeper analysis far more than the "metrum" aspect. The phrase sociometry has a linguistic relatedness in construction to other, traditional scientific terms: biology, biometry; psychology, psychometry; sociology, sociometry. From the point of view of systematics it is preparatory to the topical fields, sociology, anthropology, social psychology, social psychiatry, etc. It is concerned with the "socius" and "metric" problems common to *all* social fields. Sociometry as a science is an ideal; in its broadest outlook it engulfs but is not identical with any particular trend. Since its conscious inception it has developed three departments of research: (*a*) dynamic, or revolutionary sociometry (representatives are J. L. Moreno, H. Infield, and, to a degree, H. Jennings); (*b*) diagnostic sociometry (J. Criswell, G. Lundberg, U. Bronfenbrenner, M. Northway, M. Bonney, L. Zeleny, C. Loomis, F. Chapin, E. Bogardus, etc.); and (*c*) mathematical sociometry (P. Lazarsfeld, S. Dodd, L. Katz, J. Stewart). The three divisions overlap, and some workers (like the writer) have made contributions to each department.

Every science refers to a constellation of facts and the means of their measurement. Without adequate means of how to discover the facts and without adequate means of measurement a science does not exist. The preliminary step in the development of every science is to realize the conditions under which the significant facts emerge. How to accomplish this differs from science to science. How to realize the conditions under which physical and biological facts emerge (their description, careful observation, and study) is comparatively well known. The problem of creating the conditions under which the significant facts of human relations emerge is far more complicated. It requires nothing short of a revolutionary method. The reasons why there should be such a great difference between the preliminaries required for the social sciences as compared with the physical sciences is not immediately obvious. In the physical sciences, since the subject is inanimate, most of the emphasis has been placed upon the mechanical, physical aspects of the situation. We do not expect the subjects, stone, water, fire, earth or planets, suns and stars to contribute anything themselves to the study of their own selves; except in the mythologies, we do not ascribe to them any soul or personality, or at least we do not do it anymore. Therefore, the metaphysical relations which might exist between the planets and stars, to each other, as mythological soul-bearing actors, do not concern the science of physics. This problem does not change much when it comes to infrahuman organisms, e.g., in experiments with rats, guinea pigs, and the like. The social investigator, the one who sets up the experiment and interprets the data, is a human being and not a guinea pig or a rat. The rats or guinea pigs, so to speak, have no part in such experiments as actors in their own behalf. All such experimental designs are human designs and not designs of guinea pigs or rats. If a poetic mind à la Swift could describe how rats feel about each other and what the experiments which men make on them mean to them, it would probably be within our artistic comprehension but outside of our scientific comprehension. One could say here that we are trying to measure the behavior of rats as it "is" and not what rats feel it is, but this does not change the methodical difficulty which we encounter when we apply the same techniques of observation to the relationships of men among themselves. With animal societies one can take the stand that they are given and preordained just like the individual animal organisms are, but human society is not automatically given and preordained. Although deeply related to physical and biological conditions, it has a structure whose creation and development is initiated and can be studied from within.

The Material Aspect of the Psychological Situation

Now that the conflict between the material and the logical part of an experiment is nearing clarification, we may say that it was already noticeable throughout the last century in the development of the psychological analysis of personality—which we call in short the psychological situation. Let us consider here one of the chief ideas of this period, the notion of association of ideas. Wundt took over the notion from Locke—that ideas which belong together tend to stay together in the psyche. Freud was the first to revise it, not so much as to what associations logically are, but as to how associations can be materially produced for scientific purposes. For Wundt the individual was to an extent still a response mechanism which can be studied and measured coldly with a minimum of his participation, approximately as the animals in the maze. The psychological situation, the relation of the investigator to his subject matter, was for him as for his predecessors, Weber and Fechner, of an extreme artificiality. But Freud was more concerned with how to get the significant kind of association than how to get *any* associations or responses. Experiments in the logical sense, he felt, although he never made it explicit, must be postponed until more is known about the material structure of the psyche and about how to elicit genuine evidence from an individual. In his judgment, the experimental approach of the 1850's was premature and futile and its results were trivial. Freud already insisted upon the voluntary and spontaneous participation of the individual clients in the act of reporting and analyzing their ideas. His skepticism for the psychological experiments of the logical schools is due to his intuitive anticipation that the study of human nature is difficult if not impossible without the comprehension of what I have called "the nature of the warming up process." But Freud traveled only half of the way. It took more than a quarter of a century after his first publication (1895) until with the advent of psychodrama (1923) (10) the material part of the psychological situation was fully rescued and a deeper comprehension was reached, and it has taken another twenty-five years for this awareness to impregnate psychological literature. Freud's position underwent a deep revolution with my theory and practice of psychodrama. His notion of the associations to be elicited for scientific analysis, although called "free," was limited to an association of *words* (and, in addition, limited by the interpretation of the analyst). The spontaneity of the individual's body was not included in the operation. The psychological situation in itself was to a degree still artificial, a conversation in a doctor's office between a physician and a patient, which was bound to limit and distort the natural flow of associations. Psychodramatic methods tried to correct this; the contrived psychoanalytic physician-patient relationship was abandoned and the individual returned to the place where he actually lives and acts, back into the natural atmosphere of his existence, to that which situation literally means, in situ, the place where he thinks, feels, and acts naturally, spontaneously, and to a degree, creatively. This return to the natural setting would have been a regression if we had not been able consciously to deepen and extend the material part of the psychological situation beyond Freud's achievement. I modeled the experimental situation in such a manner that it could be for the individual a design of living, a miniature of his life situations. The subject was not only asked to speak about himself, to let go verbally, but to act, to live out, to be an actor. The association of words was extended by an association of acts. These chains of words and acts were themselves related to each other and to a concretized life situation; all the verbal ghosts were now materialized as the roles of the people in his psychodrama. The process of association of acts was still further extended into the association of interactions between various individuals. It is perhaps because of this maximal externalization of the full personality that the psychodrama is making the experimental method directly applicable to human personality by means of the psychodramatic test. In many forms of psychodramatic productions, also, the artificiality of the contrived experiment is overcome, the experiment in situ and the life setting are one and the same thing. Early types of psychodramatic procedure were experiments in situ. The transfer of a psychodrama to a "theater," a laboratory, or a treatment room was a secondary and later development. The natural social process is, of course, not all spontaneity, it produces its own restraints. If the experiment in situ, however, is kept in mind as a model, the artificialities of the contrived experiment can be kept at a minimum. Recorders, observers, and analysts are made natural parts of the group process: they are given a function of immediate usefulness for every participant (14).

Because the psychodramatic method is giving full consideration to the nature of the warming up process of human beings it is able to elicit the maximum spontaneity and co-operation of the participating subjects. It is because an advance has been made in bringing to consciousness the material part of the psychological situation that the hope perists that the logical part can and will be applied to it more adequately and with less triviality than in the past.

However complex the material structure of a single individual's life situation is, it is still possible to observe him apart from the rest of the universe. You can talk to him individually and he can talk back to you, but the material structure of the life situation of the *group* is increasingly more complicated. The larger the size of the group the more involved and impenetrable is this material structure. You cannot talk to the group and the group cannot talk back to you. It has no ego. The nature of the warming up process of the group is, if possible, a greater mystery still than that of a single individual, and unless methods are invented by means of which the drama of the group can be mobilized from within and by itself, all efforts at getting to a science of the group may fail more fundamentally than has been the case with the science of the individual.

THE MATERIAL ASPECT OF THE SOCIAL SITUATION

The dynamic logic of social relations is particularly intricate and has remained unconscious with Man because of his maximal proximity and involvement in his own situation. For millennia therefore, the activities of human society perhaps have been a greater mystery to him than every other part of the universe. Because of their greater distance from him he could see the movement of the stars and planets, or the life of the plants and animals, more objectively. Therefore, the science of human society is today hardly as far developed as physics and astronomy were in the minds of Democritos and Ptolemy. It takes enormous sacrifice and discipline to view and accept himself as he is as an individual man, the structure of the individual psyche, its psychodynamics; but the degree of invisibility of the structure of human society, of its sociodynamics, is much greater than that of the single individual. The effort of becoming objective toward the socius encounters many more obstacles than to be objective toward his own individual mind. The involvement of the ego he can still grasp, perhaps he can pretend to know it because it operates within him. The involvement of the socius, however, he cannot pretend to know as it operates outside of him; but it is an outside to which he is inescapably tied.

Sociometry has taught us to recognize that human society is not a figment of the mind, but a powerful reality ruled by a law and order of its own, quite different from any law or order permeating other parts of the universe. It has therefore invented methods called sociometric, by means of which this area can be adequately defined and explored.

The internal, material structure of the group is only in rare instances visible on the surface of social interaction; and if it is, no one knows for certain that the surface structure is the duplicate of the depth structure. In order, therefore, to produce conditions by means of which the depth structure may become visible—operationally—the "organisms" of the group have to turn into "actors"; they have to emerge presently in behalf of a common goal, a point of reference (criterion), and the "environment" or "field" has to turn into specific, action-filled situations, charged with motivating provocations. As even our most minute observations of the interaction may be incomplete, meaningless, or useless to the actors, we must get our actors to act as they would when engaged in actual living. Indeed, we must enter the movement of social living itself and aid them on the spot and in action to increase their flexibility and productivity, to extend their range of reality perception beyond its present orbit. The only productive way to make them reveal their true selves to each other—in reference to a vital criterion—is to find methods by which they can be induced to cocreate naturally. Sociometry has produced several methods of this type. Two illustrations are the sociometric experiment in situ and the sociodrama in situ. They are dynamic forms of social operationism, they define their processes in terms of the action taken by the social actors as they share in common objectives.

Sociometric methods are a synthesis of subjective with objective methods of investigation. A sociometric experiment in situ brings into realization in an unprecedented degree (a) the autonomy of the individual characters, (b) their observation and evaluation by others, (c) measurement of the subjective *and* the objective aspects of their behavior, (d) the autonomy of individual groups and the interaction between them. The same is true about sociodrama; it is a synthesis of subjective and objective methods of investigation: (*a*) the protagonists portray their own experiences in their words and actions but also, (*b*) they are observed and evaluated by others, and (*c*) measurement and recordings of the combined subjective and objective phases of production are made.

The sociometric experiment aims to change the old social order into a new social order. It is a design to rebuild the groups, if necessary, so that the official surface structure is as near as possible to the depth structure. The sociometric test, in its dynamic form, is a revolutionary category of investigation. It upsets the group from within and its relation to other groups; it produces a social revolution on a microscopic scale. If it does not produce an upheaval in some degree, it may arouse suspicion that the investigator has modified it so—in respect for an existing social order—that it becomes a harmless, poverty-stricken instrument.

"One of the reasons why sociometry has been so productive and why it promises more in the future is because it is immediately *useful*. Being useful, it avoids the fictitious flavor of most so-called 'sociological experiments'. . . . A second reason for its success and promise is that it deals with concrete, observable data, with *small social systems*. . . . It would be nice to know all about complicated social systems but it is safe to say that we never shall know very much about them until we have mastered the structure and functioning of simple systems. Then our more inclusive generalizations, which always must be more or less inferential, can be derived, tested, and revised from what we veritably do know about simple, observable, manipulable social systems. . . . Thus it has been, still is, and ever shall be in the physical and biological sciences; thus must it also be in the social sciences" (2).

The Nature of the Warming Up Process and the Experimental Method

We speak, often incautiously, of sociometric generalizations and laws, obviously assuming that there are certain regularities operating in human relations as in other parts of the universe. What justifications can we offer for such a claim? The official arbiter of validation has been the canon of the experimental method, but in the area of human relations the material and the logical part of its inquiry show a conflict difficult to reconcile due to the nature of the warming up process. We shall try now to discuss its nature, how the weakness of the experimental method can be overcome and a new model replace the old.

The warming up process can be defined as *the operational expression of spontaneity.* (Spontaneity is the variable degree of satisfactory response an individual manifests in a situation of a variable degree of novelty.) When undertaking research on the warming up process of the person it is profitable to view the process from the top down: first is the actor, then the organism, and then the act. You cannot produce acts unless you have an organism, and you cannot make your organism productive unless it becomes an actor. (*The organism in the field becomes the actor in situ.*) You cannot study the actor in reverse if he is unable to act in reverse. You cannot study him but along the lines of his productivity emerging at the time of your study. If you induce him—for research reasons—to warm up in a direction for which he is not ready or which is contrary to his inclinations, you introduce an element of artificiality into your "control" which cannot be ironed out adequately by inferential and logical argumentation. The human actor may lose his spontaneity in an instant, and a few moments later he may have a hard time to recall the experience during the act. In order to be adequate in a particular act he should begin to warm up as near to the act as possible and you ought to know when he begins to warm up. (*Rule of the warming up process or active productivity.*) In the warming up process of the group it is best to view all the coactors in situ and to view them in the direction of their productivity. In order to view them you have to move with them, but how can you move with them unless you, the experimenter, are a part of the movement, a coactor? The safest way to be in the warming up process yourself is to become a member of the group. (*Rule of "coaction" of the researcher with group.*) But by becoming a member of the group you are robbed of your role of the investigator who is to be outside of it, projecting, creating, and manipulating the experiment. You cannot be a member and simultaneously a "secret agent" of the experimental method. The way out is to give every member of the group research status, to make them *all* experimenters and to agree with them in the carrying out of a social experiment. If a group has a hundred persons there are now a hundred experimenters and as each is carrying on his "own experiment" there are a hundred experiments and a coordination of each single experiment with every other is required. Sociometry is the sociology of the people, by the people, and for the people; here this axiom is applied to social research itself. (*Rule of universal participation in action.*) But the experimenter, by giving up his identity—what has he gained for the logical part of his inquiry? At first sight it does not seem that he has gained anything. It does not seem that he can set up, in order to prove a hypothesis, two controlled contrasting situations more easily than he could before. But socratically speaking he has gained something: he is having experience, experience in situ; he is learning. As a dialectic movement toward a genuine socioexperimental method of the future he is making slow but real progress. Instead of hurrying to test a hypothesis by quickly constructing a control group versus an experimental group, a pseudo-experiment with pseudo-results, he takes his time for thinking his new situation through. A hypothesis might still be true although never validated. It is better to wait until it can be truly validated instead of unvalidated by validating it prematurely. As time goes on he may become better adjusted to his double role, since he shares it with every member of his group. But when he plans an experiment he may watch his step and not impose it too hastily on the group. Indeed, he should not assume the allures of an experimenter more than any other member. Living in the group he will soon discover that there is a deep discrepancy between the official and the secret behavior of members, that they are in a perennial conflict between official and secret needs, official and secret value systems. (*Rule of dynamic difference in group structure, peripheral versus central.*) He will also soon discover that the individuals are driven at times by private, at other times by collective aspirations, which break up the group into another line of cleavage. (*Group cleavage produced by psycho- and sociostructuring.*) Before any experimental design or any social program is proposed he has to take into account the actual constitution of the group. In order to give every member *adequate* motivation to participate spontaneously, every participant should feel about the experiment that "it is his own cause," that "it is itself a motive, an incentive, a purpose primarily for him (the subject) and not for the one who promotes the idea (the tester, the employer, or any other power agent)," that "it is identical with a life goal (of the subject)," that "it is an opportunity for him to become an active agent in matters concerning his life situation" (13). (*Rule of adequate motivation.*) As his learning expands to knowing how to bore with research ideas from within he may get the idea of being a member of two or more groups, one serving as a control of the other. This should not be an experiment of nature but one consciously and systematically created and projected by the total group. All this, of course, could only happen if the warming up processes of *all* human characters and all participating groups coalesce naturally into an experiment. (*Rule of "gradual" inclusion of all extraneous criteria.*) There are many steps and more barriers which a sensitive crew of coexperimenters might encounter on the way to a scientific utopia. However little or far they advance they never fool themselves and never fool others; they prefer the slow dialectic process of the sociometric experiment in situ to social experiments which are based on inference and logic only.

The sociometric experiment does not base its discoveries upon the interview or "questionnaire" method (a frequent misunderstanding); it is an action method, an action practice. The sociometric researcher assumes the position of the "status nascendi in research"; he is interiorating the experimental method, a participating actor. He insists on sticking to the material inquiry and does not permit himself to step out into the logical part unless he can safely do so. He tries to measure what can be measured, to validate what can be validated, but he disdains measurement and validation for their own sakes. However, measurement is an inherent part of sociometric dialectics. He looks for validation which springs from the material itself without referring to extraneous criteria. The sociometric index, for instance, is a validating index of choice-rejection behavior. Criswell (4) points out that "the patterns obtained are intrinsically meaningful and do not have to be validated by reference to outside criteria." The experimental method could not prove anything beyond what the sociometric index proves.

The fundamental contributions which sociometry has made to the social sciences are its *methods of discovery* in their central area, one in which knowledge was practically nil, the area of interpersonal and intergroup relations. Mill's experimental method is concerned with methods of proof only. In a healthy, developing natural science, methods of discovery come first, methods of proof later. Methods of proof should grow naturally out of the methods of discovery. Mill's canon of the experimental method has grown out of physics, constructed to meet the needs of *its* methods of discovery. The social sciences need to invent methods of proof indigenous to the structure of its material. The sociometric methods of discovery are numerous and still growing. (1. Acquaintance test—acquaintance index—acquaintance diagram. 2. Sociometric test—sociometric index—sociogram or sociomatrix. 3. Role test—role index—role diagram. 4. Interaction test—interaction index—interaction diagram. 5. Spontaneity test—spontaneity quotient—spontaneity scales. 6. Psychodrama—recording—process analysis. 7. Sociodrama—recording—process analysis. 8. The living newspaper. 9. The therapeutic motion picture. 10. Total action research in situ.)

In sociometric group analysis *several factors* are jointly used. Sociometry is not a single factor method. The sociometric test explores only *one* factor, attraction, rejection or tele; the spontaneity tests explores spontaneity, the S factor; the role test, the role factor. Through painstaking, direct investigation of small groups we may learn to explore smaller and smaller systems (microsociometry) and gradually tackle larger and larger social systems (macrosociometry), until the whole of human society can be treated like a single system. Sociometry is to a large extent a classificatory science, and generalizations can be made on the basis of such classifications. Geography and geology are examples of other classificatory sciences. Their counterpart within sociometry is psychological geography or sociography. Some day a psychological geography of our planetary human population will be drawn without any reference to outside criteria. In fact, as soon as the whole field can be tackled as a unit, the cause-effect relation as well as any other relation may be visible; then there will not be any criterion left outside of it and the experimental method will not be necessary for proof. It can be hypothecated about God that He gets a picture of the whole universe in an instant. Metaphorically, God might be called a sociometrist on a cosmic scale. All criteria which are for men exterior are for Him interior. God does not need an experimental method in order to prove a hypothesis about a cause-effect relationship; He can see it with His own eyes.

In the course of sociometric research we often encounter naturally contrasting situations of which we take advantage. But the dilemma of the warming up process comes into play when the experimenter is trying to *create* contrasting situations, a combination of factors desirable for logical inquiry, arranging the conditions in the community so that they fit the requirements of precise control. As sociometric consciousness grows, the people and their governments will co-operate and participate in social research. But human beings cannot be manipulated like rats and forced into the combinations required without a gross error being introduced into the experiment. By the experimental conditioning the individuals may be *changed,* their warming up processes may be distorted. Therefore, the experiment does not measure what it intends to measure. Sooner or later the individuals, due to the spontaneous inclinations and the constellations of the warming up process, may regress to their pre-experimental state of mind.

The sociometric method offers a solution to this dilemma. In the sociometric experiment a new set of rules has been generated. (1) The experiment has to be carried out in situ, that is, in their localities, in the setting in which the human characters are most spontaneous, to which they are most intensively warmed up and about which they know most from their own experiences. Because of the nature of the warming up process, if the human characters are forcibly removed from the scene of their loves and crimes, the value of their communications—even if they are made in honesty—cannot be considered as of equal value. This condition may change in a sociometric society as spontaneity training becomes integrated into its institutional processes. (2) All human characters of the group or the community are investigators of the situation they have in common. As such they may assume different functions in the experimental setup but no individual is left out from the research crew, just as nobody should be left out from receiving food and shelter. This is in total contradiction with a current fashion in experimentation that there is no need for the people themselves to be present as part of the experiment and that there is no need for the experimenter himself to perform the actual experiment. The ex post facto design is not an experiment in the true sense of the word. The exponents of this type of research, shrinking away from the difficulties of the direct action approach, fearful of the involvements of the present and that they may not be able to get a precise answer from nature when meeting it face to face, retreat into the graveyards of the past. This is the greatest triumph for Mill's dictum that the social sciences are unable to apply the experimental method to their data. The physical autocrat has been able to order around and manipulate to his scientific pleasure physical objects, plants, and lower animals. But his successor, "the social autocrat," the higher he went up the evolutionary ladder, the more unremunerative the research became.

It is therefore not due to the inferiority of social science as a natural science that Mill's canon cannot be applied; he offered the wrong model. The new model, the sociometric experiment in situ, is in its infancy but it holds great promise. Mill, like many of his modern followers a spectator sociologist, looked at the social universe with the detachment of an astronomer who looks at the universe of stars and said: No. Marx, an actor sociologist, little conscious of experimental designs said: Yes. Whence come these two diametrically opposed positions? The reasons are about as follows: the great religious experimenters in situ, Buddha, Christ, and Ghandi, the social utopists, Fourier and Owen; the social realists, Marx and Lenin—however unreconcilable their various approaches—knew something about the nature of the warming up process, the spontaneity of the individual and of the masses. They knew intuitively that an experimental design of society to be successful must follow closely and anticipate a design of living which is in a dreamlike way inherent in the people. Although they never had the intention of validating their hypothetical social orders, they contributed infinitely more to whatever knowledge the social sciences have accumulated to date than all the artificially constructed social experiments put together.

In the widest sense of the word there are two types of social research: the peripheral, external, indirect, pseudo-objective versus the central, internal, direct, subjective-objective type. There are two extreme sociological imperatives: (1) Mankind may *passively* wait for the day when the scientific utopia project of social research has completed its task; (2) Mankind may, now and here, *actively* take its social destiny in its own hands—initiate experiments and simultaneously check their validity.

THE OLD AND NEW MODEL OF THE EXPERIMENTAL METHOD

The transition from the old to the new model of experimentation is no easy task. Some of the problems which the material structure of the new model imposes upon the imagination of the investigator are here, because of their importance, illustrated in detail by a comparison between two sociometrically oriented studies ("Advances in Sociometric Technique," Moreno-Jennings (19), and "An Experimental Approach to the Study of Autocracy and Democracy," Lewin-Lippitt (7)). The theoretical and experimental background for a crucial phase in both studies was Moreno's "Who Shall Survive?" (13), one of whose chief concerns was to show by means of sociometric tests the contrast between authoritarian and spontaneous group structure in all the classrooms throughout a school community, and in a reformatory throughout all the homes and workshops. The appearance of the Moreno studies ranged from 1931 to 1936. The last study concerned with authoritative and sociometric structure appeared in February, 1936. The first report of Lewin and Lippitt appeared early in 1938. One would expect, therefore, some progress or change in approach. The comments to the Lewin-Lippitt study are here strictly *limited to the use of sociometric and role-playing methods,* the relevance they may have for the problem of the equation of groups and the creating of new experimental groups. It is beyond my intention to judge as to the significance of other variables (teacher ratings of social behavior, school records, socioeconomic status, etc.) and as to the final value of the brilliant study. For the sake of brevity, I will refer to the two studies by mentioning the initials of the collaborators, M-J and L-L.

The initial procedure in both studies is similar, "A preliminary sociometric survey was made of the affinities and rejections existing in the two classrooms. . . . Such data might always be analyzed with a double frame of reference, that of the individual group member and of the group as a dynamic unity." (L-L) The objectives are similar: to study, among other things, the difference between "autocratic and democratic" (L-L), "authoritative and sociometric" (M-J) group structure. The *difference* begins with the following proposition of Lewin-Lippitt, "Instead of utilizing the groups in schools, clubs, factories, one should create groups experimentally. . . . With a sociogram of each group at hand the groups were selected (one from each schoolroom) from the available volunteers so that the groups would be as nearly equated as possible on the number of potency of friendship and rejection relationships. . . . Instead of choosing a clique of close friends five children were chosen in each case who had expressed little relationship with each other, either in the school situation or in playing together in nonschool groupings. . . . In a ten-minute preliminary meeting with each group the leader made it clear that the aim of the club would be to make theatrical masks (a new activity for all of the children). . . . Two half-hour meetings a week were held with each group, the same experimenter being the leader in both clubs." (L-L) It appears that Lewin-Lippitt followed the sociometric model up to a certain point but then returned to Mill's model of the experimental method. By doing this they were caught in a tailspin of unreality and artificiality. In comparison, let us take a look at Moreno-Jennings' study. It dealt with the grouping of children in a dining room. This situation was not "created" by the experimenters, but it was in the nature of the situation that the children had to be arranged in some manner for their meal. An authoritatively run community (a reformatory for girls) was submitted to a sociometric experiment. The sociometric test took place in the living quarters, workshops, schoolrooms, and among other places, in every dining room. Every sociogram showed how the democratic process would run in dramatic contrast with the existing authoritative organization. In the specific dining room in which this study was made there were twenty-one girls and they were just getting ready to eat. A record was made of the order in which they were seated, as we expected to find here the results of a dictatorial policy, an authoritative structure of grouping. A "technique of placement is one applied strictly from the point of view of the authoritative supervisor of the dining room. She places them in such a fashion that they produce the least trouble to her, without regard to the way the girls themselves feel about the placements." (M-J) Tabulation A is a record of the authoritatively determined grouping. A second experiment was made in order to discover the most spontaneous structure of the group, a "complete laissez faire" (M-J) in which the authoritative supervisor was removed from the dining room and the girls were told to feel entirely unrestrained and to sit down wherever they wished; a laissez faire structure resulted: "We may let them place themselves as they wish and watch the result. A girl 'A' seats herself at Table 1; eight girls who are drawn to her try to place themselves at the same table. But Table 1 can hold only three more. The result is a struggle and somebody has to interfere and arrange them in some arbitrary manner. A girl 'B' runs to Table 2, but nobody attempts to join her; thus three places at the table remain unused." (M-J) The laissez faire test produced confusion: "We find that the technique of letting the girls place themselves works out to be impracticable. It brings forth difficulties which enforce arbitrary, authoritative interference with their wishes, the opposite principle from the one which was intended, a free, democratic, individualistic process." (M-J) A final experiment was set up, a sociometric, democratic

TABULATION A
Original Seating Arrangement — Authoritarian

Table 1	Table 3	Table 5
Belle	Flora	Anna
Dorothy	Pearl	Harriet
Angeline	Ida	Grace
	Evelyn	Edith

Table 2	Table 4	Table 6
Beth	Clarissa	Kathryn
Rose	Helen	Lena
May	Gladys	Ellen
		Mary

TABULATION B
New Seating Arrangement — Sociometric

Table 1	Table 3	Table 5
Belle	Kathryn	Dorothy
Anna	Pearl	Mary
Edith	Grace	Beth
Harriet	Ida	

Table 2	Table 4	Table 6
Helen	Flora	May
Angeline	Ellen	Rose
Gladys	Lena	Clarissa
	Evelyn	

EXPLANATORY NOTE

The placement analysis of the two tabulations A and B shows that of the twenty-one girls seated under the influence of the authoritative supervisor, only three (14%), Belle (Table 1), Ida, and Pearl (Table 3) sit at the same table after the results of the sociometric test were considered. See Sociograms, p. 79 and 80.

Note that in the laissez faire test Table 1 was crowded by nine girls although it could not place but four; Table 2 had only one girl although it could have seated three more. See Sociogram, p. 77.

method of procedure: "to ask the girls with whom they want to sit at the same table, and, if every table seats at least four, to give every girl three choices; to tell them that every effort will be made that each may have at her table at least one of her choices, and, if possible, her first choice. . . . The structure of affinities one for another is charted. The best possible relationship available within the structure of interrelations defines the optimum of placement. (Tabulation B) . . . It is a matter of principle to give every girl the best possible placement regardless of what her record may be or what experience the housemother may have had in regard to any two girls who want to sit together at the same table. We do not begin with prejudice but wait to see how their conduct turns out." (M-J) Our hy-- pothesis was that by means of this method we may get an insight into the spontaneous democratic structure and will be able to compare the deviations from the laissez faire and the authoritative structure of grouping, as portrayed in the sociograms of each. The experiment was carried on longitudinally; the test was repeated at intervals of eight weeks. The sociometric data were quantified and the sociometric indices between the intervals compared.

Let us now examine critically both experiments. In the Lewin-Lippitt experiment a sociometric test was applied to the children in the classrooms. The experimenters do not specify clearly what criterion was used, an unfortunate omission. A superficial reader might get the impression that it is *not* important which criterion is used, that it is comparatively easy to arrive at a sociogram of attractions and rejections. However, using *no* criterion or a very *weak* criterion, the findings portrayed in the sociogram may not reveal sufficiently the structure of the group. They proceeded then to nearly *equate* the groups on the basis of the sociograms. Five children who showed as little relationship as possible were chosen from each group. From the point of view of a rigorous analysis of what a sociometric equation entails, Lewin-Lippitt's effort was unsatisfactory. One gains the impression that their experience with reading sociograms was too small to warrant an effort at equating the two groups. In addition, they did not attempt the "positive" equation of two groups (that is, the comparison of their actual configuration) but what might be called a "negative" equation, calling two groups of individuals nearly equated because "little relationship" was found between them in the sociogram. That leaves the whole idea of sociometric equation hanging in the air. What does "little relationship" mean, sociometrically? These two sets of individuals might have shown in regard to a dozen other criteria a great deal of relationship which the experimenters should have tested before they called the two groups equated and made them the basis for a serious application of the experimental method. Individuals who form one structure in a home group may form a different one in a work group and a very different one again in a recreational group. The experimenters do not imply that they have compared the sociograms of the two groups in reference to sociograms resulting from other criteria. A number of vital criteria should be used before any opinion can be reached that the children chosen for each club have little or no relationship, particularly before such a gravely loaded word as "equated" is in science can be used. One can say that the foundations of the study were not well laid, thus making the conclusions drawn from the whole experiment spurious, even from the point of view of logical inquiry. Another negligence is the omission of sociometrizing the two clubs of five individuals before the experiment was begun. If one "creates groups experimentally" he should know what he has created. The experimenters might have found that the two groups of children, when sociometrized in reference to the new criterion of making masks, would have produced sociograms which would have shown a great many relationships among them. Furthermore, differences in sociometric structure in reference to the maskmaking criterion itself would have been found. Some of the children may have had a greater skill for the activity of maskmaking, some may have shown little skill or interest. Such an analysis suggests how dangerous predominantly logical manipulation is and how easily an experimenter, when moving away from the material structure of the group, loses contact with its realities and is tricked by a game of words and numbers. It also stands to reason that the sociometric tests should have been repeated before every experimental phase, to see what changes had taken place in the structure of the two clubs before, after, and between sessions. It appears as if the experiments have been done without the currently operating dynamics of the group being known. Even if interviews and observations of the children were used, their feelings for each other and the picture of the total structure of their relationships would not have been attained without repeated sociometric surveys. Such surveys might have revealed that maskmaking Club 1 and maskmaking Club 2 produced sociograms which were far from being equated. The experimenters may have found, for instance, that one of the maskmaking sociograms was from the start characterized by an autocratic type of structure, one of the children being the center of choices; the other set might have shown to have started with a more democratic distribution of the choices and rejections. The initial sociometric picture of the two clubs might have influenced or resisted the experiment of autocratic and democratic atmospheres in one or another direction. The negligence of omitting these sociometric tests to start with clouded the validity of the conclusions. This does not exclude the possibility that the hypotheses of autocratic and democratic atmospheres could be true. In fact, it had already been fairly well demonstrated by my own study in Hudson, showing the contrasting structure between authoritatively arranged and sociometrically arranged groups. It was the unsatisfactory manipulation of sociometric data by Lewin and Lippitt which was at fault, and this brings us straight back to the problem of the warming up process of the children before the experimental situation of maskmaking was initiated. We know from reading sociograms that if you take one or more individuals out of a group—depending, of course, upon their positions within it—the rest of the sociogram does not remain the same but undergoes almost instantly a revolutionary change. By taking out five individuals the remaining members redirect their outgoing attractions and repulsions and a considerable struggle between the key individuals might be the result. On the other hand, the five individuals going out of a group and forming a new one, being cut out of an older group in which they may have had strong attractions or rejections towards certain individuals, redirected their own warming up processes toward the individuals who were available in the new group. They had no choice but to operate or interact with the individuals available in the maskmaking club. This restraint was not one of their own choice, but imposed upon both the autocratic and democratic clubs by the experimenters.

Now let us examine the two maskmaking experiments themselves. Several experimenters were used in each of the two cases to assume either an autocratic or democratic role toward the participants of each club. This resembles psychodramatic work on the reality level. The difficulty here again is not in the logical manipulation but just the opposite; there is an excess of logical manipulation, one of the weaknesses of Lewin's experiments with human relations. The difficulty is chiefly in a lack of directness and concreteness as to the material structure of the experiment. The first loophole is the playing of two opposite roles by the same person. This is in psychodramatic work known as an "auxiliary ego" playing at two different occasions different roles. It is known among psychodramatists that it requires considerable training for an auxiliary ego to stick to a persistent pattern of one role over a period of time. The difficulty is increased if the same person is to embody two different roles alternatingly. Lewin and Lippitt do not state that the auxiliary egos or leaders had received role training as autocratic or democratic leaders, that they had learned to remove their own private biases and spontaneous inclinations, that they had learned to keep the two roles neatly apart. They may have done so, but at the time of their publication the ideas of role training and the warming up process, the private involvements of the auxiliary ego and the effect of a role production upon group structure, in other words, psychodramatic theory and practice, was known to a small group of students only. The question is therefore, how adequately were the experimenters *able* to perform in these roles? How were they selected and trained in the taking of roles? This is a grave omission because auxiliary egos often have deep involvements in regard to some roles and little in regard to others. What guarantee do we have that the experimenters were not excellently disposed for the role of the democratic leader, but very poorly disposed for the role of the autocratic leader, or vice versa? Thus they might have influenced the outcome of the experiment by their role behavior, being stronger in the presentation of one or the other role. Depending upon his own role structure, the weight of his personal influence might have favored the autocratic or the democratic atmosphere of the experiment. In addition, many performers, in the process of role taking, give lip service to democratic principles but in their gestures and bearing are autocratic—or the reverse may be true. A careful description of these psychological problems was therefore required.

Summing up the critique of the Lewin-Lippitt experiment, they must be commended for having recognized the problem; they failed because of insufficient material inquiry into the sociometric situation. With the advent of sociometry the group as a dynamic structural unit was discovered. In the equating of two groups this had to be taken into account. The equating in the old manner on the basis of individual characteristics and traits of their members—like intelligence, economic status, nationality, sex, religion, occupation, and so forth—had become unsatisfactory.

Let us in turn examine the Moreno-Jennings experiment. The problem of sociometric equation was not new at the time of Lewin-Lippit's research. I dealt with it in my studies of sociometric group structures as they deviate from chance (20). To my surprise I found then that sociometric equation is full of loopholes which one has to learn to avoid. The same two social configurations, which appeared nearly equated quantitatively in number of choices received or given, appeared structurally unequated in number of isolates, unreciprocated pairs, chains, triangles, leader structures. Furthermore, a careful inquiry into the material situation indicates that the equation of two groups from the point of view of their dynamic structure is not sufficient if a single factor only, the sociometric index, is considered. The dynamic structure of groups is far more complex. Their respective acquaintance diagrams (13), role diagrams (15, 16, 21), action diagrams (10), spontaneity scales, have to be explored with a view of equating them in regard to the basic dimensions which determine their living structure. Such rigorous insistence upon *precision of the "material" inquiry* makes logical manipulation and "matching for precision of control" (3, 6) difficult. But it is better that we face the problem than that we delude ourselves. "The social configurations portrayed in our sociograms are elementary and rough in texture compared with the complex relationships, rhythms, and tempos operating within a living social aggregate. With the devising of new sociometric techniques and with the improvement of the present instruments, the more subtle and more mature processes—the economic milieu, the religious milieu, the cultural milieu, which operate within social aggregates—will be made increasingly comprehensible. It is our contention that these entities (economy, religion, or culture), whatever the logic of their existence may be, cannot be so impersonal as to exist independent of the societies in which the persons actually think, live, and act. These processes must express themselves within living social aggregates although their interaction may be more difficult to trace. It is to the comprehension of these richly textured, integrated, and fully matured configurations that sociometric work aspires" (20). That may explain my ever groping for and inventing of new instruments as psychodrama, sociodrama, axiodrama, in order to gain a more complete picture of the social systems nearest to ourselves.

It is significant that the two groups which Lewin and Lippitt tried to equate consisted of five children each, the two groups of Moreno and Jennings of 21 children each—in both cases extremely small groups; and at both times the equation ended in failure: in the first instance because of premature logical manipulation, in the second because of insistence on further material inquiry, postponing the equating indefinitely until it could be tried with a reasonable expectation of validity. Looking from here at a vast number of projects in social research now under way in many places which pretend to be of particularly high scientific order because the experimental method of inquiry is used, we notice that these projects usually deal with large numbers of people and the analysis of many factors and that they neglect in their matching of individuals the sociodynamic effects of group structure. But what is true about the miniature groups described above must be equally true for large groups, and probably more true the larger the groups are. I do not doubt for a moment the earnestness of such students and their hope that someday, somewhere, what they do will be helpful. But when a science is young and in need of elementary information, logical elegance can be just as tragi-comic as a child crying for food and the mother feeding him with dolls instead. As an illustration for this trend in research I may quote from F. Stuart Chapin's recent book (3)—it is an ex post facto experimental design which he describes—"The working hypothesis of this study was: A greater degree of progress in high school leads to a correspondingly higher degree of economic adjustment in the community. . . . This experiment was based upon the high school records and community experiences of 2,127 boys and girls who left four St. Paul high schools in the school year of 1926, as graduates or after having completed from one to three years of their high school course. . . . In this study an attempt was made to hold constant six factors that would influence eventual economic adjustment if they were allowed to vary. . . . *we have made approximately equal* six factors—fathers' occupation, parents' nationality, neighborhood status, sex, age in years, and average high school grades. . . . The purpose of the Christiansen study was to isolate the presumed cause-and-effect relationship between length of exposure to high school education as a cause (from 1922 to 1926) and economic adjustment as the effect (as found in 1935.)"

The structure of the socius has no place in such studies. The "relevant" factors are individual and social traits which often are chosen as arbitrarily as the trivial hypotheses themselves (for instance, low housing standards and rentals as cause, increased tuberculosis death rate as effect; length of high school education as cause, high degree of economic adjustment as effect). The experimenter himself is replaced by an examiner of files and records, the "experimentees" are left out, and replaced by the social ghosts of their vital statistics. It is a refined form of population research and an ingenious exercise in logical manipulations—it could be called therefore "demometry" (Demos-people, metrum measure), but it has nothing to do with the most vital form of sociometry in which the socius and the metrum are treated with equal intensity. (Sociometry, broadly considered, includes, as Ernest W. Burgess pointed out in his "Sociological Research Methods" in the Special Semicentennial Issue of *The American Journal of Sociology,* Vol. L, No. 6, May 1945, besides the group of chief exponents of sociometry (J. L. Moreno, Helen H. Jennings, Joan H. Criswell, George A. Lundberg, Charles P. Loomis, Leslie D. Zeleny, Merle E. Bonney, Mary L. Northway, Stuart C. Dodd, W. I. Newstetter, among others) the work of F. Stuart Chapin, Emory S. Bogardus, and the field theoretical approach of Kurt Lewin. Bogardus' opinion in "Measurement of Person-Group Relations," SOCIOM-

ETRY, Volume 10, Number 4, p. 306, coincides with that of Burgess, "The social distance approach may be viewed as a form of sociometrics . . . " Chapin considers his work as a form of sociometry, *Ibid.*, pp. 23-28. I am taking exception here, however, to Chapin's change in definition of what sociometry is. By identifying it with social measurement at large he deflates its meaning. When I coined and defined sociometry, the study of the socius was given the central position. In Chapin's definition the metrum moves into the center, and the socius is pushed into the periphery, or entirely out of material existence. Dialectically speaking the sociometry which treats socius and metrum with equal intensity should be considered as the nucleus of all sociometric inquiry. In its periphery belongs the work of Bogardus as a projective method in *sociometry,* Chapin's work as a form of *demometry*.)

Florian Znaniecki has clarified some aspects of this problem, "There seem to be two reasons why sociologists have been more susceptible to the influence of mathematical dogmatism than biologists, chemists, or experimental physicists. In the social field mathematics was applied first to demographic statistics, whose original assumption was that the human individual is an ultimate 'indivisible' entity and that consequently every collective phenomenon is a mere sum of individual phenomena. The majority of sociologists, however, are by now fully aware that the human individual as member of a collectivity is not an independent unit but a participant in collective systems and processes and that the main task of mathematical methods in sociology is the quantitative analysis of such systems and processes. A step toward the final elimination of this old source of confusion is the recent development of sociometry—a method of research with important, though as yet only partly realized, possibilities."

THE SOCIOMETRIC MODEL OF EXPERIMENT AND MARXIAN SOCIOLOGY

In his "Theses on Feuerbach" Marx coined a phrase, "The philosophers have only *interpreted* the world in various ways; the point however is to *change* it." This quotation may lead us straight into his theory and practice of social revolution. But we are not interested here in this aspect of Marxism (18). It may also lead us to consider what contribution Marxian sociology has made toward the experimental method. This is our concern. We may give this phrase a new slant by saying: the only sure way of finding out *the basic structure of human society* is by trying to change it. But Marx was, at least consciously, not interested in finding out what "the basic structure of human society is;" he did not know that it had one. He wished to change it by applying the instruments of social revolution as he had constructed them. He possessed too honest an intellect and was too great a realist not to wish to know the full truth about the problems of social relations to which he had dedicated his whole life; but he thought that he knew already what human society needs. The changer in him was at times more powerful than the researcher. Throughout his writings there is a conflict visible between the two. His critical mind did not stay contented with any particular blueprint of a social revolution. He was revising his theories continuously. It would be worth while to explore the anti-Marx in Marx. Because of this wavering between the two extremes, Marx came in fleeting moments of intuition closer to the idea of a genuine social experiment than many of his adversaries. Marx did not realize, however, that human society had a structure of its own which can be investigated and determined with a high degree of precision. For him human society was like an immense target, a vast field seething with human action. He explored the forces and ideologies which "entered" into this field. But human society as such was for him an amorphous, undifferentiated mass of individuals and events, exposed to these powerful ideological forces he had discovered. Economic institutions like capitalism; cultural institutions like religion, family; political institutions like forms of government, their origin and evolution throughout history and the social stratifications they caused—they were the foci of his dialectic materialism. But that human society had a social structure of its own which required special instruments for investigation and for change did not enter into his mental perspective. He could see only the reflection of an intense struggle between two ideological forces, capital and labor. It may be said that he, perhaps the greatest realist of the evaluation of social forces impinging upon human society from the outside, was an irrealist and an illusionist as far as the "inside" structure of human society is concerned. But it is from this plane that an explanation can be derived for the irrational character of the social revolutions which he, Engels, Lenin, and Trotzky have instigated.

Marx proposed to deal with real people in the actual world and to cure their most pressing problems. As we see, unfortunately for the world, he did not engage himself deeply enough with material inquiry. He had little respect for the individual and for small social units. He suffered from an excess of revolutionary dogmatism, just as some contemporary sociologists suffer from an excess of logical dogmatism. His faith in social change and social justice was greater than his desire for patient investigation of the delicate and detailed material structure of the human situation. Marx had a practical idea of what genuine experiment is like, but he resembled the prescientific physician who had to apply remedies to the ailing body without knowing its anatomy, histology, and physiology.

The Marxist revolutionists do not wait for the "event" to happen. They fear delay of the uprising of the masses, or even that this may never happen, and so they *produce* it by instigating and arousing them (and they call this process the "will" of the masses). Therefore, up to a certain point, the social revolutionists create unconsciously the atmosphere of a sociometric experiment: they turn the collective life situation—where it is, in situ— into a social laboratory. But the revolutionary operation is carried out in the dark; the interindividual and sociodynamic structure of the masses involved in the action are unknown—except for certain ideological premises and the role structure on the surface—certain key individuals in the "role" of the laborer versus others in the "role" of the capitalist. The danger of the Marxist actionists is that when they instigate and arouse the masses they may stir them up to *more* action than they are spontaneously inclined and to more than they can eventually control. The result is that not only the revolutionary gains (if there are any) are of doubtful value—they do not know when a relapse or a regression to a prerevolutionary or worse state might take place, but also the social analysis itself is bound to be faulty and full of indissoluble implications because they do not know when the revolutionary action was started, what structure the masses had in statu nascendi, nor the specific dynamic factors operating within them.

II.

GROUP FORMATION AND SOCIAL DYNAMICS

THE ATOMIC THEORY IN THE SOCIAL SCIENCES
(1949)

The chief arguments of sociometry are theoretical not practical. An aspect of sociometric theory frequently neglected is the problem of *nearness*. The sociometric test is a social nearness test, a proximity test. It has often been confused with some of its peripheral developments, with social "distance" tests. But social distance is "diluted" nearness. The greater the distance, the more diluted it becomes. Distance, unrelated to nearness encourages social symbolism, social nominalism, in short, social unreality. Symbolic relations are by no means overlooked in sociometric theory but they should be seen in their proper place, within *the framework of nearness-distance polarity*.

The problem of distance is also related to the phenomenon of projection and transference; these three complement one another. Distance-projection-transference should be treated together. They have caused the pseudo-universalism and the pseudo-atomism of the past. In the physical sciences the distance of the human self from the physical atom, the infinitely small—and from the physical universe, the infinitely great, is so infinite and indefinite that it becomes unreal. The unreality of the infinitely large and infinitely small was recognized by physicists but they did not develop anything by means of which they could replace them. Einstein's relativity theory does not fill the gap, it merely points up its existence and formulates a theory of the unreality of the universalia.

In the social sciences the situation of the self is different from the situation which it has encountered in physics, it is reversed. Nearness comes first, nearness must be guarded, nearness is its first theoretical problem. The vanishing of atomism in physics and biology should be of no consequence for the social sciences. It should *not* be extended to the social sciences mechanically as it has been signalized by Gestalt and Field theorists. The atom in sociometry is not a theoretical construct of an infinitely distant event of smallness, but the scientific demonstration of the nearest, warmest, most proximate social reality. The physical atom and the social atom are at opposite poles. Microphysics and microsociology may be analogous—from the point of view of "system"—but represent totally different phenomena.

"Universalia Sunt Realia", this was the lifeline of the religious middle ages. Modern science, under the leadership of physics has destroyed the old credo. It is because of this event that we live today in a period of transition, in a world which has no universalia and no realia, no theory of the universe and no theory of the atom. But the sociometries are moving towards overcoming this calamity. By the third millennium or thereabout a new position will crystallize. It will be a reversal of the old. It will change into "Realia Sunt Universalia". With the smallest things, the social atoms, becoming real also the largest things, the universe, will become real again. With atomism returning universalism will be rediscovered. Indeed, *the leadership in scientific method and discovery which has been for nearly two and a half thousand years in the hands of physicists will pass to social scientists, and just as the social sciences were dependent upon the physical sciences for hypothesis and methods, the social sciences will some day help the physical sciences to understand and run the physical universe.*

ORGANIZATION OF THE SOCIAL ATOM

(1936)

The number of acquaintances which an individual has at the time of testing has been called by me his "acquaintance volume". A person may remember about many of these individuals only that he has met them or talked with them. Most of them, however, do not matter to him, do not mean anything personal to him. And he doesn't matter to them; he doesn't mean anything to them, at least at the moment. But among these acquaintances there is a small group who mean something personal to him, in some degree and in respect to some criterion; he is attracted to them or he rejects them. There may be in this group, whether he knows it or not individuals to whom he means something, who are attracted to him or who reject him. If we compare this acquaintance volume with the physiological cell we may say that the general pattern of acquaintances which are without individual meaning for him is like the cytoplasm, and the meaningful acquaintances like the nucleus of the cell. *Often the boundary between the outer mass and the nucleus of acquaintances may not be absolute.* There may be some individual about whom it cannot be said with finality whether he is already an acquaintance or merely a mass-symbol, whether he is a mere acquaintance or already an emotional partner. But the general demarcation line between the nucleus of emotionally related individuals which I termed the "social atom" and the rest of the acquaintance volume will be very clear. The partnership may be directly emotional or it may be occupational, cultural or spiritual, without any intensive emotionality; or it may be social, two people linked together, for instance, merely because a person to whom he is related is related to the other, in whatever fashion.

The point of transition from being a mere acquaintance to becoming an emotional partner in a social atom is theoretically significant. A study of numerous social atoms reveals a definite line of demarcation between the acquaintance volume and the social nucleus proper, the "social threshold". We can say that the moment that I wish a certain acquaintance—an individual whom I have just met or whom I may have known for some time—to become closer to me, to enter into a relationship with me, more or less permanent in respect to some criterion, work, love, or whatever, this person has passed the social threshold of my social atom. The same can be said about individuals who wish to enter into a relationship with me, whether I reciprocate their desire or not. They also have passed the threshold of my social atom. To my social atom evidently would belong all individuals to whom I am bound by an invisible desire which may be little or not at all manifest; also those individuals to whom I am tied in actual overt relationships. Indeed, we here see the social atom itself further subdivided into two parts: the outer part of the nucleus formed by the "wished" for relationships and the inner part of the nucleus formed by the actualized ones. These may have been once wished for or they may once have been neutral and now found desirable. This indicates that the two sociometries, the one on the spontaneous level and the other on the reality level are closely interwoven and in continuous interaction. However small and inconsistent the realized portion may be, within the social atom they form a natural unity. It is only within our social and cultural institutions that they appear in disconcert.

The emotional currents which, so to speak, pervade a social atom are of varying intensity. There are many levels of preference. We made a study of the factors contributing to this uneven distribution of preferences, or better said, the uneven intensity of feeling preferences. For a certain social situation (choosing of house-members), the majority of the subjects made full use of their choices. Some did not have enough with five preferences.* But a considerable number did not use the full five choices, and a very few chose but one or none at all.

In our usual procedure the individuals tested expressed five degrees of preference, but they did not suggest how many individuals they liked *equally*

---

* See *"Who Shall Survive?"* p. 94 concerning the exercise of full, unrestricted spontaneity of choices.

well. Therefore a series of tests was subsequently made in which the emphasis was slightly differently placed. The subjects were instructed: "As you choose, weigh carefully whether you would like two or three individuals to live with you equally well. You may like two or three persons 'first choice,' or two or three persons 'second choice'; or all the persons to whom you are attracted may be the same degree of choice; or there may be just one 'first choice' and the rest in other degrees, perhaps each at a different degree of preference." The results showed again several levels of preference but often *several individuals at the same level of preference.* In regard to work a certain young woman named one person first, a man; three persons second, two women and a man; in regard to living in the same house she named no one, preferring to live alone; in regard to love she named one man first and four men second; in regard to social and cultural contact she named ten persons with whom she liked to associate equally well.

RELATIONS TOWARD THINGS VS. RELATION TOWARDS PERSONS

Evidently there are individuals whose feelings of preference are more articulate than those of others. Also, some may have more articulate preferences in respect to one criterion, for instance, work. However, it seemed to us that the wide differences of preferential feeling which individuals reveal who are of similar intelligence and under similar environmental influences cannot be explained satisfactorily by simply calling them more or less articulate. There must be other factors of persistent influence.

Now there are besides the preferences for individuals the preferences for things, objects, values, and objectives, like sex, food, money, ideas, etc. A sociometric test was constructed in which the subjects spontaneously reveal in order of preference the things to which they are attracted: for instance, money, sex, clothes, automobiles, books, etc. An analysis of the results and their comparison with the type and degrees of preference for individuals which these subjects showed raised the question: What bearing has the greater or lesser affinity toward individuals upon the classification of character? Are there any definite quantitative classifiable relationships between the affinities which an individual has toward persons and the affinities he has toward other things? Does the sense of affinity of an individual for other individuals diminish as his affinity for things and ideas increases, or vice versa?

To illustrate, let us consider one of the subjects who cares for money most of all and exclusively, being indifferent toward all other things and giving as a reason that with money he can buy all that he wants. It can be

SOCIAL ATOM

Nucleus of persons emotionally related to the subject
(outer and inner nucleus)

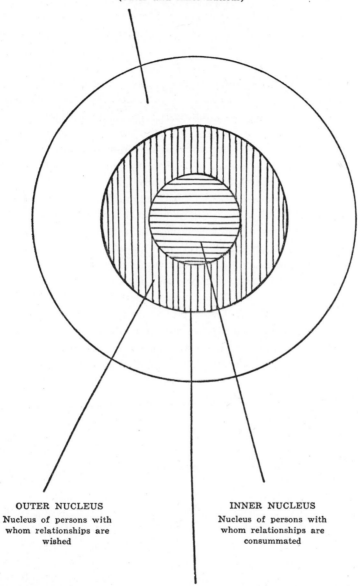

OUTER NUCLEUS

Nucleus of persons with
whom relationships are
wished

INNER NUCLEUS

Nucleus of persons with
whom relationships are
consummated

ACQUAINTANCE VOLUME—Acquaintances which are without emotional meaning for
the subject; it is the larger area of "social" contacts from which he can draw his emotional
partners; "outside" of the acquaintance volume extends the area of symbolic-mass contacts.

well seen that in the case of a person who has such an affection for money
the persons with whom he would like to work would matter little; that he
would not feel any special preference for one or another person so long as
these persons equally support his affection for money. He may divide the
persons into those who aid him in getting money and those who are of dis-
advantage to him in this respect.

The sociometric test for interrelations with persons is modified in the
manner described so that it becomes a sociometric test for interrelations with
things. The two tests will provide for two measures: the affinities of an
individual for persons and the affinities of the same individual for things.
The correlation of these two types of affinities will gradually develop a
measure of the *sociometric character* of an individual. So much for the
individual. In regard to the group, and society as a whole, it promises
to accomplish a dream, cherished by many but discarded as futile and
impractical: the synthesis of the socio-organic concept of society with
the economic concept of society, the inclusion of economics into sociometry.

It is probable that there will be found a close relation between the
tendency to have a strong affinity for persons and the tendency to have a
weak affinity for things; and vice versa, the tendency to have a strong affinity
for things and a weak affinity for persons. It is from such studies that we
shall be able to estimate the quantitative difference between levels of preference, as for example the difference between a first and a second choice.

An individual may show strong interest in the ideal of love, and urged
by it may act with equal kindness toward everyone regardless of his specific
individuality. An individual may show a great interest in power over things
and people—for instance, for money as conferring the power to buy—and
he may act with equal eagerness to gain money for himself regardless of the
specific individualities of the people from whom he has to wrest it. An
individual may show a great interest in sensuous pleasures, for instance, sex,
and a slight interest in the specific individuals involved. What is, sociometrically speaking, the affinity, the positive or negative "tele" for each of
these things as compared with the tele for the persons whom one meets in
pursuing life's goals?

We find that individuals who have a slight interest in *specific* individuals
in regard to sex are far from being disinterested in personal characteristics;
they may have a great interest in certain *group characteristics* in regard to
sex. Such individuals develop little attachment to a specific individual, but
may be intensely drawn toward individuals possessing certain physical and
mental attributes regardless of their individuality. Such a person craves a

certain complex of attributes and little, or not at all, the individual carrying them. He uses the individuals; he is not in love with them. He can emancipate, free, separate himself from a specific individual in regard to sex because he was attached to a *combination of attributes* which exist and grow elsewhere also. His sexual impulse is independent of individual persons. Therefore he may be free of attachment to a pattern of individual traits. The more universally distributed these attributes are or these combinations of attributes, the larger will be the number of persons belonging to the group toward which he is drawn. His "freedom" from a specific individual will be relatively greater, the larger the number of individuals who belong to this group.

In the sociometric tests we may find the dominating preference for sex as an impersonal thing suddenly interrupted if a person of group S complex competes with a person of group Non-S. And in general, the feeling-preferences for various things, values, ideas, objects or objectives may at certain points be interrupted, distorted, and complicated by feeling-preferences for individuals. In regard to money, or the equivalents of money, an individual may proceed to accumulate it undisturbed by the individual differences between its owners until he hits upon an individual or individuals to whom he is sensitive (persons whose association he craves because of their social, intellectual, or "racial" superiority, etc.). Then his emotional energy, hitherto directed toward money, may be interfered with and slowed up by personal elements which are wrongly called subjective. This energy may even be transformed and turned in the opposite direction, into the losing of money, the desire to buy with money the association with this person or these persons who have social standing, political influence, sexual appeal, etc. In regard to race as a thing, an individual may find a dominating preference for individuals of a certain race not because of their specific individuality but because of their "race", suddenly interrupted if a person of the group to which he is sensitive competes. This person may not belong to the race required and demanded by him in principle. A monk, subscribing to a certain idea of conduct, may act toward everyone he meets with the same "equalized" affection until this attitude is suddenly interrupted by an individual to whom he is sensitive. It may be useful to differentiate between attraction to individuals for their exclusive individual characteristics—which cannot be "replaced" at least in the thought of the person attracted—and attractions for their group characteristics.

III

GENERAL SOCIOLOGICAL IMPLICATIONS

The imbalances arising can be harmonized, to some extent at least, through constructive rearrangement of people and of things. But this is only a palliative measure. The true solution would be a spontaneous balancing of all these factors. The question is what is the next stage in the evolution of human society, what kind of society will finally crystallize, perhaps aided in finding its destiny by sociometric guides? Theoretically I can visualize three solutions.

The first possibility is a human society in which the preferences for things entirely dominate the preferences for persons; a society in which attachments to persons are extinguished. Attachments exist only to things independent of persons, and to persons only so far as they carry certain things, since the optimum of satisfaction will depend only upon things and things can be indefinitely "replaced" by other things. The individual being may reach a degree of happiness and balance he has never known heretofore. It would be a technological panacea. The emotional currents between persons would be reduced to zero. A certain kind of love would still matter, but not whom one loves; work would matter but not with whom one works; food would matter but not with whom one eats; ideas would matter, too, but not who embodies them. A society would arise in which individuals become symbols and things the only reality. It may bring an optimum of happiness with the extinction of the interrelation strains. The solitaire, the saint, and the schizophrenic are psychological pioneers in this direction. Feeling-for-things would replace feeling-for-persons.

A second outcome would be a human society in which the preferences for individuals would entirely dominate the preferences for things; a society in which attachments to things in themselves would be extinguished; attachments would exist only to individuals and to things only as they are an expression of individuals, social or personality panacea.

A third resultant would be a human society in which the preferences for individuals and the preferences for things would be extinguished; it would not matter whom you love or what you eat. All attachments are extinguished: the Buddhistic panacea.

THE SOCIAL ATOM AND DEATH
(1947)

The gods and immortals which men have cherished for millennia have lost a great deal of the dignity and value which they were supposed to have. Is the idea of immortality entirely a figment of the human mind? I believe that in the future it will become fashionable again and find new attraction for the philosopher and the dreamer. We have been thrown down from the heavens and have a hard time to keep midway between heaven and hell.

You all know that one of the basic concepts which sociometry has developed is that of the social atom. (Atom is derived from a Greek word "atomos" which means the smallest thing. The term has been introduced by Democrites into scientific language. He used it to indicate the smallest particles in the physical universe. However, the physicists have no priority on the word; many words introduced by early philosophers describing physical phenomena as gravitation, atom, attraction, saturation, have a poetic-symbolic character; they are metaphors for psycho-social experiences and belong rightly in our social vocabulary, whence they have been taken.)

Sociologists have used the term socius in a vague way for a long time. It has never meant anything specific until sociometry discovered and defined it as the social atom. People usually thought of the individual as the center of the social universe, of the family as the next larger unit, then the neighborhood, the village, etc.; from the point of view of surface experience sociologists accepted tacitly a scale starting with the individual and ending with the entire universe. We sociometrists challenged this view. The social atom is the smallest social unit, not the individual.[1] The social atom is involving an individual *and* the people (near or distant) to whom he is emotionally related at the time. We have shown that these configurations function as one unit. They may not be the same people with whom a person is officially related and who are in turn officially related to him, but they are always people to whom he has a feeling relationship. It is like an *aura* of attractions and rejections, radiating from him and towards him. These social atoms change from time to time in their membership, but there is a consistency about their structure, the way our bone

---

[1] See "Psychodramatic Shock Therapy," Psychodrama Monograph No. 5, Beacon House, New York, p. 29. From a philogenetic point of view "the individual" appears to be a more recent development than an aggregate of individuals.

structure has a certain consistency. I predicted this would be found true of the social atom in 1931 when I first "saw" a psychological geography of a whole community. Sociometric findings confirmed this prediction. An individual has from birth on already a structure of relationships around him, mother, father, grandmother, and so forth. The volume of the social atom is in continuous expansion as we grow up; it is within it that we live most concretely.

I am now coming to the topic which I intended to discuss in this paper: the consistency of these social atoms changes as we get old, especially the ability to replace loss of membership. Although the social atom is changing intermittently as long as we are young and more resourceful, when one individual member goes out of it another individual fulfilling a similar role takes his place. As one friend steps out, the old friend is rapidly replaced by a new one; social repair seems to take place almost automatically. But when an individual fulfilling one function is lost rarely more than one steps in to replace him. It is as if the central individual cannot sustain two or three of the same kind. There is, simultaneously, a continuous pull from millions of other social atoms, equally craving for replacements. The total effect is as if the emotional economy of the social atom is operating in accord with an unconscious postulate—to keep the social atoms in equilibrium, what I have also called their "sociostasis." Thus a certain range of emotional contacts always exists and remains fairly constant. Their frequency of emotional exchange tends towards balance. This is the reason why what I have called the "emotional expansiveness"[2] of an individual can be measured.

But as we grow older replacements of lost members in significant roles take place with greater difficulty; similar as repairs are more difficult to our physical organism in the course of aging. It is the phenomenon of "social" death, not from the point of view of the body, not in the individual sense of the psyche, not how we die from within but how we die from *without*. A man or woman of sixty may be related to twelve or fifteen individuals, so many women and so many men, of various age levels representing various interests, in such roles and in such counter-roles. Social death throws its shadow upon him long before physical or mental death. An individual may begin to lose in the cohesion of his social atom for various reasons: a) loss of affection, b) replacement by another individual not as well suited, and c) death. The death of an

---

2 *Who Shall Survive?*, p. 73 and 134.

individual member is usually a more permanent loss, the shock coming from it is rarely considered in its full significance. If we happen to survive the ones we love or hate, we die a bit with them as we feel the shadow of death marching from one person of our social atom to another. The people who move in to replace them do not always substitute the lost ones, even the very fact of substitution represents a certain loss. Therefore we feel from childhood on through the networks of our social atom, the meaning of death long before it actually comes with the signs of physical and mental disability. Maybe that we sociometrists will find the predeterminants for social death, a syndrome quite different from the one pointed out by the physician and psychiatrist. We were warming up to the death of the people whom we loved or hated or who loved or hated us. It should be possible to find remedies against the social death shock.

It is probable that the minute shocks coming from social death experience paves the way to premature aging, old sickness and physical death. Old people should learn not to give in to this curse, they should find friends, someone to love again. They should first try to restore the youth of their social atom. It is probably easier to treat the social atom disorders by sociatric devices than to treat their physical and mental complaints. The idea that love and spontaneity is for the young only, that old people should prepare themselves for death, is an antiquated cruelty. A new breath of hope should come to geriatrics, the science of the old age, from the recognition that we do not live only within ourselves, but that there is a "without" of the self which is highly structured, and responsive to growth and decay. Death is a live function, it has a social reality. The death of one person is connected with the death of many others. The people towards whose death you are sensitive and who are sensitive towards yours make up the last social atom you have. We are all surrounded continuously by people with whom we die. Physical death is something negative, we don't experience it, the other fellow does, the fellow who is a member of our social atom. Social death is a *positive* force. Death is among us, like birth. Just as the infant—to an extent —pushes himself into birth, we push ourselves into death, *and each other,* often prematurely. As the s (spontaneity) factor operates throughout pregnancy towards birth, it warms up the sparks of fear in the social atoms and pushes its members towards death. We see how birth progresses during pregnancy, from conception on. Similarly we see how death progresses, from its conceptions in the social atom, the first people whom we have experienced as dying, and the little shocks we received from it.

When we will know more about the processes going on in the social atom of individuals we may invent means of repairing its disorders. Maybe a new profession will develop in time, the sociatrists, who among other matters will treat socio-atomic disorders.

I recall the case of twelve individuals who were sensitive for each other's death expectancy and so infected each other. They belonged to the same profession, they were all physicians, and their respective social atoms crossed and overlapped each other's. One pioneered with a coronary thrombosis. Five of the group succumbed to the same ailment, the other six of the group lived in fear of it. At this writing two of them have died from it, three have recovered from an actual attack, the balance of the group are increasingly worried, the first thing they read in the newspapers are the death notices and they are frequently going for physical check ups. We sociometrists are aware that more important than printed matter are the psychosocial networks. News travels through them, but also death news. If you don't have a coronary thrombosis, or any other physical or mental ailment which appeals to you because it has appealed to your socio-atomic associates, you may pass without a mental attack of it. But another may be sensitized by such news and hasten the onset of such an attack if, of course, there are some somatic conditions inviting it. I had an opportunity to put on the psychodrama stage people who were chained to one another by mutual love and death fears. Some of the individuals knew one another only through a link but they had high regard for each other. To their surprise they found out during their work on the stage that what happened to one meant a great deal to the other. The work out on the stage seemed to bring them relief, a sort of death catharsis. Mirroring each other's death awareness awakened their sense of humor. Another case concerns eight air pilots. The subject was the ninth. As he was enacting on the stage shocks from death experience a scene suddenly occurred to him which he had felt more keenly than the death of his grandfather and of a younger brother: with eight other candidates for air service, he was undergoing a physical checkup. They were all accepted except himself, he did not pass. He saw them there for the first time in the examination room. Before he left they arranged to keep in touch with each other. He wrote them and they wrote back, but after a while, from every one of them in succession his own letters returned, stamped "Missing in action." These new and rather incidental members of his social atom were apparently dead. As he was re-enacting the situation on the stage he said: "There, but for the grace of God, go I."

The eight men were not quite dead yet, they were beckoning him to follow. The life of men extends beyond their physical death through their social atoms. A man dies when his social atom dies. Physical and individual death are not the end of life, they can be viewed as functions of an older unit, of the socio-atomic processes in which they are both embedded.

RE-GROUPING OF COMMUNITIES AND ACTION RESEARCH "IN SITU"*
(1936)

The need of some population analysis, sociometric or otherwise, is proverbial in the field of community organization. Innumerable times a new settlement is started but decays. Of the many that are begun, few settlements survive and develop into villages and cities.

The federal government is at present occupied with the resettlement of people in new areas. Large investments are made to start the new settlements. How many will survive a decade or two hence? To prevent an unfavorable outcome of such settlements a carefully worked out plan is presented here which illustrates the sociometric process of selecting and settling the people from the old community to the new.

In a federal plan the job of selecting the people for a new settlement is up to the government. It is the opposite of the *laissez faire* of spontaneous migration by independent persons. The methods currently used in choosing the members of a new community are social case methods, at best based upon the opinions of a participant observer, at worst more or less arbitrary. There can hardly be conceived a greater contrast than that which exists between the planned arrangement of people in a community and an arrangement based upon the spontaneous inclinations of these people. In a plan the procedure tries to attain the optimum of satisfaction for a fictitious aim, the "idea" involved, or the optimum of satisfaction for the metaphorical "whole" of the group, or indeed the optimum of satisfaction for the *authoritative* person who tries to shape it in accord with his personal aims.

The ruthless "planners" are often so fascinated by an idea of order and system which they think the total collective ought to have that they

---

*"In Situ" means, the places where people actually live and work, and not a 'Research' or 'Treatment' situation outside of them.

believe it can be attained, so to speak, wholesale over the heads of the ego
participants, without any detailed account of the actual spontaneous situation of every individual concerned. However efficiently their plan may
work on the surface, it must fail in the end because of too crude and too
universalized an image of the individual ego.

The aim of a sociometric project is to enable every individual in a
certain group to attain his optimum of satisfaction within it. We must
first uncover the wishes and aims of every individual in regard to the other
participants, and of all other individuals in regard to him, that is, the
sociometric position of every individual of a group. The material, statistically or graphically arranged, discloses to us totalities of relations, the intricate organization of interrelation patterns—information which the un-
critical totalist never attains because he tries to recognize the universe
without recognizing the atoms first. In our sociometric chart we see every
individual in a struggle for a psychologically balanced position. And we can
read from it, quantitatively and qualitatively, what *the optimum of satisfaction for every ego and for the group as a whole* may be. A technique which
offers all the advantages of a pioneering enterprise of self-reliance and free
development combined with all the advantages of an organized movement
which allows for preventive measures and social control, is the sociometric
test.

An example of a re-settlement situation which is typical for many concrete projects at present underway is the following one. The government
has purchased land and provided housing facilities for five hundred families
in area X. However, there are seven hundred and fifty families who have
applied for a new home and been found eligible. Two hundred and fifty
families live in village A, two hundred and fifty families in village B, two
hundred and fifty families in village C. A, B, and C are some distance apart.
The people of each village do not know those in the other villages. Some
selection has to be made because there are two hundred and fifty applicant
families too many. But even if there were not more applicants than
houses available, the question would still arise whether they would make a
well balanced kernel likely to produce a live community.

The sociometric investigator assembling the applicants of one community, village A, says: "You may have something to say about the people
with whom you would like to live. No outsider can ever guess these wants
of yours accurately."

Everyone writes down the family which he would like to have *as a
neighbor* in the new community. He is asked the reason for his choice.

Mr. McCormick chooses Mr. Mitchell and gives his reason: "My daughter is engaged to his son." The sociometric investigator asks them to make a further choice, a second, third, fourth, and fifth *or more* and to arrange them in the order of preference. They always add the reason for each choice. The results are assembled in a sociometric chart. It is a social map of that community. It shows some families isolated; no one wants them. Here and there a family or its head appears as a potential leader of a large group. This is not necessarily because the family or the individual has received many first choices, but on the map appears a series of significant chains leading finally to this head. For instance, Mr. McCormick appears directly or indirectly as the center of seventy-five families.

The map also shows structures important for social balance. Mr. McCormick and Mr. Mitchell give their first choices to each other. As Mr. McCormick is the potential leader of seventy-five families, and Mr. Mitchell is the head of sixty-two families, they make a combination of much strength and influence. These are groupings which have taken years to build and cannot be replaced. Their breakup might precipitate failure in the new community. Such groups may be transferred bodily in the migration.

The map shows one or two small groups of families which choose one another but are isolated or rejected as a whole. The map shows a few scattered families which command little popularity but provide the stimulus of progress in the community. It also shows families who have little education but can perform the necessary hard physical labor.

A careful analysis of village A suggests the most desirable combination of families for community X. The same procedure is repeated for village B and village C. The results are again assembled in sociometric charts.

Now however excellent the groups selected from the three villages may be, throwing them together may lead to clashes. They cannot live successfully if their leaders are antagonistic. Therefore, before the final selection is made, the potential leaders from villages A, B, and C are picked from their respective maps, three from A, four from B, and six from C, more or less as may seem necessary. These leaders come together in a face-to-face meeting. Each man meets each other man individually. They express their preferences for one or another in the manner developed at Hudson in the Family Test. Mr. McCormick from A may feel attracted to Mr. Brown from B, who is there the leader of a minor group. But he may reject Mr. Smith from B, who is the potential leader of more than half of this community. This evidence may weigh heavily against throwing the Mr. Mc-

Cormick coterie with the Smith group without careful consideration. The reason Mr. McCormick gives for not liking Mr. Smith is: "His ideas are too radical for our crowd. I am afraid quarrels may result."

In this manner the evidence as presented in the three community maps and the leader map is carefully analyzed with the ultimate aim in mind of selecting from the seven hundred and fifty applicants five hundred for the new settlement.

A simple consideration shows the three maps in a new light. The nationality and race of each applicant is known to the investigator. The evidence usually shows that there is no real prejudice until the saturation point for that particular minority group is reached. This saturation point —the rejection of additional persons of a particular race, creed, or nationality —arrives when the dominant group no longer has need for more of the minority group. Thus the test shows that Negroes are often welcome additions to migrating communities. The map of village A shows nine Negro families. Seven of them choose one another, but they are isolated from the rest of the community. Yet two of the Negro families are chosen second and third by three families which in turn are chosen by one of the potential leaders. It is apparent from the map that these two Negro families are fairly well adjusted and have become an essential part of the community. The sociometric saturation point is fluid. It changes from time to time. With it, prejudices ebb or rise.

Before selection, the sociometric investigator makes critical use of all supplementary material available, case studies of each of the families, information and advice as given by intelligent observers who have lived in these communities for some time and know their own people.

Another typical re-settlement situation arises when the applicants are so widely scattered over so large an area that practically no family knows the others. Then, of course, the technique described above cannot be used, as it is practicable only for compact groups who are well acquainted. Two hundred families are applicants, of whom one hundred and twenty-five can be selected. The problem area within which the two hundred families are scattered is divided into ten regions, twenty families coming from each region. The heads of the twenty families are brought to a face-to-face meeting. The results of the meetings of every region are mapped. From the ten maps the potential leaders appearing are picked, and are brought to a face-to-face meeting. The results are again charted. The total evidence is analyzed and the selection is made.

There is no re-settlement situation in which some sociometric procedure cannot be devised and used to advantage. It is an individualistic, demo-cratic process of selection. The settlers are given the feeling that they are not moved like cattle, but take an immediate part in a matter which is immensely important to them.

The most intelligent and penetrating observation or case-study cannot serve as substitute for sociometric procedures. The larger the size of the population to be considered, the less adequately can observation or case work enable us to form an idea of the whole.

"Centerville* is unique. For the first time in twenty years since Moreno began to develop the application of his sociometric techniques in European resettlement programs during the First World War, sociometric principles have been applied to an *open* community."

"As a psychological preparation for community life, as well as for edu-cational and informational purposes, frequent group meetings for about fifteen families at a time were held in a large city accessible to the appli-cants during a period of almost one year before the project was ready for occupancy. One hundred and ninety-eight families (the project was pre-pared for 250 families) participated in these meetings, which, of course, included the thirty-five families considered here. The group meetings, often attended by the whole family, served to foster personal and social contacts, with their fabric of criss-cross attractions and repulsions. Lines of cleavage were noted. Friendships were formed on the basis of the spirited discussions usually generated by the Family Selection Specialist or other project officials."

"With the completion in July 1936 of the first 35 houses, thirty-five families totaling a hundred and fifty-four persons were chosen for occu-pancy. The determination of these first thirty-five families was based pri-marily on the need for satisfactory personnel for factory operations."

"In the pre-settlement situation in Centerville all of the thirty-five families accepted as prospective settlers were unknown to each other before applying for membership to the colony, except in a few cases where the family heads had had common employment contacts in the industry. All the families were residents of a large neighboring city."

"In approaching the problem of assignment of houses to the individual families, the Family Selection Specialist deemed it advisable to apply sociometric principles and procedures as far as conditions would permit. In consideration of the personal and family welfare of the colonists, the popu-lation test, a form of sociometric testing, was utilized in the determina-

---

*See SOCIOMETRY, Vol. I, 1937, p. 220-254.

tion of the house assignments to the first thirty-five homesteaders. The test was based on *the criterion of the neighbor preference* of each family."

"Leader individuals and their following were noted. The former included several applicants who had long been identified with the project in its early struggles for realization. Some others were highly regarded for their ability to uphold their convictions in discussions, and others were favored for their personality characteristics. On the whole it may be said that, in spite of the low acquaintance volume and the limitations on vital criteria in the relationships of the future colonists during the pre-settlement period, there was adequate basis for assignment of houses based on a sociometric population test. The thirty-five prospective settlers were agreed that a test based on their neighbor preferences was both an individualistic and democratic process of selection. They felt that they were not to be moved like cattle, but were taking an active part in a matter of great importance to them."

"The families were asked to submit a secret ballot indicating three neighbors in the order of choice, at the first, second, and third level. The Family Selection Specialist stressed the fact that the preferences were to constitute a composite reaction of the whole family. Sociogram I expresses graphically the choices of the families. The structure of affinities of one family for another becomes clear. Individual centers of attraction, mutual and unreciprocated attractions, and unchosen families are all indicated in the chart. A veritable network of forces, attractions and repulsions are delineated. The sociogram expresses the spontaneous activations that came out of the group meetings."

"Motivations that were evident within the whole group before the settlers were on the ground were, of course, personal and social likes and dislikes. A few ambitious souls made more or less successful attempts to influence certain family heads in the neighbor preference vote."

"Psycho-geographical Map I shows the *actual* geographical assignment of houses, with all degree of mutual choices and unreciprocated choices of the neighborhood selection test superimposed. It should be noted that the houses are set about a hundred feet apart (except in seven cases where two are connected by adjoining garages), and all are in one line, about the same distance from the roadway. In the map the houses are offset merely for purposes of clarity in drawing the lines of expressed choices."

"The thirty-five available houses were divided into six geographical units, five units containing six houses and one unit containing five houses. Every family was assured a location if not next door to its choice at least within a restricted area along with the other definitely related families of his group."

"After the houses were allocated it was agreed that all the thirty-five families were privileged to exchange houses among themselves. No exchanges of this kind were made. A serious limitation to an ideal distribution of houses based on choices of the inhabitants was the fact that most of the houses had five rooms while some had six. As a result, in three instances, families of two or three people, finding themselves in possession of six-room houses, on the basis of the above procedure, voluntarily relinquished their houses to larger families. Each change, of course, involved the removal of two families from their related sub-group."

"*After six months of living in Centerville a second survey of the same first thirty-four families was made to ascertain the psycho-geographical position of the families and to note progress, regression or standstill of community interrelations.* The criterion used in this test must be classified as a 'near sociometric' criterion, since it was not based on an interrelational situation which could be changed in order to satisfy the choices expressed in the test. The families were asked to assume that they might be able to enjoy a reassignment of houses, and that therefore they had the opportunity again to choose three neighbors beside whom to live. In contrast to the criterion in the pre-settlement test when the houses were still to be assigned, this second criterion is 'weak.' "

"The preferences of the colonists were not discovered by calling them to a meeting of *the entire group** for that purpose. The data for the second sociogram was gathered for the most part in the course of informal conversation with individual homesteaders. In several instances older children in the families cooperated by getting the exact information required. Each family again was asked to make three choices at the first, second and third level of choice."

"In comparing Sociograms I and II it is discovered that from the first to the second tests there is observable a considerable diversion of tele from the most popular leader group. The tele goes to more obscure individuals, potential leaders who may become the kernel of a minority group. The observation of recent developments has clearly shown that in the course of the economic development of the community such a minority group is growing up. Now it is merely in negation of the cooperative ideology, but

---

* It was done in the first test. The assembly of the whole group is a preferable procedure.

under favorable circumstances it may develop into opposition around an ideology which is more individualistic and more conservative."

"The fact that a decrease from six to four unchosen families occurred from the first to the second test may well be significant. Since we regard the project as a lifetime affair, the bringing about of a greater mental happiness to two families has great import. If in the course of the next few years through sociometric technique, and whatever means natural to the situation, one more of the four "unincluded" families wins an acceptable position, there will be built up gradually a strong human collective, as well as a strong economic collective, if indeed the latter ever can become truly strong unless the former lays a basis for it. We know from control studies that the building up of reciprocal relations and the gradual integrating of one newcomer after another into a community in process of formation has a cumulative effect."

THREE EXPERIMENTAL PROJECTS: LAISSEZ FAIRE, AUTOCRACY AND DEMOCRACY
TESTS (1936)

A simple illustration of the three approaches is the grouping of children in a dining room.

I. LAISSEZ FAIRE TEST OF GROUPING

In a particular cottage of our training school live 28 girls. In their dining room are seven tables. The technique of placing them around these tables can take different forms. We may let them place themselves as they wish, and watch the result. A girl "A" seats herself at table 1; eight girls who are drawn to her try to place themselves at the same table. But table 1 can hold only three more. The result is a struggle and somebody has to interfere and arrange them in some arbitrary manner. A girl "B" runs to table 2, but nobody attempts to join her; thus three places at that table remain unused. We find that the technique of letting the girls place themselves works out to be impracticable. It brings forth difficulties which enforce arbitrary, authoritative interference with their wishes, the opposite principle from the one which was intended, a free, democratic, individualistic process.

A LAISSEZ FAIRE SOCIOGRAM (A)
(Seating arrangement in a dining room)

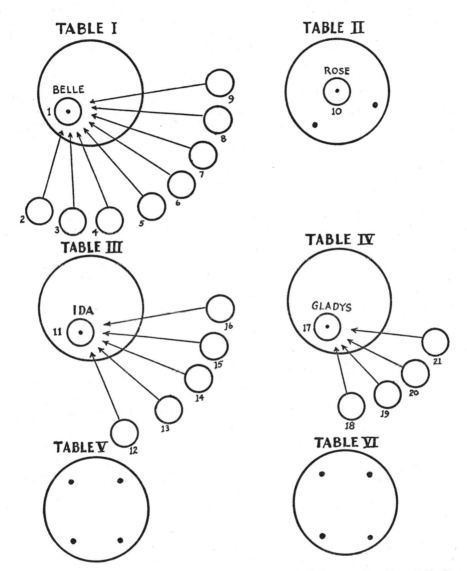

Twenty-one girls place themselves as they wish. A girl, Belle, seats herself at Table I; eight girls who are drawn to her try to place themselves at the same table. A girl, Rose, runs to Table II but nobody attempts to join her, etc. The result is a struggle and somebody has to interfere and arrange them in an arbitrary manner. (Sociometric Review, 1936)

II. Autocracy Test of Grouping

Another technique of placement is one applied strictly from the point of view of the authoritative supervisor of the dining room. She places them in such a fashion that they produce the least trouble to her without regard to the way in which the girls themselves feel about the placements. Or she picks for each of the seven tables a leader around whom she groups the rest without regard to the leader's feelings about them and without consideration of whether the "leader" is regarded by the girls as a leader.

III. Democracy Test and the Sociometric Method of Grouping

A more satisfactory technique of placement is to ask the girls with whom they want to sit at the same table, and, if every table seats at least four, to gve every girl three choices; to tell them that every effort will be made that each may have at her table at least one of her choices, and, if possible, her first choice. Every girl writes down first whom she wants as a first choice; next, whom she wants as a second choice if she cannot receive her first choice; and last, whom she wants as a third choice if she cannot have her first or second choice. The slips are collected and analyzed. The structure of affinities one for another is charted. The best possible relationship available within the structure of interrelations defines the *optimum of placement*. This is the highest reciprocated choice from the point of view of the girl. The order is as follows: a subject's first choice is reciprocated by a first choice, 1:1; a subject's first choice is reciprocated by a second choice, 1:2; a subject's first choice is reciprocated by a third choice, 1:3; a subject's second choice is reciprocated by a first choice, 2:1; 2:2; 2:3; 3:1; 3:2; 3:3. Where there is no choice that meets with a mutual response, the first choice of the girl (1:0) becomes her optimum, that is, from the point of view, the best placement for her available within the structure.

The three groups contrasted in sociogram A, B, and C consist of the same individuals. It is as if we would have three test tubes, A, B, and C each containing the same material, but only C is exposed to reagent X. The reagent is the sociometric test. Sociogram A and B tabulate the seating arrangement of a group of 21 girls around six individual tables, just before the test is given, Sociogram C *after* the test is given. A and B represent the control groups, C the experimental group.

The *laissez faire* group A can be considered an "experiment of nature." However wild and incongruous the grouping is strong telefactors must have operated between the individuals and the criterion, sitting at this or the

AN AUTOCRACY SOCIOGRAM (B)
(Seating arrangement in a dining room)

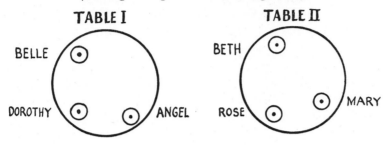

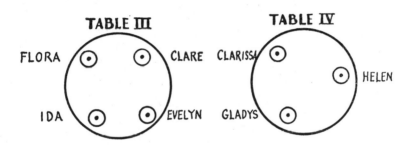

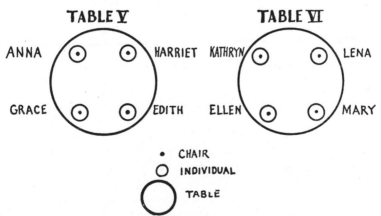

The authoritative supervisor of the dining room places 21 girls. She picks for each of the seven tables a leader around whom she groups the rest without regard to the individual feelings. (Sociometric Review, 1936)

DEMOCRATIC SOCIOGRAM (C)
(Sociometric seating arrangement in a dining room)

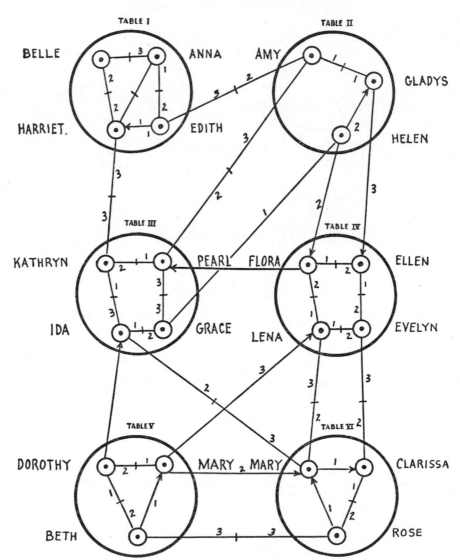

The sociometric test promotes a free, democratic, individualistic process of placement. It gives every individual an optimum of satisfaction and *it provides the group with the optimum structure in regard to the particular criterion.* (Sociometric Review, 1936)

TABLE A—Section 3

SOCIOMETRIC FINDINGS

	No. of girls	Pct. of girls
Population 21		
Number of girls receiving in the test:		
3 reciprocated choices	3 or	14.3%
2 reciprocated choices	3 or	14.3%
1 reciprocated choice	7 or	33.3%
No mutual choice but chosen	1 or	4.8%
Isolated (unchosen)	7 or	33.3%
	21	100. %

TABLE A—Section 4

PLACEMENT ANALYSIS

Population 21		
Number of girls receiving in the placement (at her table):		
One reciprocated choice (or more)	11* or	52%
Unreciprocated first choice (or more):		
No mutual choice but chosen in the test	1 or	5%
Isolated (unchosen in the test)	6 or	29%
Number of girls who receive "optimum"	18 or	86%
Of the remaining three girls,		
Number who received 2nd from optimum	1 or	5%
Number who received 3rd from optimum	2 or	9%
	21	100%

*Twelve reciprocated choices were satisfied in the placement but one of these (Helen's) was not the girl's optimum choice.

TABLE A—Section 5

NEW SEATING ARRANGEMENT

TABLE 1	TABLE 2	TABLE 3
Belle*	Helen***	Kathryn*
Anna*	Angeline* (Ang or Amy)	Pearl*
Edith*	Gladys*	Grace**
Harriet*		Ida*

TABLE 4	TABLE 5	TABLE 6
Flora*	Dorothy*	Mary (2)*
Ellen*	Mary*	Rose*
Lena*	Beth*	Clarissa***
Evelyn*		

*Denotes the individual is receiving optimum placement.
**Denotes the individual is receiving 2nd choice from optimum.
***Denotes the individual is receiving 3rd choice from optimum.
Note—Of the isolated girls all but one receives optimum placement.

other table. The authoritative Group B can be considered as an "experiment of culture" an "axio normative experiment." Several factors may have entered into producing *this* particular seating arrangement. The use of authority by the housemother, however pronounced it may have been, is only one factor influencing the seating order; a fair degree of influence of the girls upon her decisions may have been exercised. Favorites of the housemother may have had on and off a perversive influence in passing privileges to their own favorites among the girls so that they could sit wherever they liked. However rigid, it is a natural situation in which some of the spontaneity of the subject-individuals passes through as it is often observed in autocratic regimes. It can be assumed that the larger the number of individuals is, the weaker is the housemother's hold upon them and the more she has to give in to let them have their own choice. Some "tele" must have operated in the situation.

As the hypothesis to be tested is the degree to which a hypothetical factor, tele, operates in the formation of groups, it was assumed that some tele must operate in every natural grouping, therefore also in grouping A and B. But it was not possible to differentiate without further inquiry who among the girls sitting around the six tables were tele choices, positive or negative, and who were not. Sociogram C shows a grouping of the same individuals vastly different from the Sociograms A and B. Via the sociometric test the truly wished arrangement, the genuine tele choices have been made fully visible. The twenty-one individuals disclose twenty-four different ways of preferred pairing, a fact which is used in the arrangement around the tables itself, to give every individual an optimum of satisfaction.

A comparison of the Sociogram B in the authoritative situation with the Sociogram C in the experimental situation can now be made in order to determine how much tele operated already in the authoritative situation. It discloses that two times a pair of individuals wish to be seated together as if they would have been given their choice. It indicates, however, that the tele factor operates in the experimental group in a degree seven times greater than in the authoritative situation. We consider here only the factor of pair formation. It is much greater if the total table structures or the whole dining room structures are compared. Compare Sociogram B with Sociogram C. From Sociogram C one can see that there are only two pairs in Sociogram B involving three individuals (Beth-Mary and Beth-Rose in Table II) to which happens to be given satisfaction, in Sociogram C there are 15 pairs to which is given satisfaction (Table I, 3 pairs; Table II, 1 pair; Table III, 4 pairs; Table IV, 4 pairs; Table V, 2 pairs; Table VI, 1 pair).

TABLE A—SECTION 2
Choice Analysis*

	Individual Analysis of Reciprocated Choices									Individual Analysis of Outgoing Unreciprocated Choices			Individual Analysis of Unreciprocated Choices Incoming**														
													Firsts					Seconds					Thirds				
	1:1	1:2	1:3	2:1	2:2	2:3	3:1	3:2	3:3	1:0	2:0	3:0	1	2	3	4	5	1	2	3	4	5	1	2	3	4	5
Belle	1	—	—	—	1	—	—	—	—	—	—	1	1	—	—	—	—	—	—	—	—	—	—	1	—	—	—
May	1	—	—	1	—	—	—	—	—	1	—	—	1	—	—	—	—	—	—	—	—	—	—	—	—	1	—
Mary	—	1	—	—	1	—	—	—	—	1	1	—	—	—	—	—	—	—	—	1	—	—	—	—	—	—	—
Flora	—	1	—	—	—	—	—	—	—	1	1	1	—	1	—	—	—	1	—	—	—	—	—	—	—	—	—
Lena	—	—	—	—	—	—	—	—	—	1	1	1	1	—	—	—	—	—	—	—	—	—	—	—	—	—	—
Dorothy	—	—	—	1	1	—	—	—	—	1	1	1	1	—	—	—	—	—	—	1	—	—	—	—	1	—	—
Kathryn	—	—	—	—	—	—	—	—	—	1	1	1	1	—	—	—	—	—	—	—	—	—	—	—	—	—	—
Ida	—	—	—	—	—	—	—	—	—	—	1	1	—	—	—	—	—	—	—	—	—	—	—	—	1	—	—
Edith	—	—	—	—	—	—	—	—	—	1	1	1	—	—	—	—	—	—	1	—	—	—	—	—	—	—	—
Beth	—	—	—	1	—	—	—	—	—	1	—	1	—	1	—	—	—	—	—	—	—	—	1	—	—	—	—
Ellen	—	—	—	—	—	—	—	1	—	1	1	1	—	—	—	—	—	—	—	—	—	—	1	—	1	—	—
Anna	1	—	—	—	1	1	—	—	—	—	—	1	1	—	—	—	—	—	—	—	—	—	—	—	—	—	—
Helen	—	1	—	—	—	—	1	—	—	1	—	1	—	—	1	—	—	—	—	1	—	—	—	—	1	—	—
Evelyn	—	—	1	—	—	—	—	—	—	—	1	1	—	—	—	1	—	—	—	—	—	—	—	—	—	—	—
Angeline	—	—	—	—	1	1	—	—	—	1	1	—	—	—	—	—	—	—	—	1	—	—	—	—	—	—	—
Rose	1	—	—	—	—	—	—	1	—	1	1	1	—	—	—	—	—	—	—	—	—	—	—	—	—	—	—
Harriet	—	1	—	—	—	—	—	—	—	1	1	1	—	—	—	—	—	—	—	—	—	—	—	—	—	—	—
Pearl	—	1	—	—	—	—	—	—	—	1	1	1	—	—	—	1	—	—	—	—	—	—	—	—	—	—	—
Gladys	—	—	—	—	—	—	—	—	—	1	1	1	—	—	1	—	—	—	—	—	—	—	—	—	—	1	—
Clarissa	—	—	—	—	—	—	—	1	—	1	1	1	—	—	1	—	—	—	1	—	—	—	1	1	1	1	—
Grace	—	—	—	—	1	—	—	—	—	—	—	1	—	—	—	1	—	—	—	—	—	—	—	—	—	—	—
Total	4	3	1	3	6	2	1	2	0	13	10	18	4	2	3	4	0	2	2	6	0	0	6	2	6	4	0
Total	8			11			3				41			13					10					18			

Note: The larger "1's" are used to indicate that these choices, were satisfied in the placement.

*This is the analysis of the second testing of Cottage 2. See Table C, Section 2.

**1, 2, 3, 4, 5, indicate the number of incoming choices, firsts, seconds, or thirds, which are unreciprocated by the person chosen.

TABLE B
Efficiency of Placement Attained Through Sociometric Technique
FIRST TEST

Cottage	Population	No. who could receive optimum placement without sociometric aid*	No. receiving optimum placement through sociometric aid**	Efficiency in placement	No. receiving no choice in placement
1	21	4	16	76%	0
2	24	4	17	71%	0
3	19	4	14	74%	1
4	21	6	18	86%	0
5	31	4	23	74%	1
6	29	10	24	83%	1
7	30	3	26	87%	0
8	26	4	23	88%	1
9	28	10	23	82%	0
10	38	4	38	100%	0
11	29	4	24	83%	2
12	27	6	24	88%	0
13	29	8	24	83%	0
14	25	8	21	84%	1
A	20	4	15	75%	0
B	17	6	13	77%	0
First Test	414	89	343	82%	7
Summary of Second Test	404	96	340	84%	7
Summary of Third Test	397	122	338	85%	4

*Number who receive optimum spontaneously, a mutual first choice (1:1). They could be placed without sociometric aid.

**The girls who receive second or third from optimum placement are not included in calculating efficiency, only those who receive optimum. See page 26-29.

These two simple rules guide each placement. As table A illustrates for a specific group, they can be called into effect with a high degree of efficiency. Even in instances in which a number of girls do not receive their optimum, they can receive their second very often.

This procedure has two phases: analysis of the choices and analysis of placement. The analysis of choices discloses the structure of the group and the position of every girl within it. It discloses how many girls are wanted spontaneously by all three partners whom they want at their table, how many are wanted by two of the three partners whom they want at their table, how many are wanted by one of the three only, and how many by none of the three. It discloses the high percentage of girls who have to make some adjustment to the group because they cannot get what they want.

A technique of placement has been worked out to help the girls as far as possible where their spontaneous position in the group stops them in a blind alley. Their criss-cross affinities as charted in a sociogram are simple, direct guides which a technique of placement can intelligently use. The attempt is made to give every girl of the group an optimum of satisfaction. We consider as the optimum of satisfaction the duplication for a girl of such a position in the placement as is revealed to be the most desired by her in accordance with the actual structure presented in the sociogram. (See Table A for details of application to a specific group.)

The tabulation of placement is figured out. It indicates the seating which has been calculated for every cottage. (See Table B.)

We find that sometimes it is possible to be efficient up to 100%; on the average we are able to give an optimum of satisfaction to more than 80% of the girls. Considering that the percentage of girls who would reach this optimum if left to their own devices is on the average not higher than 25 to 30%, the help coming from sociometric technique of placement is substantial.

It is a matter of principle with us to give every girl the best possible placement regardless of what her record may be or what experience the housemother may have had in regard to any two girls who want to sit at the same table. We do not begin with prejudice but wait to see how their conduct turns out.*

We have noted that the girls' own spontaneous choices may deadlock them in a certain position, and we can well visualize that they may be forced in actual life to make an adjustment which is very arbitrary and deeply against their wishes. These "deadlocks" are not something which every individual outgrows spontaneously, but are something which works like a social destiny for the majority of individuals. It was therefore of great interest not only

---

* Occasionally we see that two or more girls who have affinities for each other do not behave to advantage for themselves or for others. Then a different placement may be more desirable for them and this is based on findings as presented elsewhere. See *Who Shall Survive?*, chapters on Racial Quotient, Sex, and Psychological Home.

from a practical but also from a theoretical point of view to study whether the technique of placement would have for the girls a significance beyond the temporary aid it gives them. If, through our intermediation, they can mix during their meal times with girls who appeal to them and learn to choose better the next time, if the technique helps them to facilitate and train and improve their social spontaneity and to break the deadlock more rapidly than if left to their own devices, then the service of such a procedure may find many applications.

The sociometric test in regard to table choices is repeated every eight weeks. To estimate accurately the progress, or regression, or standstill of social interrelations, we have calculated the findings and made a comparative study. See Table C.

Table C presents the outcome of the test in three successive testings eight weeks apart, a period of twenty-four weeks. In the first test, of the 327 girls who participated, 23.9% succeeded in having their first choice reciprocated by a first choice (1:1); 11.9% succeeded in having their first choice reciprocated by a second choice (1:2); 10.4% succeeded in having their first choice reciprocated by a third choice (1:3). In the second test, of the 317 girls who participated, 27.1% succeeded in having their first choice reciprocated by a first choice; 15.1% succeeded in having their first choice reciprocated by a second choice; and 11.4% succeeded in having their first choice reciprocated by a third choice. The total success in the first test in getting a mutual choice of any sort in response to the first choice was for that population 46.2 per cent. The success in the second test, was for that population 53.6 per cent. The difference of 7.4% is the *increase* in the efficiency of the girls from the first to the second test in finding their first choices reciprocated *without* outside aid. The increase in efficiency from the first to the second test in regard to 1:1 mutual choices is 3.2%; in regard to 1:2 mutual choices it is also 3.2%; and in regard to 1:3 mutual choices it is 1 per cent. In other words, the increase in efficiency shows up most in the 1:1 and 1:2 choices but is less noticeable in the 1:3 choices. In regard to second choices, the increase in efficiency is 10.6%, and for the third choices, 1.4 per cent. The total increase in mutual choices is 19.4% from the first test to the second test.

In consequence of this increase in responses to first choices, there is a corresponding decrease from the first to the second test in outgoing choices which remain unreciprocated, a decrease of 19.4 per cent.

When we examine the findings of the third testing, we see the amount of mutuality of first choices still increasing, 2.6% more than in the second

TABLE C—Section 1

Analysis of Table Choices of the Cottage Populations

First Test—8 Weeks Later

Cottage***	Population	RECIPROCATED CHOICES*										UNRECIPROCATED CHOICES**			
		First			Second			Thirds				Firsts	Seconds	Thirds	
		1:1	1:2	1:3	2:1	2:2	2:3	3:1	3:2	3:3	Total	1:0	2:0	3:0	Total
1	21	4	4	4	4	4	3	4	3	4	34	9	10	10	29
2	24	4	3	3	3	2	1	3	1	4	24	14	18	16	48
4	21	6	2	0	2	2	2	0	2	4	20	13	15	15	43
5	31	4	3	3	3	4	0	3	0	4	24	21	24	24	69
6	29	10	3	5	3	2	5	5	5	0	38	11	19	19	49
8	26	4	2	2	2	2	3	2	3	4	24	18	19	17	54
9	28	10	2	1	2	8	2	1	2	6	34	15	16	19	50
11	29	4	3	5	3	4	1	6	2	4	32	17	20	18	55
12	27	6	3	6	5	4	3	2	1	0	30	12	19	20	51
13	29	8	5	1	3	2	5	1	5	8	38	15	17	17	49
14	25	8	3	1	4	4	3	2	3	4	32	13	15	15	43
A	20	4	4	2	3	4	2	4	3	2	28	10	9	13	32
B	17	6	2	1	2	4	2	1	2	2	22	8	9	12	29
Total	327	78	39	34	39	46	32	34	32	46	380	176	210	215	601
Average	.239	.119	.104	.119	.141	.098	.104	.098	.141	1.16	.538	.642	.657	1.84	
Sum of Averages		.462			.358			.343			1.16		1.837		1.84

*1:1, indicates a subject's first choice is reciprocated by a first choice; 1:2, indicates a subject's first choice is reciprocated by a second choice; 1:3, indicates a subject's first choice is reciprocated by a third choice; 2:1, indicates a subject's second choice is reciprocated by a first choice; etc.

**1:0, 2:0, 3:0, indicate first, second or third choices, respectively, which were not reciprocated.

***Cottages 7 and 10 are omitted because they are not comparable, being larger in population and of a different race. Cottage 3 is omitted because many vocational assignments are such that few members are in the cottage for meals together.

TABLE D
SOCIOMETRY CONTROL STUDY

With average difference between the findings of successive tests when the tests are given at intervals of eight weeks, with choices not put into operation.*

	Popu-lation	Reciprocated Choices										Unreciprocated Choices			
		Firsts			Seconds			Thirds			Total	Firsts	Seconds	Thirds	Total
		1-1	1-2	1-3	2-1	2-2	2-3	3-1	3-2	3-3	Total	1-0	2-0	3-0	Total
Sum	22	6	1	1	1	2	3	1	3	4	22	14	16	14	44
Average		.273	.0454	.0454	.045	.091	.136	.045	.136	.182	1.000	.636	.727	.636	2.000
Sum of Averages			.364			.273			.363		1.000		2.000		
Sum	23	6	0	2	0	4	0	2	0	2	16	15	19	19	53
Average		.261	0	.087	0	.174	0	.087	0	.087	.696	.652	.826	.826	2.304
Sum of Averages			.348			.174			.174		.696		2.304		
Sum	23	5	0	1	2	1	0	1	0	0	10	17	20	22	59
Average		.217	0	.044	.087	.044	0	.044	0	0	.436	.739	.869	.956	2.564
Sum of Averages			.261			.131			.044		.436		2.564		
Difference Between Averages of:															
First and Second Tests			-.016			-.099			-.189		-.304		.304		
Second and Third Tests			-.087			-.043			-.130		-.260		.260		
First and Third Tests			-.103			-.142			-.319		-.564		.564		

*For routine purposes we have carried totals to the 3rd decimal place, but it was not considered wise at this time to apply the more complex statistical methods such as the computation of critical ratios.

test, but a falling off for second and third choices. What this means is the accumulation of benefit going to the first choices, as we see when we examine the number of unreciprocated first choices in the first testing, 53.8%, and number in the third testing, 43.8%, a difference of 10 per cent. See Table D.

To see whether these choices are being more broadly spread throughout the various cottage groups we calculated the percentage of isolated girls in each group for each period. For the first period the isolated girls are 17.6% of the total number, and for the third period, 14.8%, a decrease of 2.8 per cent.

The question is whether the findings in this period of twenty-four weeks presents a significant trend. This question cannot be answered except through further testing. It appears reasonable to assume that the placement technique should increase the spontaneous efficiency of choosing. The procedure brings a number of isolated girls into contact with popular girls who under normal circumstances may not pay any attention to them. The unchosen girl sitting beside her favorite has an opportunity to show herself to better advantage and to win the person she wants as a friend. Similar relationships of all sorts develop through our "shuffle", which lays the ground open for potential clickings to take place. Without the use of this placement technique the girls who know each other well get to know each other still better and the newcomers tend to be excluded.

A *control series* of tests given at intervals of six weeks over a period of eighteen weeks to one cottage, with a population of 22 girls at the time of the first testing and 23 at the time of the third testing, is reported in Table E.

The placement procedure was not allowed to go into effect during this period. The findings indicate a continuous fall in the mutuality of choices —for first choices a decrease of 10.3%; for second choices, 14.2%; and for third choices, 31.9%—together with a continuous rise in unreciprocated choices amounting to 56.4 per cent. While this is a very small group, it suggests the needs for sociometric placement technique and supports the trends mentioned above.

A problem which often recurs is that sometimes girls remain over to whom no satisfaction can be given in the placement. In placing a population of 412 girls on the basis of the first testing reported here, only seven girls (or 1.7% of the population) received none of their three choices. (In the second testing, 1.7%, and in the third testing, 1% of the population received none of their three choices.) To these seven girls individually an explanation is given that to give them any one of their choices would block the choices of a great many other girls in the cottage; they are asked to accept the situation with the understanding that at the next choosing (8 weeks later) if it is necessary that any girl go without her choices for the sake of the majority of the girls, other girls than they will be asked to do so. The girls are told who these girls are who want to sit with them but whom they did not choose. They are glad to find themselves thus chosen, and take with a good spirit the placement they are asked to accept. They render a service to less well adjusted and little chosen or isolated girls who choose them.

The argument may be raised that it matters very little with whom a girl sits at the table. The question whom one has at his table during meal time may rightly seem so very insignificant to a person who lives in a great city and has the opportunity to mix freely with everyone and has plenty of time at his disposal. But in an institutional community where the number of acquaintances one can make is strictly limited, and where a certain amount of routine is necessary, free association during meal time with the person you desire to be with is of great social value. We have made similar observations in the dining rooms and dormitories of colleges.

Another argument may be raised that for most people what they eat is more important than with whom they eat. This is partial truth which is valueless as long as it remains unqualified by quantitative analysis. Our social atom studies showed that there are people in whom the preferential feelings toward other *persons* are especially articulate and that there are people in whom the preferential feelings toward *things* are especially articulate. This we have observed frequently also in our placement studies. We found here and there girls who craved to sit at a table where they know that the waitress is in the habit of giving special favors.

Another argument may be raised that a popular and perhaps superior girl, although she may have received one or two of her choices, may have to tolerate as a third partner an isolated girl who chose her but whom she violently rejects. In reply to this it can be said that the popular girl, exposed to chance, may not have received even the two friends whom she wanted; also it may be an important part of her training to expand her emotional experience also toward people who do not appeal to her so much as others. An increase in emotional flexibility should not decrease her preferential sensibility.

Sociometric techniques of placement overcome the lack of system which is seen in the picking of roommates generally, especially in colleges. A haphazard procedure appears satisfactory to the individuals who associate themselves readily, but it is totally inefficient for the majority of those who have a hard time to find the partner they want. The following explains the technique as applied to *colleges*.

Let us suppose that the whole student population is 240, and that their dormitory arrangements are such that to each bedroom are assigned two students. Each student is given three choices. The choices are analyzed and charted. Sixty students, let us say, form first choice mutual pairs. They are eliminated from the contest. The remainder of one hundred and eighty are called to a second meeting. They go through the same process. This time, let us say, one hundred and twenty students form first choice mutual pairs. They are then eliminated. The remainder of sixty students are called to a further meeting. They go through the process again. Should still some of the students remain unchosen, these are called to a further meeting, and so forth, until everybody has found a partner.

In this variation of our placement procedure, the "adjuster" is eliminated. He doesn't interfere; he does not make any suggestion beyond stating the actual findings. He states the positive findings, the pairs formed. He does not state the negative findings. The adjuster here is merely a charter. He gives information beyond stating the pairs only when he is asked to do so. One or another student who did not succeed in receiving his partner may want to know what his position is in the group. He may find, for instance, that although his first and second choice remain unreciprocated, he is chosen first by two and second by three students to whom he had paid little attention. This may urge him to think more clearly about his relation to his co-students and also prepare him better for the next shuffle. The charting is repeated, of course, after each meeting.

This variation of sociometric technique seems a happy combination of complete *laissez-faire* and of placement aid. Information or aid is only given if a student asks for it. Otherwise it is withheld. The same procedure can be used in every type of group.

PSYCHODRAMA *WITH* CHILDREN
VERSUS PSYCHOANALYSIS *OF* CHILDREN
(1945)

The psychoanalysts in play situations with children *do structure* and do help in the production. Obviously, they do not only observe and analyze the *material* but they operate as "auxiliary egos" to the children. It is therefore an intellectual dishonesty to proclaim, as some psychoanalysts do, that the child should not be "pushed", that the play situation should not be "structured" because in the actuality of the playroom they do push, influence and structure. What advantage is there in leaving these important processes which take place between analyst and child or teacher and child and among the children themselves *unconscious and unanalyzed*. It appears that psychoanalysts insist on rigorous analysis only in areas in which they have a conceptual framework but whenever they enter a new area for which no conceptual framework has been developed by them they either apply concepts from other areas automatically or they belittle the dynamic importance of the new. Psychoanalysts contradict here their own dictum "to analyze". But there is a parallel to the counter-transference in the adult situation. The analyst becomes in the play situation a *counter-producer*, a *co-producer*. This means, of course, that structuring takes place in a lesser or greater degree. Once this fact is openly recognized, instead of secretly practiced the new factors entering the play situation, a) the other persons, the therapist, the teacher and other children, like untrained auxiliary egos, b) their inter-personal relations, c) the dynamic group structure emerging from their relations, their spontaneities and creativities and the productions emerging, they all can be systematically developed and controlled.

The toys, the dolls and the inanimate objects of the old-fashioned playroom are welcome guests in the psychodramatic playroom but the unconscious play analyst has to turn into a "conscious psychodramatist in order to correct the constant threat to the healthy development of children; the world of toys and dolls is a poor substitute for the open world outside and the real people they are going to encounter. Toys, dolls, and objects should therefore be "animated with reality by auxiliary egos" representing them.

---

* See, Homo Juvenis (1909 and 1914—page 19-22, in "Einladung zu einer Begegnung") ; Die Gottheit als Komoediant (in "Daimon" Vol. II, 1919) ; Der Koenigsroman (1923) ; Das Steigreiftheater (1923), published by Gustav Kiepenheuer, Berlin, Germany.

The resistance of psychoanalysts, "orthodox" or "oriented", against play psycho-therapy, and especially against its most complete and determinate form, the psychodrama, is the still widely prevailing dictum—just to look at children and to analyze them at a distance, to leave the play situation amorphous, as the children have them, to leave the spontaneity of the children unstimulated, permitting them as little and no more than the cultural milieu, in which they grew up, has permitted to pass, to be as non-directive as possible which is often another word for non-committal and non-responsible. This resistance goes from the base of psychoanalytic theory, a resistance which I strongly felt between 1911 and 1914 when I began to use play techniques with children and again when I opened the Stegreiftheater in Vienna in 1921. *The play principle was then treated as the very opposite, as the antithesis of psychoanalysis.* Although many years after I had proposed in theory and practice in a spectacular form the principle of play, analysts like Melanie Klein (1926) and Anna Freud began to argue for its acceptance as a psychoanalytic technique, it took considerable persuasion during the late twenties and early thirties to give the play idea appropriate hearing at psychoanalytic meetings and it is even today, in the year 1950 far from being truly accepted by the "old timers". The reason is simple: the play is a foreign body in psychoanalysis, accepting it fully means the capitulation of the total psychoanalytic framework of concepts and replacing it by a new one. It means replacing the theory of analysis by the theory of play, or more specifically, the theory of psychoanalysis by the theory of psychodrama. The play method was in my writings from its beginning closely allied to "Experimental Method" ("Das Stegreif Experiment"). Psychoanalysis was from its beginning opposed to experimental methods, it stood only for analysis. Play, spontaneity, creativity, production, play catharsis, psychodrama, sociodrama, role playing are parts of a natural continuity, they are branches of the same tree, they have the same roots in common. Psychoanalysis and all the analytic derivates belong to a different continuity and have different goals.

ROLE PLAYING IN SOCIOMETRIC RESEARCH
(1934)

When our attempt to adjust Elsa to the group with which she was living —treatment by suggestion, analysis of her conduct, change of her function within the house and of her associates within the group—had not succeeded in effecting a change in her behavior we considered creating an entirely new setting for her. But the question was where to place her and with whom. The sociometric test was at this point a useful methodical guide which indicated to us the individuals in the community to whom her spontaneous affection travelled, housemothers, teachers, or other girls. When we found that her interest revolved more or less persistently around certain persons in three different cottages, we began to pay attention to these individuals, especially to the motives Elsa had in seeking association with them and how the latter responded to her affection. As her acquaintance volume in the community was small, we thought that there may be many other individuals besides these who might have a beneficial effect upon her and we tried to enlarge the number of her acquaintances by having her meet others in the role playing groups.

Elsa took part in one of the Impromptu play groups and she was often given occasion to act out different roles—the role of a daughter or a mother, of a girl friend or of a sweetheart, of a housemaid or of a wealthy lady, of a pickpocket or a judge. She acted these parts in a great variety of standard life situations as they impress themselves upon an adolescent who grows up in the slums of a great industrial city. In these situations she is faced with a home conflict—mother and father in a heated argument which leads finally to their separation, with a work conflict in which she gets fired from a job because she stays out late, with a love conflict in which she loves a boy who is as poor and rejected as she is. An analysis of the text and gestures produced in these Impromptu situations gave us clues to understand better her early family life and the emotional tensions which gradually brought about her present status.

Through this technique we had the opportunity to see her acting opposite the individuals chosen by her in the sociometric test and also opposite other girls whom she had not known before and in roles self-chosen or chosen by us. When the sociometric test was repeated after four weeks, she added three others to the number of girls with whom she wanted to live and she was in turn wanted by four. The girls for whom she displayed attraction we divided into those who showed attraction in return, those who rejected her, and those who were indifferent to her. To gain an insight into which associations gave promise to be more enduring and beneficial, we placed her to act with the various other persons, whether these rejected or were attracted to her, in standard life situations in order that we might surmise what their conduct towards her would be in actual life. It was our principle to let the girls work out by themselves any situation which may turn up in life and which they may one day have to meet. A comparison of a series of 82 situational records indicated that only two of the seven girls Elsa had chosen released from her spontaneous expressions which contrasted favorably in articulation of emotion and judgment with her daily behavior and which overcame certain petty habitual trends which she had demonstrated in speech and action when acting with the other girls. It seemed that she wanted to win the sympathy of Jeanette and Florence when acting with them. After a gradual elimination of the cottages unfit for Elsa and a close scrutiny of her relation to these two girls and to the housemother of C11, cottage 11 appeared as the most auspicious assignment for Elsa.

THE STRATEGIC FUNCTION OF ELECTRIC RECORDING FOR CLINICAL PSYCHOLOGY AND PSYCHOTHERAPY

(1944)

Now that electric recording of therapeutic sessions is universally accepted, and used by the psychotherapies of all denominations, it may be worthwhile to narrate the story of how it originated in my mind. Every new idea has a special genesis, usually in a personal thinker, no idea comes out of nothing, although it may appear so to the uninformed who do not know of the birthpangs of the pioneer.

Between 1921 and 1925 I was engaged in two parallel activities, first the study of electromagnetic fields and the invention of an instrument for recording and second the study of spontaneity-creativity and of instruments for the advancement of "spontaneity research", (See "Das Stegreif Theatre", 1923). The two ideas seemed incompatible with one another but it is due to their combination that the idea of electric recording of therapeutic sessions was born.

In collaboration with Frank Loernitz, we started where the Danish engineer Paulsen had left off. We suggested the following improvements: a) the replacement of Paulsen's wire tape by a *steel disk*; b) the use of both sides of the disk, one for acoustic, the other for optic impressions; c)

besides its use as an "electro-magnetic phonograph", to connect the instrument to radio and television, and so develop a tele—and radio conserve. This is the reason why the invention was called "radio film". The
news of the invention was cabled from Vienna by the Associated Press and
the New York Times brought the first report of it to American readers.
(The New York Times, Friday, July 3, 1925, *Invent Radio Records;
Viennese Scientists Catch Broadcaster on Phonograph Discs;* Copyright,
1925, by The New York Times Company; By Wireless to The New York
Times. Vienna, July 2.) "An innovation in broadcasting was announced
today by The Vienna Press. It is the invention by the Austrian scientist
Moreno and the engineer Loernitz, which they say makes possible the fix-
ing of broadcast sounds as if by a gramophone record and the rendering
of them later at will any number of times. The principal part of the invention consists of discs on which the broadcast sounds are recorded by a
spiral consisting, not of deeper or shallower impressions as on a gramophone
record, but of a continuous line of points more or less strongly magnetized
according to the strength or quantity of the sound. It is also possible to
down only certain parts of this record, skipping others. The discs are
demagnetized by a simple process and may be used again. The inventors
do not declare they have discovered any new principle but have combined
known elements into something decidedly novel". An American concern
sponsored the invention, and brought us with the model to the United
States in October, 1925. I came to the U. S. A. therefore, not because of
sociometry or psychodrama, but because of our invention of an electric
device of recording. The idea of making records of therapeutic sessions
came immediately to my mind as a possibility of the greatest importance
for making therapeutic research more accurate and objective and of the
greatest usefulness to mental patients. In the beginning I persistently rejected the idea for the following reasons: It was in discord with the
hypocratic oath to make *public* the case histories of the patients, especially
revelations of an intimate nature. The making of electric recordings of
thereapeutic processes and the replaying of them afterwards appeared to
be unethical, entirely against the spirit of the hypocratic oath. In addition
to that, the idea was prevalent and still is in many places that patients who
come for advice to a psychotherapist would be greatly disturbed or hindered
in their cure if they would know that recordings of their utterances are
made. It was thought that this might interfere with the spontaneity of
their utterances and so reduce the value of the therapeutic effect of counseling. It appeared also that a patient would have a just reason to pursue

a physician legally for libel for disgracing his private life and ruining his social status by making and displaying such recordings. Therefore, my first reaction to the idea was, "No, it can't be done". Meanwhile when organizing a laboratory for spontaneity research in the Theatre for Spontaneity (Stegrif Theatre) in Vienna, I encountered independently a problem which was in a way parallel. In a theatre of spontaneity there is no script whatsoever. Indeed, in the old drama research the problem of recording did not exist because the manuscript of the playwright and the rehearsing instructions of the producer were already given as a record in *advance*. Every performance was supposed to be a one hundred percent duplication of the record already made by playwright plus producer. There was no additional recording necessary, of a production in development. But in a theatre of spontaneity some means of recording became indispensable so that the creations of the moment might be preserved for students and patients as well. An effort in this direction was my charting of interpersonal productions by means of *the interpersonal and the position diagrams*. Although a good device for measurement, they were too incomplete and lifeless. The electric recording permits the reproducing not only of the literal words and dialogue but of the living voices of the participants.

In addition, once the total acoustic picture of a session is preserved, possibilities of analysis suggested themselves to the clinical investigator which did not suggest themselves so easily, if only fragmentary notations of what occurred were made *after* a session had taken place. The ideas which came to me later were a logical consequence of recording: a) to make a content analysis of the word volume of each participant; it was hypothecated by me that *the volume of words* spoken in a situation are a measure of the aggression or non-aggression of that individual; b) quantitative analysis of the emotional and ideological content of the production; (See "Who Shall Survive?", pp. 186-190); c) duration of a session and the relation of acts to pauses.

I suggested, therefore, that *"a talking machine should photograph the process" and "that we should make systematic use of this machinery of personality recording."* And further that *"any reactions witnessed by the psychologist and revelations given by an individual during a course of interviews, casual or planned, are, at least from the point of view of cooperative, controllable research, of little value since they are after the event merely memory impressions of the observer. The multiform interpretations offered by the subjectivists in psychology are without proper demonstration and reconsideration as long as they do not conserve the moment."*

And again *"occasions to study the use of electrical recording have led the writer and his collaborators to lay emphasis upon the recording of spontaneous behavior in especially assigned situations which are unprepared and unexpected by the person to be tested."**

I suggested also that by *"recording of* mimetic *expression, reactions which may have been undervalued in the haste of presentation are available for study. Signs which are preferred by the psychologist and consequently stressed by him are present together with signs which he may have overlooked. A level of 'intelligence' which is indicated in a rich aptitude for mimic expression may then be observed simultaneously with a comparatively poor aptitude for verbal expression, or vice versa, and properly considered in the rating. These inconsistencies of verbal expressions with other expressions of the subject imply that free-word-association by itself is frequently a deceptive basis of study. Many gestures and movements, unintentional or intentional, pass unobserved by the testers during the test due to the fact that their attention is absorbed by the process. These actions have often a definite bearing on the subject. During the review of the film later, any subtle deviations in behavior may become prominent along with clues to conflicting tendencies within the acting persons."***

DISCUSSION OF SNYDER'S "THE PRESENT STATUS OF PSYCHOTHERAPEUTIC COUNSELLING"***

(1947)

Psychiatrists have frequently claimed that psychologists are not "fit" to practice psychotherapy, but their attitude is changing in recent years. Psychologists, in turn, often assert that they are superior to psychiatrists in the use of scientific methods. However, an objective approach and understanding—from both sides of the fence—is of the utmost importance if we are ever to attain a united front among the psychotherapists. By articles like the one of Snyder the existing chaos in psychotherapeutic

---

* See for these quotations "Application for the Group Method to Classification" published by National Committee of Prisons, 1931 and 1932, p. 16-18.

** Conserves of the tests can be repeated (playback) and not only are certain striking symptoms stored for duplications at will but the otherwise unrecordable scale of mimic expressions" (combination of acoustic recording with motion pictures).

*** Snyder, W. U. The present status of psychotherapeutic counseling. *Psychol. Bull.*, 1947, **44**, 297-386.

counseling will be increased and the cleavage between psychiatrists and psychologists further widened. The author frequently stresses that psychiatrists are commonly inclined to be unscientific, subjective and intuitive in approach, whereas psychologists believe in experimental methods and scientific validation; that psychiatrists indulge in esoteric terminology, but that psychologists use terms which are universal, that is, accepted everywhere by the scientific fraternity. Such bias, which runs intermittently throughout the review comes to a head in the statements directed against Freud and Moreno. In the chapter on psychoanalysis he says:

> One difficulty for the nonpsychoanalytically trained reader is that the vocabulary of psychoanalysis is so esoteric that it frequently has little meaning. . . . the majority of psychiatrists in this country and almost every psychologist are more likely to agree with Blanchette (?) that psychoanalysis is a medical psychology without adequate roots in or connections with scientific medicine or scientific psychology.

In the chapter on psychodrama he says:

> Moreno himself is unscientific and intuitive in approach. . . . Moreno postulates relationships and behavior patterns which are explainable only in terms of his esoteric system. In this regard his method is similar to Freudian psychoanalysis (p. 333).

It is common knowledge that psychoanalysis is rooted in French psychiatry, the school of Charcot. If it added some original ideas to medical psychology, this in itself should not make it unscientific. To treat Freud in an article on therapeutic counseling as if he would be a dead dog is ridiculous. He was a great empiricist, he formulated his hypotheses with care and discarded them when new observations seemed to warrant it. Because he was pre-experimental, this does not mean that he was unscientific; as the psychology of the individual was in its infancy when he approached it, he was as scientific as its stage of development permitted. Unfortunately, the words "scientific" and "esoteric" are used by Snyder in a moralizing, almost schoolmasterly way. All scientific terms have once been esoteric and many are now universally accepted. Should one hesitate to introduce new ideas and coin new terms because they are bound to be considered esoteric by our contemporaries? It should not be permitted that fear of new ideas and resentment of originality raise their head under the guise of a narrow concept of science and of how new ideas emerge.

The treatment which psychodrama and sociometry receive at the hand of Snyder is intuitive and esoteric, to use his own terminology. If he would have studied the subject more thoroughly he would have learned that the outstanding development in counseling in recent years is closely linked to sociometric and psychodramatic methods. It has nothing to do with the controversy "directive-nondirective" which psychiatrists have been carrying on for more than fifty years. In "sociometric counseling" the counselor may be anonymous; the counselor is not only nondirective but may be altogether *absent* from the scene when the therapeutic choice process takes place. The sociogram, mapping the emotional currents operating among the members of a group, becomes the objective reference upon which his recommendations as counselor are based. The process of involvement is in principle removed from the counselor-client relationship to the client-client relationships.

Psychodramatic counseling is more complex; practically all problems which appear singly in each of the current psychotherapies reappear in a psychodramatic session magnified or in new combinations. Because there are many types of problems which the clients bring to us there are many versions of psychodrama. There has not been found a single method which can be applied universally. The oldest and most popular form of psychodrama is the *self directed* form, in which the self of the client directs the production exclusively, director and auxiliary egos assisting him in the production if he wishes. In another version of psychodrama the director is outside of the situation, the therapeutic process takes place between the two or more clients involved in the conflict.

There can be no greater contrast than the one between the nondirective interview and self-directed psychodrama production. Nondirective puts a premium on a *minimum of self expression of the counselor;* psychodrama puts a premium on the *maximum of self expression of the client.* The word nondirective is often misleading. It is a negative term, implying that the spontaneity of the client should be permitted to express itself without interference from any source. Nondirective writers talk often the language of spontaneity in reverse; they are worried about making the counselor as unstimulating to the client as possible but not worried about whether the subject is stimulated to be himself. Various interviewers have been observed in practice; it was found that, however cautious they may be in their questionings, on the action level they assumed various attitudes which appealed to the subject in uncontrollable ways. One counselor may have a fatherly way of taking the role, smiling approvingly; the other a businesslike way; the third may be withdrawn and indifferent; all three may use the same technique of questioning but they have a different effect upon the client. It was evident that the very physical appearance of the counselor was bound to influence the client; it has, as we sociometrists phrase it, a tele effect.

Mr. Snyder refers to one of my papers "Scientific foundations of group psychotherapy." He is unaware that this article is just a summary, that it refers back to fifteen years of research in which several hundred workers have collaborated, contained in nine volumes of SOCIOMETRY, books like *Who Shall Survive?*, about fifty monographs. The climax of ignorance for the meaning of psychodrama and group psychotherapy comes forth in Snyder's statement: "In evaluating psychodrama it is perhaps of significance to note that Moreno himself performs for the public at two weekly sessions in New York where admission is charged" (p. 334).* This is obviously a derogatory remark. Snyder seems to believe that it is unworthy of a psychotherapist, perhaps also unscientific as well as undignified, to give sessions "for the public."* The fact is that the most revolutionary change in therapeutic counseling since psychoanalysis is linked with the *open* sessions for the public. My giving of open sessions had enormous consequences because it broke with two sacred cliches, first that of the counselor being closeted in a secret chamber with the client and no other client or counselor sharing in the experiences evoked in the session; it was and had to remain strictly confidential. The public session opened the door wide for the participation of larger and smaller groups in a common therapeutic experience. Second, not making any record during the session which was to remain sacred and discreet for the sake of the client. But once the privacy of the one-to-one therapeutic relationship was broken it became a foregone conclusion that simultaneous observation and recording of the therapeutic process should be permissible. This marked the way towards the objectification of the interview. The clinical advance inaugurated by the public session meant automatically also an advance in objectively recording and analyzing its operations. The principle of electric recording taking place simultaneously with the therapeutic process was announced by me seventeen years ago and followed since then throughout my writings and fre-

---

*At the New York Psychodramatic Institute a ten weeks' seminar, one session weekly, is given by me as is customary for experts in a specialty. The fee for the entire seminar is $15.00. The fee for a single admission is $1.65. The public consists of students of the universities and colleges in and around New York.

quently practiced—it is curious therefore that Snyder should give the non-directive counselor priority in this:

> Reactions witnessed by the psychologist and revelations given by any individual during a course of interviews, casual or planned, are, at least from the point of view of cooperative, controllable research, of little value since they are after the event merely memory impressions of the observer. The multiform interpretations offered by the subjectivists in psychology are without proper demonstration and reconsideration as long as they do not conserve the moment. I suggested frequently therefore that "a talking machine should photograph the process" and that we should make a systematic use of this machinery of personality recording.*

Psychodramatic procedure, being an offshoot of sociometry, has to be viewed and evaluated with sociometric methodology and experimentation as a background. Concepts like *sociodynamic effect, social atom* and *tele* can appear esoteric and intuitive only to one who has not acquainted himself with the methods by which they have been explored.

PSYCHODRAMA AND GROUP PSYCHOTHERAPY I

(1946)

Two thousand years ago mankind underwent, as we do today, a crisis of the first magnitude. To the broad masses catharsis came from Christianity, due to the universality of its methods and the practicality of its instruments, love and confession, charity and hope, instead of from the philosophical schools of Egypt and Greece. In our time the social and mental sciences aim at a similar accomplishment as religion once attained. Mankind's masses suffer from social and mental unrest. Catharsis will probably come again from instruments which combine universality of method with great practicality. One of the most promising methods developed in the last twenty-five years and fulfilling these demands is the psychodramatic method.

Drama is a transliteration of the Greek δρᾶμα which means action, or a thing done. Psychodrama can be defined, therefore, as the science which explores the "truth" by dramatic methods.

---

* Moreno, J. L. *Application of the group method to classification.* New York: The National Committee on Prisons and Prison Labor, 1931, p. 16. (Current edition: *Group method and group psychotherapy.* New York: Beacon House, p. 16.)

The psychodramatic method uses mainly five instruments—the stage, the subject or patient, the director, the staff of therapeutic aides or auxiliary egos, and the audience. The first instrument is the stage. Why a stage? It provides the patient with a living space which is multi-dimensional and flexible to the maximum. The living space of reality is often narrow and restraining, he may easily lose his equilibrium. On the stage he may find it again due to its methodology of freedom—freedom from unbearable stress and freedom for experience and expression. The stage space is an extension of life beyond the reality tests of life itself. Reality and fantasy are not in conflict, but both are functions within a wider sphere—the psychodramatic world of objects, persons and events. In its logic the ghost of Hamlet's father is just as real and permitted to exist as Hamlet himself. Delusions and hallucinations are given flesh—embodiment on the stage—and an equality of status with normal sensory perceptions. The architectural design of the stage is made in accord with therapeutic requirements. Its circular forms and levels of the stage, levels of aspiration, pointing out the vertical dimension, stimulate relief from tensions and permit mobility and flexibility of action. The locus of a psychodrama, if necessary, may be designated everywhere, wherever the patients are, the field of battle, the classroom or the private home. But the ultimate resolution of deep mental conflicts requires an objective setting, the therapeutic theater. Like in religion, although the devout may pray to his God in his own chamber, it is in the church where the community of believers attain the most complete confirmation of their faith.

The second instrument is the subject or patient. He is asked to be himself on the stage, to portray his own private world. He is told to be himself, not an actor, as the actor is compelled to sacrifice his own private self to the role imposed upon him by a playwright. Once he is warmed up to the task it is comparatively easy for the patient to give an account of his daily life in action, as no one is as much of an authority on himself as himself. He has to act freely, as things rise up in his mind; that is why he has to be given freedom of expression, spontaneity. Next in importance to spontaneity comes the process of enactment. The verbal level is transcended and included in the level of action. There are several forms of enactment, pretending to be in a role, re-enactment or acting out a past scene, living out a problem presently pressing, creating life on the stage or testing oneself for the future. Further comes the principle of involvement. We have been brought up with the idea that, in test as well as in treatment situations, a minimum of involvement with other persons and objects is a most desirable thing for the patient. An illustration of this is the "Rorschach." The Rorschach situation is reduced to ink blots. In the Rorschach the subjects change but the situation is always the same. It is thought to be its greatest virtue that it is pure and therefore offers an "objective" test. The psychoanalytic interview in its orthodox form too, tried to be pure and objective, by reducing the involvement with the analyst to a minimum. In the psychodramatic situation a maximum of involvement with other subjects and things is not only possible but expected. Reality is not only not feared but provoked. Indeed, in the psychodramatic situation all degrees of involvement take place, from a minimum to a maximum. In addition comes the principle of realization. The patient is enabled not only to meet parts of himself, but the other persons who partake in his mental conflicts. These persons may be real or illusions. The reality test which is a mere word in other therapies is thus actually made true on the stage. The warming up process of the subject to psychodramatic portrayal is stimulated by numerous techniques, only a few of which are mentioned here: self presentation, soliloquy, projection, interpolation of resistance, reversal of roles, double ego, mirror techniques, auxiliary world, realization and psycho-chemical techniques. The aim of these sundry techniques is not to turn the patients into actors, but rather to stir them up to be on the stage what they *are,* more deeply and explicitly than they appear to be in life reality. The patient has as dramatis personae either the real people of his private world, his wife, his father, his child, etc., or actors portraying them, auxiliary egos.

The third instrument is the director. He has three functions: producer, therapist and analyst. As producer he has to be on the alert to turn every clue which the subject offers into dramatic action, to make the line of production one with the life line of the subject, and never to let the production lose rapport with the audience. As therapist attacking and shocking the subject is at times just as permissible as laughing and joking with him; at times he may become indirect and passive and for all practical purposes the session seems to be run by the patient. As analyst he may complement his own interpretation by responses coming from informants in the audience, husband, parents, children, friends or neighbors.

The fourth instrument is a staff of auxiliary egos. These auxiliary egos or therapeutic actors have a double significance. They are extensions of the director, exploratory and therapeutic, but they are also extensions of the patient, portraying the actual or imagined personae of their life drama. The functions of the auxiliary ego are threefold: the function of the actor, portraying roles required by the patient's world; the function of the therapeutic agent, guiding the subject; and the function of the social investigator.

The fifth instrument is the audience. The audience itself has a double purpose. It may serve to help the patient or, being itself helped by the subject on the stage the audience becomes the patient. In helping the patient it is a sounding board of public opinion. Its responses and comments are as extemporaneous as those of the patient, they may vary from laughter to violent protest. The more isolated the patient is, for instance because his drama on the stage is shaped by delusions and hallucinations, the more important becomes, to him, the presence of an audience which is willing to accept and understand him. When the audience is helped by the subject, thus becoming the patient itself, the situation is reversed. The audience sees itself, that is, one of its collective syndromes portrayed on the stage.

The stage portion of a psychodramatic session has opened the way to action research and action therapy, role test and role training, situation tests and situational interviews whereas the audience portion has become the common ground of the better known forms of group psychotherapy, as lecture methods, dramatic methods and film methods. Scientific foundations of group psychotherapy require as a prerequisite a basic science of human relations, widely known as sociometry. It is from "sociatry," a pathological counterpart of such a science that knowledge can be derived as to abnormal organization of groups, the diagnosis and prognosis, prophylaxis and control of deviate group behavior.

Now that we have described the five basic instruments required to run a psychodramatic session we may ask ourselves: to what effect? We will limit ourselves here to the description of a single phenomenon, mental catharsis (stems from the Greek, it means purging, purification).

Breuer and Freud were ignorant of the psychotherapeutic implications of the drama milieu to which Aristotle referred. It remained for psychodrama to rediscover and treat the idea of catharsis in its relation to psychotherapy. We picked up the trend of thought where Aristotle had left off. We too, began with the drama but *reversed* the procedure. It was not the end phase but the initial phase of the drama towards which we directed attention. *Mental* catharsis was when we entered the scene with our investigations to be found only in dramatic literature, in faded memories of Aristotle's old definition and the term itself practically out of circulation. The psychoanalysts, after a flare up in the early 1890's had pushed it aside. As practically every human activity can be the source of some degree of catharsis the problem is to determine in what catharsis consists, in which way it differs for instance, from happiness, contentment, ecstasy, need satisfaction, and so forth, and whether one source is superior in the production of catharsis to another source; indeed, whether there is an element common to all sources which operates in the production of catharsis. Therefore my aim has been to define catharsis in such a way that all forms of influence which have a demonstrable cathartic effect can be shown as positive steps within a single total process of operation. I discovered the common principle producing catharsis to be: spontaneity.

Because of the universality of the act and its primordial nature it engulfs all other forms of expression. They flow naturally out of it or can be encouraged to emerge, verbal associations, musical associations, visual associations, color associations, rhythmic and dance associations, and every other stimulus which might arouse or inhibit the emergence of one or another factor, for instance, the use of psychochemical starters like sedatives, as barbiturates, sodium amytal, sodium pentotal; or shock methods as insulin, metrazol or electricity; or endocrinological medications as thyroid are fully within the scheme of total catharsis; they may condition and prepare the organism for psychodramatic integration. The need for the drama can be temporarily choked, for instance, by sleep or shock therapies. But the fundamental need for the realization of certain fantastic imageries can not be "shocked away." Unless the subject is reduced to a brain invalid by surgery or prolonged shock treatments, the temporarily scared patient is bound to relapse and reproduce the same type of mental syndrome he had before treatment began. It is into the stream of action catharsis that all the rivulets of partial catharsis flow.

The treatment of audiences has become an important alternative to individual treatment. The relationship of the audience to itself in a psychodramatic session, being treated by its own spokesman on the stage, gives us a clue as to the reasons of the cathartic effect of psychodrama. According to historians of the Greek drama the audience was there first, the chorus, musing about a common syndrome. There were "keynoters" among them but they remained within the chorus. Aeschylos is credited with having put the first actor upon a social space outside of the chorus, the stage, not speaking to them, but portraying the woes of their own hero. Euripedes is credited with having put the second actor on the stage, thus making possible the dialogue and interaction of roles. We may be credited to have put the psyche itself on the stage. The psyche which originally came from the group—after a process of reconversion on the stage—personified by an actor—returns to the group—in the form of the psychodrama. That which was most startling, new and spectacular to see and to feel on the stage appears to the participants after thorough exposure as a process which is familiar to them and intimately known—as their own selves. The psychodrama confirms their own identity as in a mirror.

PSYCHODRAMA AND GROUP PSYCHOTHERAPY: II
(1948)

In the last two centuries, three revolutions have taken place in the field of psychotherapy. Each was characterized by *a specific change of operation*. In each case, the new practice gradually compelled an overhauling of theory, but in each successive case the new method was broader in scope and, to a degree, included the previous form.

The first, in the middle of the eighteenth century, is connected with the name of a Viennese physician, Mesmer. The operation, *hypnosis,* consisted in putting the patient into a state of trance. Mesmer thought that the hypnotist is responsible for the state of the "hypnotizand" and developed a theory about animal magnetism according to which a fluid travels from the physician to the subject.

At the end of the nineteenth century, another Viennese, Freud, brought about a new revolution by discarding the hypnotic sleep as a means of treatment and establishing another form of operation. Patient and physician faced each other in full consciousness, the patient was told to tell the doctor whatever came to his mind. The physician expected to attain by this method, which he called *psychoanalysis,* all the results which had been attained previously by means of hypnosis and many more things to which the hypnotized state of the patient closed the doors. The psychoanalytic method of operation brought Mesmer's theory of animal magnetism and all its intellectual modifications *via* Charcot, Bernheim, and others into discard, and it was replaced by the well-known system of psychoanalytic theories.

During the crucial years between 1900 and 1925 in which psychoanalytic theory and practice developed, there have been many widely discussed differences between psychoanalytic schools. However, the conflict between Freud, Jung and Adler was due to different views of analysis and interpretation, and there was no conflict between them as to *operation*. The Freudians emphasized libido and its cathexis as chief determinant of human behavior, while Adler preferred inferiority organs and inferiority feelings as the core of his analysis, and for Jung it was the collective unconscious and the extrovert-introvert types of personality which seemed to matter. But if we could have entered the office of a Freudian, an Adlerian or a Jungian between 1910-1930, the operation would have been about the same: a physician and a patient alone, in a doctor's office strictly private and sealed from observers. There were slight modifications: in one case a patient relaxing on a couch, in another case facing him, the patient sitting in front of the doctor, in still another case the procedure being more informal and the duration of the treatment shorter. But in all cases the patient would have been found talking freely about himself and the physician giving an analysis of the material elicited. However great the contrast may have been in the ways of interpretation and in its depths, there was no difference in operation.

In our time, in the last twenty-five years, a new revolution took place when the first therapeutic theatre was started in Vienna. It was again due to a radical change of operation. The method has become known as psychodrama, sociodrama, role playing, and action taking. *The patient is now an actor on the stage, acting before a smaller or larger audience of other patients.* The physician-patient relation has become subsidiary. Again, we are in the midst of an overhauling of theory. With the new operation, new concepts and theories are emerging. It consists of two procedures: (*a*) treatment of the audience (group psychotherapy); (*b*) representatives of the group portray on the stage the problem from which the audience ails (action therapy). The group is facing the mirror of itself (in many versions) on the stage. It looks into this mirror and sees itself. The responses coming from the shock to the audio ego (members of the audience) and to the auxiliary egos (actors on the stage) are systematically followed up.

SUMMARY

"Psychoanalysis . . . only began with my rejection of the hypnotic technique" (Freud "Autobiography", 1935). I could paraphrase this by saying: Psychodrama began with my rejection of the couch and the free association technique, and their replacement by an open, multidimensional space (the stage or any other open field) and the psychodramatic techniques.

GROUP PSYCHOTHERAPY AND SOCIAL COHESION

(1948)

I have frequently raised the question as to the cohesion of the group and the possible relation of cohesion to therapeutic success. But in order to determine what group cohesion is, the more inclusive question has to be answered: *how* are groups formed? What factors enter into group formation *in statu nascendi* and which factors produce changes from poorly structured to highly structured groups? In the course of the last two decades a large number of experiments have been set up by sociometrists in various communities. Our premise was that groups have a structure of their own and that special instruments have to be constructed in order to explore effectively this new area. The psychologic, psychiatric, psychoanalytic and sociologic instruments generally applied at that time when our work was started were utterly unfit. The new group procedures are now commonly known as sociometric—sociometric test, acquaintance test, spontaneity test, action test, situation test, psychodramatic and sociodramatic approach, to mention a few. By means of these instruments it has become possible to study group structure empirically and to isolate factors which enter into their formation. The most important factor which we tried to identify was called "tele," a Greek word meaning "projection into distance." Tele was assumed to be responsible for the cohesion within groups. The tele hypothesis has been tested by the following experiment: Seven sociometrically tested groups consisting of real individuals were compared with seven equally large chance groups consisting of chance individuals. The finding was that the groups consisting of real people showed constantly specific social configurations of interaction formed by them—a high number of mutual attractions or mutual hostilities and more complex structure as triangles, quadrangles and chains; whereas the chance groups excelled in a high degree of unreciprocations and a low number of mutual relations whether positive or negative. This deviation of the structure of actual groups from chance groups and the changes from poorly structured to highly structured groups must be ascribed to a specific factor: tele. The cohesion of the group, C, is therefore a function, f, of tele, T. $C = fT$. A number of experiments have been set up in order to investigate when and how a *change* in group structure takes place, the change of a group of a low cohesion into a group of a high cohesion. Cohesion was defined by the structure a given group discloses when submitted to a sociometric test, the number of isolates, pairs, triangles, chains, networks, stars, positive or negative. By moving individuals of a low sociometric status out of the group and moving into it individuals of a high degree of sociometric status the cohesion of the group improved, as demonstrated by sociometric tests before and after the assignments and reassignments were made. By using sociometric tests at two points in time of the group development the change in its cohesion could be measured. But the dynamic change in structure may be a spontaneous one, that is, autonomously occurring in the group without any interference by an outsider and without any conscious manipulation. Therefore, an additional experiment was set up in which spontaneous group development was compared with sociometrically manipulated grouping. This experiment proved decisively that by means of sociometric group technics the cohesion of the group advances faster than if the spontaneous conditions of the group remain unharnessed.

Groups of patients participating in a treatment situation should be submitted to a diagostic test each time they meet for treatment. The test would disclose the structure of the group at the moment, the changes in structure which have taken place since the test was last given. On the basis of the findings recommendations can be made (a) as to the size of the group (eliminating certain patients or adding new ones); (b) as to the *frequency* of sessions (if treatment sessions are held too far apart the cohesion of the group may slow up—if they are too frequent the saturation point for optimum benefit may be passed); (c) as to the *medium* most useful and effective for producing therapeutic change—lectures and what type, discussion and what topic, introducing a patient's problem to the group, psychodrama, etc.; (d) as to the relationship of the participants to the conditions "in situ," that is, outside of their treatment sessions, in the places where they live and work.

The need of group psychotherapy can be thus established. Failure as well as success of group psychotherapy can then be carefully measured, indications and contraindications as to type of group psychotherapy can be established and termination of treatment can be determined.

THE PREDICTION AND PLANNING OF SUCCESS IN MARRIAGE*
(1941)

One of the greatest of the methodological difficulties which the social sciences have had to face has been the discrepancy between verbalized behavior (as expressed in interviews, free-association tests, the answers to questionnaires, etc.) and behavior in life-situations (the action-patterns of individuals) in which verbalized behavior is but a minor component and in which the meaning of the verbal content, itself, undergoes a profound change, due to the influence of the action-pattern from which it springs. The more fundamental and central a situation or relationship may be in family and marriage relationships for example, for the individuals concerned, the greater is the social tension if such discrepancy arises. In "pre-marriage" situations, a neglect of this discrepancy must account for grave errors in the analysis of the material, in the prediction of failure or success and, last but not least, in the rational planning of future relationships.

It seems to me that the most important major research in family and marriage problems must focus, in the next few years, upon the devising of theories, procedures, methods and tests which are able to bring this problem nearer to solution. The difficulty confronting the researcher in the field of inter-personal relationships has always been that there seemed to be but two main approaches available: studies based upon verbalized behavior and the observation of people in life-situations by such means as participant-observer techniques. Both methods have and have had their merits, but when it comes to actual planning of inter-personal relationships and the prediction of their development, these methods do not appear to be adequate. It is necessary, therefore, to find a middle way between these two extremes which is capable of coming closer to the action-pattern of the inter-personal relationships, themselves. In the course of dealing with many marriage problems by means of psychodramatic techniques, we have developed, I believe, a method which can diagnose with ease and accuracy the reasons for the

---

* *Needed Research in Marriage and the Family.*—Not only have the members of the Research Committee been submitting memoranda on what they consider to be established knowledge in the field of marriage and family relations, but some of the members have agreed to set forth what they regard as important research problems which should occupy the attention of workers for the next several years. The first of these memoranda to be submitted is that by J. L. Moreno in which he emphasizes the desirability of applying psychodramatic techniques to the analysis and treatment of problems in these areas. Leonard S. Cottrell, Jr., Chairman.

failure of many marriage relationships as well as offer a means whereby future maladjustments may perhaps be prevented.

The psychodrama—and its ally, sociometry—open up fields of action research which should make a great appeal to the young sociologist because of the almost unlimited possibilities of experiment in new devices which go far beyond the methods and tests worked out to date. Psychodramatic methods permit the researcher to observe inter-personal relationships *in action*. Sources of conflict, past, present or future, come to light in a milieu where they can be diagnosed and treated, foreseen and dealt with, often with the result that, if and when they occur in a relationship, their importance is minimized, and they are viewed with the "proper" perspective. If conflicts in an inter-personal relationship can be prevented, it would follow that this relation-ship has a good expectation of success. It is therefore upon the prediction and prevention of inter-personal conflicts that the researcher should con-centrate.

Psychodramatic procedure, in this field of research, deals first and fore-most with actual life-situations. The researcher can focus his attention upon the situation, itself, as well as the people in it. The psychodrama does not have to rely upon interviews, questionnaires or reports. The subjects are studied, singly or in pairs, as they actually move and speak and act in a situation. The approach is a three-dimensional one and takes place in the present, not removed in point of time. In this way, the researcher can observe, simultaneously with the subjects, the spontaneous reaction of both partners in a relationship as they come face to face with the actual life-situations.

The factor of spontaneity is a very important one. Confronted with a life-situation which is often unexpected and provocative, the subject is called upon to react spontaneously. Observation will enable the researcher to arrive at the "spontaneity quotient" of the subjects. One partner, for in-stance, may be slow in his or her reactions, while the other, quicker one may grow increasingly impatient. A realization that the other's "spontaneity quo-tient" is greater or less than his own may help each partner to allow for this in the future, and an unconscious source of irritation may thus be mitigated.

Based on the principle that each partner in a relationship is *playing a "role"* for the benefit of his or her *vis-à-vis*, and that everyone sees himself, at various times and on various occasions, in a variety of these roles, the psychodrama offers them an opportunity to play out these roles, together. In the course of psychodramatic investigation of the structure of marriage relationships, we have been able to discern certain typical conflicts which appear in almost every marriage. Different solutions are arrived at by different couples; in fact, one might say that a great part of the success or failure of a marriage depends upon the solution arrived at and the ease and speed with which it is attained. Accordingly, psychodramatic procedure establishes a number of typical situations which are standardized for use in the various relationships which come under observation. These situations, of course, are based upon actual psychodramatic experience with many married couples. Each situation simulates an experience which could occur in almost any marriage relationship; it contains the seeds, at least, of a conflict and invariably leads up to some critical point at which one or both partners will be called upon to respond in some way which will work toward a resolution of the crisis which has materialized.

Thus, not only are the prospective bride and bridegroom warned, so to speak, of some of the difficult moments they will, in all probability, have to go through in the course of their married life, but their solutions for these difficult moments are analyzed with them and their mistakes and inadequacies pointed out. Not only do they see one another in the rosy glow usually prevalent in such pre-marital states, but they are forced to face some of the more unpleasant realities which are likely to come and of which they are probably ignorant, as yet. Each partner is revealed to the other in a variety of roles: as a husband or wife, as a home-maker or provider, as a father or mother of a family which is still far in the future, as an errant husband or wife, the other reacting as jealous, complaisant or in whatever spontaneous manner the action calls forth, and *not* solely as lovers anxious to show their best sides to the loved one. In the course of this procedure, hitherto hidden roles will emerge. Many undiscovered facets of both the personalities will appear and are made use of in the education of the couple and the enlightenment of the researcher. The two are able, in a remarkably short time, to learn to know one another and to be prepared for similar situations in the course of the projected relationship.

Psychodramatic treatment of marriage problems has emphasized the importance of the part played by hidden roles in the personalities of the two partners. Many cases of failure have been noted in which the cause could be traced to the emergence of the role, say, of adventurer or poet, at a time which may be even years after the wedding. Had the other partner been aware at the outset of the presence of such potential but undeveloped roles, these roles could have been allowed for, and some counter-roles provided. In every case of failure through this kind of cause, it was the lack of the ability to satisfy a role of this sort which lay at the basis of the marriage's failure. The hidden role emerged, found no satisfaction in the marriage-partner and sought gratification elsewhere. How much happier would the outcome have been if the hidden role had been brought to the surface by psychodramatic means, then perhaps allowed to lie dormant until some later date when it could emerge to find satisfaction in the marriage partner, rather than in someone else.

To set up the psychodramatic milieu in which an experiment of this sort can be conducted is an easy task. The results are two-fold and simultaneous: unlimited research material on a level of actuality and real life, together with practical preparation of and by prospective married couples for their life together.

FRAME OF REFERENCE FOR TESTING, OBJECTIFYING AND MEASURING THE SOCIAL INVESTIGATOR*
(1940)

The problem of investigating a social situation has two fundamental aspects, the first of which is the question of how to achieve a close and accurate approach to the social process to be investigated so that the truly real and valid facts are harvested and not, perhaps, illusionary and unreliable ones. Sociometry in communities and the psychodrama in experimental situations make a deliberate attempt to bring the subjects into an experimental state which will make them sensitive to the realization of their own experiences and action-patterns. In this "spontaneity state" they are able to contribute revealing material concerning the web of social networks in which they move and the life-situations through which they pass. This conditioning of the subjects for a more total knowledge of the social situation in which they are is accomplished by means of processes of warming-up and by learning to summon the degree of spontaneity necessary for a given situation.

---

* This study carries on the discussion of testing which was begun with some material on spontaneity tests in "Application of the Group Method to Classification" (1932), on the analysis of the social investigator in "Who Shall Survive?" (1934), on the participant observer vs. the auxiliary ego in "Sociometry in Relation to Other Social Sciences," SOCIOMETRY (1937), on the standard situation in "Psychodramatic Treatment of Marriage Problems" in SOCIOMETRY (1940)—all by the author of this study.

In the social sciences, the subjects must be approached in the midst of an actual life-situation and not before or after it. They must be truly themselves, in the fullest sense of the word. They must be measured in a real and natural situation; otherwise we may find ourselves measuring something totally different from the situation we set out to measure. If we have not a clear picture of the problem, it may result in our measuring the subjects at a time when they are half in and half out of the situation, before they begin to act in it or long after they have lived through it and the situation has grown "cold", a social conserve. It is evident that *the situation to be measured must be caught in statu nascendi and the subjects warmed up to it.* This emphasizes the enormous importance of the concept of the Moment for all conceptual thinking relevant to the preparation of truly genuine experiments in human societies.

The need for investigating a relationship or a social situation in a manner which adequately portrays every phase in its development (an early phase, a later phase and an end-phase) is crucial in every field within sociology. Sociometry has made this end its particular objective. Sociometric techniques which are known today are probably but a small part of the tools which a future sociometry will make use of, and they are by no means to be confused with sociometry as a general theory in the social sciences.

The other fundamental aspect of the problem concerns the investigator himself. In the social sciences, the problem of the investigator and the situation in which the experiment or study is to be carried out have been of the gravest concern. However, the methods for dealing with this fundamental difficulty have been most unsatisfactory, to date. Let us consider two of the most advanced of these approaches: the method of the participant observer and the method of the psychoanalyst.

The participant observer, in the course of his exploration, enters into contact with various individuals and situations, but he, himself—with his biases and prejudices, his personality equation and his own position in the group—remains unexamined and therefore, himself, an unmeasured quantity. The displacement in the situation to be investigated which is partly produced by his own social pattern does not appear as an integral part of the findings. Indeed, we have to take the inviolability of his own judgments and opinions for granted and *the "uninvestigated investigator" constitutes, so to speak, an ever-present error.* This is, of course, only true for social studies in which the investigators are, as individuals, essential parts of the investigation. It is different in social studies which investigate finished products— processes which have become stereotyped and stationary, lending themselves to actuarial study and the development of scales. Social measurements of such processes are, of course, a part of sociometry in its broader sense, but they have a limited practical meaning without the frontal approach—the direct measurement of interpersonal phenomena.

The psychoanalytic investigator is also an unknown quantity in the situation in which he operates as an analyst. Any educational psychoanalysis which he may have undergone at an earlier date does not alter the fact that he is not measured during the process of interviewing and analyzing any individual. Indeed, in order to accomplish the evaluation of both analyst and patient, a third person—a super-analyst—who is in equal relationship to both, would have to be present during the treatment-situation—and yet aloof from it. The direction of his treatment and his interpretation of the material gathered is totally subjective. At the time there is no frame of reference in the situation except his own opinion, which can provide a basis for determining whether the material has been secured in the proper fashion or whether the significance he assigns to it is scientifically valid.

In order to overcome the grave errors which may arise in and from the investigator himself, we resort to a sociometric approach which is especially adapted to the microscopic study of social phenomena. The participant observer—in one particular form of this work—does not remain "objective" or at a distance from the persons to be studied: he becomes their friend. He identifies himself with their own situations; he becomes an extension of their own egos. In other words, the "objective" participant becomes a "subjective" one. As a *subjective participant* he can enter successively or simultaneously into the lives of several individuals, and then function as a medium of equilibration between them. This is the first step.

If we consider the investigator who gives out questionnaires as being in a situation of maximum *formal* objectivity then the investigator who identifies himself successively with every individual participating in the situation approaches *a maximum of subjectivity*. A professional worker acting in this fashion produces excellent therapeutic effects, but the method does not improve upon the intended objectification of the investigator, himself.

A step beyond this is *the psychodramatic method, a situation which provides an experimental and a therapeutic setting simultaneously.* Here, the director of the theatre is present, but outside the exploratory situation, itself. The investigators to be tested are placed in life-situations and roles which may occur in the community or in their own private lives until their ranges of roles and their patterns of behavior in these life-situations has been adequately gauged. This procedure is carried on until every one of the investigators is thoroughly objectified. Re-tests are made from time to time in order to keep pace with any changes which may have taken place in their various behavior-patterns.

In the course of such work, the range of roles and the range of expansiveness of each investigator become clearly defined and the stimulus which he may be to the subjects of his investigations has become a known quantity. Thus, the psycho-dramatic procedure provides a yardstick by which we can measure and evaluate an indefinitely large number of subjects in specific life-situations and in specific roles. The paradox is that the investigator, although he has become objectified by this process—a "controlled participant observer," so to speak—still continues to be what he originally started out to be: a subjective participant.

The process of objectifying the investigator takes many forms in accord with the situation which he is to explore and it has, also, many degrees of perfection. An ideal situation of this kind is obtained with a psycho-dramatic group in the experimental setting of the therapeutic theatre. For the members of a psychodramatic group, a range of spontaneity is permitted in roles and situations which far surpasses that of any actual community and yet may include all the roles and situations which exist there. At the same time, the behavior of every member of the community—however spontaneous it may be—is recorded in addition to the interaction between the members of the group both on the stage and off it. Thus, the ideal background is constructed for the task assigned to testers within the psychodramatic group, itself.

When the investigator has been tested in this manner, we are able to use him as a tool for testing any group of subjects in typical situations, as described above. In addition to this, he can be used for the treatment of subjects in his new qualification as a subjective participant who is objectified to a point where he can be considered a known quantity in the procedure. He has become an auxiliary ego whose behavior in the process of guidance on the psychodramatic stage is within some degree of control. The treatment is thus freed from the biases and emotionalisms of the therapist. An essential advance upon the psychoanalyst as an investigator as well as a therapist is thus presented by this method. It is obvious that teachers, social workers, nurses and others in their respective treatment-situations can profit greatly from preparatory training of this sort.

Finally, this method can be used to advantage as an improvement upon the participant-observer technique of investigation. As a result of careful gauging of the personalities of the investigators who are to be employed as sociometrists or observers in the community at large, a frame of reference is established at the research center to which the investigators return with their data and findings. The use of this frame of reference provides a more objective basis than has heretofore existed for evaluating the reflection of the investigators' own behavior-characteristics upon their findings in the community. *The social investigation of any community, when based upon sociometric principles, is equipped with two complementary frames of reference. The one is the objectified investigator so prepared and evaluated that his own personality is no longer an unknown factor in the findings. The other frame of reference consists of the members of the community who are brought to a high degree of spontaneous participation in the investigation by means of sociometric tests, and therefore contribute genuine and reliable data.* Thus, the social structures which actually exist in the community at the moment of investigation are brought to our knowledge with a minimum of error on the part of both the investigators and the investigated, counseling through tele or double technique as against interview.

SOCIOMETRY AND THE THEORY OF ROLES
(1947)

I like to go to the cradle of an idea, its *status nascendi,* in order to find out what it is. The final form of an idea is often deceptive. I found this method useful in understanding others. Here I apply it to myself. It is an illusion to think that an author knows his own works well because it is he who has written them; an author of fifty may be more distant from himself at twenty than from another man of fifty. When I am doubtful, therefore, of whether I am on the right or wrong track with an idea which I started, I look back at the moment of my first inspiration, and when I gave it its first form, when the flame of the thought was bold and undisturbed.

I am taking the reader, therefore, to one of my first writings, a pamphlet which appeared in the spring of 1914, a few months before the outbreak of the First World War. The title contains the whole idea: "Invitation To A Meeting", or, as in the German original "Einladung zu einer Begegnung". It meant literally what it said, invitation of me (the author) to meet you (the reader). It meant to cure a false or derivative meeting, that between author and reader (the reader reading a book), by a real meeting, the person of the author meeting the person of the reader, actually. Because this plan was truly intended, before it became an experiment in action, it became an experiment in my thought; it filled the book with the reflections on what is involved in the process of one man meeting another and the preparations for this goal. The imperative expectancy of the meeting had consequences. The author was on the way to change his role, he was to be transformed into an actor, and the reader or readers, were similarly on the way to change their roles, to be transformed into actors. The author warmed up to meeting the readers and they warmed up to meet him until at last the meeting was to take place, the preliminary step towards the formation of genuine association. It appeared to me that only people who "meet" one another, or who are on the way towards a meeting of one another can form a community. The meeting was a category of realization and on a different plane from intellectualized derivations as inter-human or inter-personal relations. I tried persistently to move from a fictional plane to a reality plane of production, without leaving out anything which the intellect could offer to enhance the spontaneity and creativity of the meeting when entering into the plane of reality. The outcome of such an approach to people and things was the development of a social method which can be called the *analytical-actor method,* in contrast to the analytical observer method, action research in contrast to observational research.

I turned myself into an actor in order to learn more about my thoughts (choices and decisions) and my fellow men into actors in order for them to learn more about their thoughts (choices and decisions), and reversed their roles in order that they may learn more about each other. In a broad sense here is the methodological seed of what became later known as inter-personal systems, sociometry and psychodrama. It is not the unconscious human actor of old, it is not the analyst of old, it is a synthesis of both— one analytic actor meeting another. The analytic element does not interfere with the spontaneity and creativity of the actor, it is a part of him. In the course of development the analytic element can differentiate itself within the personality of the actor as an analytic self observer, a further synthesis, one between the analytic actor and the analytic observer method, takes place.

George H. Mead is a classic example of the keen analytical observer. He belonged, like other thinkers of the early twentieth century as Sigmund Freud, Henry Bergson and John Dewey, to the class of spectator-philosophers.

This is one basic difference which I see between Mead and my own work and it probably reflects throughout everything which each of us has done. There is nothing more elevating than confirmation of ideas. A great service is done to the propaganda of truth if similarities are pointed out where they exist. But differences should be equally strongly pointed out. However, disagreement in approach does not necessarily mean disagreement in goals. The next question is therefore whether Mead and I were aiming at the same goals. Yes, I believe we were both preparing for a creatively emerging and sociometrically directed society.

A comparison of Mead's "philosophy of the present" with my "philosophy of the moment" suggests another difference of opinion, perhaps more than this—of spirit. I formulated this difference at another occasion as follows: "Mead's present is a universal, static and passive 'category', it is a correlate of every experience so to speak, automatically. As a transition of the past to the future it is always there. The present is a *formal* category in contradistinction from the *moment* which is a dynamic and *creative* category; it is through a spontaneous-creative process that the formal category of the present attains dynamic meaning, when it turns into a moment. A completely automatic and purely mechanical process as for instance the repetition of a film, has just as well a 'present' as the most intensive creative experience"[1] but it has no "moment". Mead has refined and extended the idea of the present but in a diametrically opposed direction. He, the analytic observer, was keenly concerned with the complex relativities of presentness within the framework of scientific method. I was concerned with the creative act and the "evolution of the creator": Apparently we both have been influenced by Bergson. But whereas Mead left out the mystic element in Bergson's "durée", I digested and surpassed it by developing action and training methods which made creativity trainable as well as measurable.

Another difference does not lie as much in method as in the form of attainment. I am referring here to the point of similarity between Mead and myself, the theory of roles, which we developed *independently*. I developed it by means of experiment, introducing concepts as role playing, role player and role testing. He introduced it as an observer, introducing terms like role taking and taking the role of the other. He was interested

---

[1] See "The Theatre of Spontaneity", Beacon House, New York, 1923 and 1947, pp. 110.111. It is characteristic too that I had coined the phrase "evolution of the *creator*" to underline the contrast to Bergson's phrase "creative evolution".

in the cultural conserve of role taking whereas I started with role playing in *statu nascendi,* experimenting from the spontaneous-dynamic production of roles towards their stereotyped formations. Mead had to struggle through a life time of observations in order to arrive at it, I got it effortlessly, "free of charge" from the spontaneous drama, the medium within which I began to work around 1910.[2] Even here a significant departure should be pointed out. It appears that Mead and I have been influenced by Wundt's ideas as to the relation of gesture to speech. But for Mead the development of gesture and language occupied too large an area of the psyche, leaving little considered and unexplored the *anti*-semantic areas. According to my hypothesis there is considerable psychic resistance against the intrusion of language and even some resistance against gestural infiltration. There is no reason to assume that the *language-free areas* are sub-human (as Mead does). These silent areas are co-existent with the vocal ones on the human level and have great potentialities for growth. There may be forms of "social" communication without gestural involvement. It is therefore an error to reduce the tele phenomenon to a mere reflection and correspondent of the communication process via language.

Last but not least, similar efforts of trying to find points of agreement between the work of others and my own, for instance of Bergson and Freud, can be made perhaps with the same amount of justification. A Bergsonian could make it plausible that my work provides the clinical foundations for "L'Evolution Creatrice" and the "elan vital". Psychoanalysts could argue that psychodrama is on the action level what psychoanalysis is on the verbal level, that the two methods have similar aims. The real and final question, however, is whether out of the social psychology of Mead, role practice and role training, psychodrama and sociodrama, sociometry and group psycho-therapy could ever have developed—whether out of Bergson's durée and Freud's libido and transference method my elaborate system of action and training methods, could ever have arisen. The answer is—in my opinion—

---

[2] The two books to which the spread of role theory can be traced appeared about a half a year apart, *Who Shall Survive?* in March, 1934, *Mind, Self and Society* in December, 1934. See in *Who Shall Survive?* pages 321-331; in *Mind, Self and Society,* pages 360-367. The undertitle of *Mind, Self and Society* is "From The Standpoint Of A Social Behaviorist". The undertitle of *Who Shall Survive?* could very well have been "From The Standpoint Of A Social Actionist". Although role theory has become part and parcel of practically every text book on social psychology or sociology, it is a rare occasion that either Mead or myself are referred to. *Sic transit gloria mundis.*

for all three men in the negative. Their contributions were enormous and prepared the ground, but I believe that it took the theorist and practitioner in one, a theory which grew out of and with practice, a synthesis of actor and observer, to give the new methodologies the peculiar concrete shape they have.

PROGRESS AND PITFALLS IN SOCIOMETRIC THEORY

Sociometric Methods and the Surface-Depth Cleavage Within Group Structure

Sociometric tests show in a dramatic and precise fashion that every group has beneath its superficial, tangible, visible, readable structure an underlying, intangible, invisible, unofficial structure, but one which is more alive, real and dynamic than the other. This was found to be true of groups which have a highly formalized institutional character as well as of groups whose structure is informal, fluid and transitory. It was found that in a work or business relationship individuals do not respond in an objective and adequate manner; an individual, for instance, who had the opportunity to choose freely among two physicians who were considered of equal skill and requiring equal monetary expenditure, chose the one whom he liked best for some "personal reason". The skill angle, the economic angle and the private preference angle were subtly interwoven, resulting in one particular, specific choice. Another individual who had an opportunity to chose partners for a recreational situation, going fishing, had to put up with a carpenter across the street instead of a musician whom he would have preferred. In conclusion we can say that formal *and* informal groupings, whatever the criterion, do not differ sociometrically; they have in common the division between an upper and an under structure of personal relations.

The "personal reason" referred to in the above paragraph is nothing mysterious. It is a *displacement* of social feeling projected into an inappropriate situation. It is imaginable that in an utopian sociometric society the tele sense of individuals will be so highly differentiated and trained that when an individual chooses an associate for working together he would be influenced *only* by the objective requirements for the work situation and not by some cultural or amatory aspirations he may have, because they will be taken care of in the other groupings in which he participates. In such a society every criterion of grouping would be equally permissible and no individual will have to look for the realization of his social feelings in situations undesigned for their expression.

One of the difficulties which we have encountered in sociometric work is the definition and analysis of social criteria. Social criteria are the foci around which individuals cluster and around which groupings of varying degrees of constancy and duration are formed. The more specific the criteria are the more care has to be taken to construct a sociometric test accordingly and the better are the chances that it will tap the most spontaneously intimate and real structures which individuals produce among themselves. There are studies which are not based on *any* criterion—"Whom do you like or dislike." They should not be called sociometric. There are studies which use vaguely defined criteria—"Who are your best friends, and who are your enemies." It is obvious that the more vaguely the criteria are defined, the less precise will be the sociometric test instrument and the less complete and more distorted will be the findings. Loosely defined criteria indicate that the aim of the sociometric investigator is not clear. A sociometric test does not merely require a subject to give a verbal response to a verbal quest. It tries to mobilize the subject, to arouse in him an action response, an action response however which he may have denied himself but which is the deepest, present expression of his spontaneity. Every sociometric test attempts to warm up the subject to act in behalf and in accord with his subjective reality level. It encourages him to act out, to be himself; it permits him to have a goal, a goal for himself, a goal of his own. If we ask a person therefore, whom do you like or dislike, he may relate to us at best some of his social perceptions but the process of self mobilization and realization is left out of the subject's world. But when we ask him in all earnestness to choose the one he wants to share a room with he is confronted with a situation, he has to make a decision, to think through the relationship, knowing that it may be consummated. In order that a test should help him in furthering the autonomy of his social relations the test has to apply to him, not he to the test.

A frequent pitfall has become the notion that by watching the activities of informal groups as playing cards, going fishing, hitch hiking, picnicking, the intimate private structure of a group comes to the surface and that sociometric test procedures are thus superfluous. This trend of thought has been particularly encouraged by the Hawthorne experiment[1] and by studies of cliques and gangs.[2] This experiment, however noble and worthy in itself tries in vain to use interview and observational techniques to supplant the

---

[1] Roethlisberger and Dixon, "Management and the Worker", Harvard University Press, 1939.

[2] W. F. White, "Street Corner Society," Chicago University Press, 1943.

sociometric test. I have warned against this pitfall in the early days of sociometry for methodical as well as practical reasons. In any effort to disclose the interpersonal structure of a group, interview and observational techniques without the sociometric test are hopeless and incomplete gestures. After the sociometric test is applied however, a focus of inquiry and a focus for action is established which intensifies the value of interview and observation many times. From the point of view of systematic sociometric research the Hawthorne experiment belongs into a class of studies using pseudo sociometric clues and a pseudo sociometric language without applying sociometric instruments and a *thinking through* the findings—and without *carrying them out* to benefit the workers. It is the animal technique of the "maze" applied to a human situation. The workers are treated like guinea pigs instead of like autonomous, mature human adults. As the main results of the Hawthorne experiment were published at a time when a well established sociometric climate existed, the laborious work must be considered a regression.

It is unfortunate that Dr. Roethlisberger and Dr. Dickson did not apply sociometric methods in their study; this is particularly deplorable because Dr. Elton Mayo, the senior exponent of their study, was appreciative of our sociometric experiments as early as 1931 and had read some of the material published (see letter from Elton Mayo in "Application of the Group Method to Classification" by J. L. Moreno, in collaboration with E. Stagg Whitin published by the National Committee on Prisons and Prison Labor, p. 82, 1931 and 1932, current edition "Group Method and Group Psychotherapy"). Indeed, *no* study of group structure can be taken seriously if it does not use sociometric methods wholeheartedly; they certainly can be improved but they cannot be *bypassed*.

A period in the development of sociometry comes to an end which may well be called "halfway sociometry". The halfway sociometrists of the last decade, especially some of the workers coming from general and abstract sociological schools, preferred broad and vast sounding questionnaires of interpersonal relations with a flair for sociometric concepts to the sociometric test itself. These questionnaires fell more easily into practicable academic methods of research but they diluted and deflated the sociometric method. The true sociometric test as we planned it is a revolutionary category of investigation. It upsets the group from within. It produces a social revolution on a microscopic scale. If it does not produce an upheaval in some degree it may arouse suspicion that the investigator has modified it so

—in respect for an existing social order—that it becomes a harmless, poverty stricken instrument.

PSYCHO-SOCIO DRAMATIC METHODS AND THE PSYCHO-SOCIO CLEAVAGE
WITHIN GROUP STRUCTURE

Psychodramatic and sociodramatic methods disclose that each individual or group of individuals belong simultaneously to a privately structured and a socially structured world. In fact, the hypothesis that a cleavage exists between private and social within every individual and in every group has been the reason why I constructed two different instruments, the psycho-drama and the sociodrama. The differentiation between psychological and social structuring takes place in every group, in home as well as in work groups, in school as well as in recreation groups, in formal as well as in informal groups. The impact of our social and cultural order is so all inclusive and penetrating that there is no grouping of any sort which is not permeated by some degree of collectivity. In turn there is no grouping able to exist without being permeated by some degree of spontaneous subjectivity because of the individual resistance to a given social order.

Helen Jennings,[3] in a report concerning the difference in sociometric structure between psyche and socio makes the following statements: ". . . a population tends to form two distinguishable kinds of groups: (I) sociogroups, *i.e.*, groups where sociometric structure is based on a criterion which is *collective* in nature; . . . (II) psychegroups, *i.e.*, groups where sociometric structure is based on strictly *private* criterion which is totally *personal* in nature;" . . . "An analysis of the sociometric data based on the 'unrestricting' criterion, leisure-time (and/or) recreation, in the same community . . . reveals that the sociometric structure of groups formed around this criterion, differs from the sociometric structure of groups formed around 'restricting' criteria (working, and/or living, in same group) to such extent and in such manner as to suggest we are dealing with 'groups' which are fundamentally different."

Jennings arrives here at a formulation which may create in readers not well acquainted with sociometric work a misunderstanding as to the meaning of our terms. The term "group" is usually reserved for the total picture of the interaction of all factors operating on the psycho-social level, similar to the term organism which is reserved for the total picture of all factors operating

---

[3] Helen H. Jennings, "Sociometry of Leadership", Sociometry Monograph, No. 14, Beacon House, 1947.

on the biological level. To divide, therefore, a population into two categories, socio- and psychegroup, adds a new, unnecessary hypothesis. It suggests the idea that there are two fundamentally different categories of groups whereas we agreed up to now that groups of every type are endlessly and continuously formed around specific criteria and as being filled with some psychic and some social structures. We can differentiate, as useful abstractions, between psycho and socio structures within a group, in situ, on the reality level as we are differentiating between psychodrama and sociodrama on the instrumental level. But just as we do not claim that we have a psycho and sociodrama per se, we cannot claim that there is a psyche and socio group per se. The possibility of miscomprehension is eliminated if we hypothecate a split between psycho and socio within the sociometric structure of a group, the psycho trend showing greater intensity in certain groups, the socio trend showing greater intensity in certain other groups.

There is no sociometric evidence for the hypothesis that there are groups which are strictly collective, dominated by a collective pattern of behavior and groups which are strictly private, dominated by a private pattern of behavior. But there is increasing evidence of a *psycho-socio continuum*. The notion of two independent worlds, a private and a social, is here challenged: a) there is no psyche which is a private product reigning in splendid isolation and there is no socius, the product of social forces only; b) it is a fallacy to assume that our social and cultural order is a devilish imposition upon our private psyches and if we could deliver ourselves from this order we would have our private psyches back undiluted, unhampered, in their original state of free spontaneity.

THREE DIMENSIONS OF SOCIETY
THE EXTERNAL SOCIETY, THE SOCIOMETRIC MATRIX AND THE SOCIAL REALITY

(1949)

It is of heuristic value to differentiate the social universe into three tendencies or dimensions, the *external society,* the *sociometric matrix* and the *social reality.* By external society I mean all tangible and visible groupings, large or small, formal or informal, of which human society consists. By the sociometric matrix I mean all sociometric structures invisible to the macroscopic eye but which become visible through the sociometric process of analysis. By social reality I mean the dynamic synthesis and interpenetration of the two. It is obvious that neither the matrix nor the external are real or can exist by themselves, one is a function of the other. As dialectic opposites they must merge in some fashion in order to produce the actual process of social living.

The dynamic reason for this split is the underground existence of innumerable social constellations which impinge continuously upon external society, partly in an effort towards its disintegration, partly in an effort towards their realization and, last not least, because of the resistance which external society puts up against its substitution or change. As the profound and chronic conflict between these two tendencies is never fully resolved, the result is a compromise in the form of what may be called the "social reality".

A position which has become axiomatic for sociometrists until proven otherwise is that the official (external) society and the sociometric (internal) matrix are not identical. The one is visible to the senses, it is macroscopic, the other is invisible, it is microscopic. In the sense of this dichotomy all groupings, whether as rigidly formalized and collectivized as an army or a church, or as casual and transitory as a meeting of people on a streetcorner, they belong, as long as they are visible to the naked macroscopic eye, to the externally structured society. One can not assume in advance that the sociogram of an army platoon, for instance is radically different from the official structure of the platoon, rigidly imposed upon the men, or that the sociogram of a casual gathering on a streetcorner is equal or nearly equal to the actually visible formation. It is easily possible that in certain cultures, widely divergent from our own, the sociogram of a rigid social institution is identical with its actual social structure on the reality level.[1] It is

---

[1] See "Some Attraction and Repulsion Patterns among Jibaro Indians", by Bengt Danielsson, SOCIOMETRY, Vol. XII, February-August, 1949, No. 1-3.

therefore methodically of utmost importance not to *mix* the sociometric position which is *neutral* (or let us say as neutral as possible) with the social order just existing and passing. Sociometry is equally applicable to every type of society which has emerged in the past or which might emerge in the future.

The structure of the external society is comparatively easy to describe. It consists of visible, overt and observable groups; it is made up of all the groups recognized by law as legitimate, of all the groups rejected by law as illegitimate, as well as of all the neutral groups permitted, although unclassified and unorganized. The shortest way to obtain a picture of the legitimate groups is to use the system of law ruling a particular society as a guide. In order to obtain a picture of the illegitimate groupings excursions into the underworld are effective. Illustrations of legitimate groups are: the family, the workshop, the school, the army or the church. Illustrations of informal and illegitimate groups are: the casual encounter of two, the crowd, the mass, the mob, the streetcorner gangs or criminal rackets. The structure of the sociometric matrix is more difficult to recognize. Special techniques called sociometric are necessary to unearth it; as the matrix is in continuous dynamic change the techniques have to be applied at regular intervals so as to determine the newly emerging social constellations. The sociometric matrix consists of various constellations, tele, the atom, the super-atom or molecule (several atoms linked together), the "socioid" which may be defined as a cluster of atoms linked together with other clusters of atoms via inter-personal chains or networks; the socioid is the sociometric counterpart of the external structure of a social group; it is rarely identical with what a social group externally shows because parts of its social atoms and chains may extend into another socioid. On the other hand, some of the external structure of a particular social group may not make sense configurationally as a part of a particular socioid but may belong to a socioid hidden within a different social group. Other constellations which can be traced within a sociometric matrix are psycho-social networks. There are in addition large sociodynamic categories which are frequently mobilized f. i. in political and revolutionary activities; they consist of the interpenetration of numerous socioids and represent the sociometric counterpart of "social class" as bourgeoisie or proletariat; they can be defined as sociometric structure of social classes or as *classoids*. The social reality itself is the dynamic interweaving of and interaction of the sociometric matrix with the outer, external society. The sociometric matrix does not exist by itself, just as the outer society does not exist by itself; the latter is continuously pushed and pulled by the structure underneath. Within a sociometric system we distinguish therefore three processes: the outer reality of society, the internal reality of the sociometric matrix and the social reality itself, the historically growing, dynamic social groupings of which the actual social universe consists. If one knows the structure of the official society and the sociometric matrix he can recognize the bits and pieces which enter from the two dimensions into the compromising forms of social reality. The greater the contrast between official society and the sociometric matrix the more intensive is the social conflict and tension between them. One may venture to formulate the following hypothesis: *social conflict and tension increases in direct proportion to the sociodynamic difference between official society and sociometric matrix.*

I have given attention to the study of the sociometric matrix because it seemed to be the key for solving many riddles. In the beginning I thought that every legitimate group has a corresponding sociometric structure. But soon I recognized that the illegitimate or informal groups too have a corresponding sociometric structure. I quote here from *Who Shall Survive?,* p. 111, "There is evident a trend to differentiate between the choices of the girls in respect to the collective and its function, *i.e.,* between those with whom an individual prefers to live and those with whom she prefers to work." But just as it seemed economical to describe the official society as a single social continuum formed by interdependent groups I preferred to consider the sociometric matrix as a single sociometric continuum with a varying discrepancy between the two continua, rarely being entirely apart and rarely being entirely identical. The sociometric matrix of a given work group may thus at times show a greater discrepancy than the one of a home group and more than the one of a play group.

Contrasts in the correlations of choices between criteria of working and living, between working and playing are therefore to be expected. My advice to define the criterion around which the group is to be formed specifically and concretely was motivated by the desire to attain specific responses. My assumption was that vaguely defined criteria are bound to evoke vague responses from the subjects. This was the reason in early sociometric work for advising against the use of "friendship" as a criterion, for instance: "Who are your friends in town?" Friendship is actually a cluster of criteria. A sociometric friendship study is possible but it requires a theoretical preparation and analysis of the multiple criteria which enter into the social phenomenon friendship. What is true about friendship is equally true about leisure which Jennings uses in a vague fashion and which may cover innumerable things. Not all leisure activities go hand in hand with maximum spontaneity and minimum of restriction. However informal a grouping may be it is to be differentiated from its sociometric structure. We cannot, therefore, compare generally and vaguely "the inter-individual expression of choice for leisure" with the inter-individual choice for living or working together. Because leisure is a cluster of criteria one must differentiate the hundreds of leisure criteria individually from one another and must compare each separately and concretely with equally specific work and living criteria. To mention a few: blind dating, going fishing, hitch hiking, going out to dinner, dancing, accosting strangers in trains, nightclub parties, meeting strangers in hotels, visiting houses of prostitution. It is obvious that leisure can include many things, like friendship. What perception is evoked in a subject when you tell him "Choose your leisure associates"? What is included in leisure, what is excluded from it? There are many, most informal situations of leisure activity: groups of people bathing together on a beach, or an adventurous hitch-hike of a few boys and girls throughout the country.

Some people think that when a group is formed casually and informally the sociometric test is unnecessary because one can see with his own eyes what the structure of this particular informal group is. The confusion of an informal group with the sociometric structure of a group has been en vogue for some time. Illustrations of this tendency can be found in Roethlisberger and Dixon's "Management and the Worker". The authors give us the impression that they have arrived at the core of the intimate structure of the work group if they compare their formation in the wiring room or in the workshop with their intimate and spontaneous grouping in recess or after work hours, when playing cards or chatting, lunching or going home together. There is no question that it is valuable to watch the interactions of the same individuals in different situations, to watch them how they interact in situations of objective responsibility, to get a specific job done in a certain time and when they act more free of such restraints in the lunch hour. But from the sociometric point of view the informal groupings must be submitted as rigorously to sociometric testing and analysis as the more rigidly structured. The fact that Roethlisberger and Dixon portray their data in a sociometric manner, using the form of the sociogram does not bring them closer to the truth. As a matter of fact, the authors do not deal with the deeper dynamics of social groups but with its external manifestations. All the truly dynamic conflicts between employer and employee, labor unions and the owners of industries, between engineers and foremen, foremen and workers are silently passed over. They are not only passed over ideologically or politically, but, what is from a sociometric point of view worse still, the instruments which are able to bring to the surface the sociodynamic forces which operate in an industrial setting are not used, the sociometric instruments of action research[2] in cooperation with the participants. It all culminates in the leaving out the workers themselves from the research undertaken. They are observed, interviewed, analyzed. But they are not given the freedom to think, choose, decide and act. As the action research is not started by them, it is not carried out and not ended by them. It is a research enterprise void of a clear goal, perhaps for the sake of a platonic-utopian science, perhaps for the benefit of employers, it is certainly not consciously constructed to give the workers themselves full participation in matters which are vital to their life. The two writers were probably in fear that by giving the workers prestige and power in the research enterprise instead of keeping them subordinate, keeping the matter nice, sweet and commonplace—and every worker in his place—might end in a bedlam and turn the factory over to a psychiatrist—or they have the still greater fear that sociometric action research will end in social revolution. They do not realize that social revolution is rather promoted than prevented by half-hearted social researches which do not go the whole way of action and analysis but permit the dynamic forces to operate uninhibitedly underground. It is, on the other hand, only the stubbornly carried out one hundred per cent sociometric process from both sides, employers and workers which may produce a true measure against revolutions and may put into the hands of man *techniques of prevention of social revolutions* in the future. Such techniques and skills are not learned in fear and cowardice but only in the course of carefully prepared experimentation. Sociometry is the only promise visible on the horizon to replace revolutions of dictatorship by *revolutions of cooperation.*

An illustration of a similar type are the streetcorner studies by Whyte. However subtle his observational studies and near-sociometric the results, they are inaccurate as well as ineffective because they do not warm up the tramps, the bums, etc., to any action of their own. His sociograms are impressionistic, put together by empathetic participant-observers but not by the participant-actors themselves.

---

2 As it is out of sociometric research that action research and action methods grew, we should watch everyone who gives lip and "print" service to the terms but avoids the operations of action.

This fundamental position is not altered by the evidence that in every group formation, besides the official criterion, for instance, living together in a particular house or working together on a special job, many "latent" criteria operate, for instance, the search for making dates with co-workers, the desire to find people of a certain political orientation in the work group, perhaps in order to form a socialistic or a fascistic club, gaining members for the Knights of Columbus or the Communist Party, making friends with those who are interested in fishing or stamp collecting. On the other hand we know from sociometric research that in highly spontaneous groups not determined by coercive social pressures as work groups various latent criteria operate which are highly restraining in character, collectivistic and compulsory. A man may pick out as associates on a fishing trip people who have a higher economic and social status than himself; going fishing may be the official criterion of a particular, informal group, but making good business contacts or increasing one's pull in the ruling political party may be latent collective criteria which may operate just as rigidly here and distort the naivete of the informal relationships, as informal criteria frequently distort the character of the more rigorous groups.

A third illustration of the difficulties which arise if the difference between external society and the sociometric matrix is neglected is a recent article[3] by Helen Jennings. It deals with the phenomenon of leisure activity. But it does not make clear to which the dimension the groups formed by leisure activities belong, to the external society or to the sociometric matrix. To this obscurity it adds a new one—from a sociometric point of view leisure, just like friendship, is a cluster of criteria and not a single criterion. As Jennings defines leisure vaguely in her test instructions the data she obtains from her subjects have little validity, as much or as little as the validity one gets if one asks an individual "Who are your friends?" As a matter of fact, she is committing here the same error with leisure activity for which we have criticized others—the use of no criterion or vague ones like friendship, which were then classified as near-sociometric researches. It is not more sociometric as ask "Whom do you choose as partner for leisure activities" without specifying the particular activity you, or better the subject, is concerned with at the time of the test. Leisure activity can be playing chess, or

[3] See Helen H. Jennings, "Sociometric Differentiation of the Psychegroup and the Sociogroup", SOCIOMETRY, Vol. X, No. 1, 1947, p. 71.

playing baseball, driving a car or boxing. These activities, although they may be leisure, are determined by rigid rules of the game which must be just as strictly observed as certain codes in a workshop or within a family setting. However great the spontaneity in the making of a choice of partners, however apparently unlimited by external coercion, it is often limited by the skill and competence of the subject and that of the partner. Engaging in sexual intercourse with casual partners may also fall into the class of leisure activities, however, it is such a singularly specific criterion that it cannot be thrown into the same basket with all the other leisure criteria, merely because they all seem to imply freedom from collective coercion. As a matter of fact, even in the choice of a sexual partner or in the pursuit of one, strictly collective criteria play a great role. A man may go out with a girl because he wants to take her away from his friend, not because he loves her particularly. It is not enjoyment which he looks for, it is revenge. A girl may choose as a sexual partner a man whom she does not love; she chooses him, not because she likes him better than anyone else but because her mother likes him, or because he is wealthy, or because he is the town hero and everyone thinks he is wonderful. Here we see collective factors determining private decisions.

The lack of sensitivity for the social criteria which so many sociometrists indicate in their writings may well be due to the circumstance that most investigations are carried out on a diagnostic level only. Therefore, for them the choices made by the subjects propelled by a specific situation are not resolutions to be turned into immediate action; they are just wishes which are to remain on the wish level, phantasies and social projections which may have induced some commentators to consider the sociometric test as a projection technique. Far be it from me to underestimate the many contributions which diagnostic sociometric research has made, but it should be remembered that classic sociometry started out as an action research on a large scale (read *Who Shall Survive?*). That was its heroic time, when choices were choices, actions were actions. Sociometry was then seen through the "eyes" of the participants. It awakened the social scientist to a new conscience and it paved the way for the revision of the experimental method in social science.

SUPPLEMENTARY NOTE ON THE DIFFERENCE BETWEEN
DIAGNOSTIC AND ACTION CRITERIA

The difference between diagnostic and action procedures has been at the very core of sociometric theory since its early days. However, there is a chronic preference of research men for diagnostic procedure as against action procedures. This preference is rooted in a veritable resistance against giving up certain deeply ingrained perceptions and habits of orderly scientific behavior. The perception of the scientist as an observer of subjects and objects and as an experimenter in the safety of a laboratory milieu seems to contradict the perception of the scientist as an actor, an *"action agent,"* with the subjects as co-actors and co-scientists, the experimental situation moving from the laboratory into life itself. Actually the older perception is not given up, it is well integrated into the newer perception of the *action scientist.* The resistance comes from another source, the confusion of action methods and action research with the old controversy between scientific and applied; to "apply" is considered to give less status to a scientist than to establish basic principles. However, sociometric action theory is not the outcome of an emphasis upon pragmatic and empirical thinking but the result of a *critique of the total methodology of social science.* The conclusion was that a theory of human relations cannot be founded without propelling human groups into action. The great misunderstanding, even among sociometrists comes from a *neglect of studying experimentally the warming up process taking place in the making of a choice, a resolution of performance and of action.* It may be useful to differentiate among sociometric criteria between *diagnostic* and *action* criteria. An illustration of a diagnostic criterion is "whom do you invite to have meals in your house."* It is specific but it does not provide the subjects with the op-

---

*Charles P. Loomis and Dwight Davidson, Jr. "Sociometry and the Study of New Rural Communities" SOCIOMETRY, Vol. II, p 56-76, 1939.

Another illustration of a diagnostic criterion is "who is quoting whom." A great deal of spontaneity enters into the choice of quoting someone, or leaving others out from a "table of references". The investigator is interested among other things—whether the subject quotes himself and how often, whether he is quoted by others, and whether he quotes others, positively or negatively, whether he quotes living or dead authors, or whether he quotes no one. The quoters and quotees may be charted by means of sociograms of the scientific societies to which they belong. (see J. L. Moreno, "SOCIOMETRY and the Cultural Order", SOCIOMETRY Vol. VI, 1943, p. 329.)

portunity to get into immediate action and it does not justify the sociometric director to prompt the subjects to act; in other words the test provides only for information but not for action. An action criterion involves a different situation. It prompts the subjects to a different warming up process. It requires different instructions than a diagnostic test. An illustration of an action criterion may be found in the paper "Re-Grouping of Communities and Action Research 'In Situ'," pp. in this publication. The settlers come to a town meeting and they are addressed by the sociometric counselor *as a group*: "You are preparing to move into the new settlement Centerville. Whom do you want there as a neighbor?" This is obviously a situation which is different from the diagnostic case. The people have an immediate goal to which they are warmed up. The choices they make are very real things, they are not only wishes. They are prompted to act at present and in the presence of the group. In the diagnostic case the reference is to the past, however crucial; the diagnostic approach can easily be changed to an actional one. Choices are then decisions for action, not attitudes.

FOUNDATIONS OF SOCIOMETRY
Concepts and Experiments With Rumors
(1941)

The Problem

The discovery that human society has an actual, dynamic, central structure underlying and determining all its peripheral and formal groupings may one day be considered as the cornerstone of all social science. This central structure—once it has been identified—is either found or discernible in every form of human society, from the most primitive to the most civilized: it is in the genesis of every type of society. In addition, it exerts a determining influence upon every sphere in which the factor of human interrelations is an active agent—in economics, biology, social pathology, politics, government and similar spheres of social action.

It seems to be established beyond any reasonable doubt that the tele factor, the social atom (with its specific types of patterns), the stages which are intermediary between atoms and more inclusive configurations, the psycho-social networks and their patternings, the principle of socio-genetic evolution—all these have always been operating in human society and will continue to do so. These concepts and structures have been either isolated or demonstrated by methods called "sociometric." Every other genuine method bent upon the study of social processes should be able to verify their existence.

In the past, as long as the individuals composing a human society remained passive agents—more or less immobile entities, carried hither and thither by fate or circumstance—these key structures could not be found. Per se, they do not become manifest in a human society. A reagent—a catalyzer—is necessary in order that they may be brought to view. This catalyzer is, on the social level, the spontaneity of all the individuals in the given society. Up to the advent of sociometric exploration of human society, we had seen the social scientist himself beginning to come into contact with the life-situation which was to be explored, but the subjects—the material of the investigation—had been left out of any participation in the study of this, their own life-situation. This meant shutting off the spontaneity of the subjects—the most important source of information. In other words, the methods used to explore the subjects were those which had been successful in physical, chemical, geological and astronomical exploration, for example, where—metaphorically speaking—the spontaneity of the subjects studied did not enter into or disturb the experiment. But in human interrelations and in human society, the spontaneity of the individual is the alpha and the omega, the crux, of every social situation and of the whole experiment.

The task of the social scientist is to invent adequate instruments for the exploration of a chosen domain. On the level of human interrelations, this domain is made up of the interactive spontaneities of all the individuals composing it. Therefore, the task of the social scientist becomes the shaping of instruments in such a fashion that they are able to arouse the individuals to the required point on a scale which runs all the way from zero to the maximum. But individuals cannot be aroused—or only to an insignificant degree—by undynamic and automatic means. The individuals must be adequately motivated so that they summon from the depths of their beings the maximum of their spontaneity. Thus, the invention and shaping of methods for social investigation, and the stirring up of the actions, thoughts, and feelings of the people on whom they are used, must go hand in hand.

Finally, knowledge of the central structure of human interrelations is essential to any general planning and construction of human soicety. In fact, this was well-nigh impossible as long as the key structures remained unknown. Man believed that the genesis of society was outside his province —even more so than the genesis of personality.

Sociometry opened up a new possibility of genuine planning of human society for the reason that the factors of spontaneity, the initiative and the momentary grasp of the individuals concerned were made the essence of the method of exploration and of the investigation itself. In a sociometric system, the essence of every process of planning is *total spontaneity*—not, as heretofore, the spontaneity of a small number of leaders or individuals chosen at random. The total sum of the individuals, by means of their spontaneities, becomes operative in determining every direction of planning and, in addition, in the selection of every key individual or leader to whom a certain function or action is to be entrusted. Thus, all the peripheral actions and functions—on every level between the periphery and the center—remain under the continuous or recurring control of the key or central structure. The new philosophy of human interrelations, sociometry, gives us a methodology and guide for the determination of the central structure of society and the evocation of the spontaneity of the subject-agents, and these two factors together supply us with a basis upon which the planning of human society may be undertaken.

Historical Background

It was during the first World War that the idea of a sociometry, in conjunction with a modern, revised theory of spontaneity,[1] had its first expression. Sociometry developed at a moment which had no precedent in the history of mankind—at a moment when, notwithstanding all the advances man had made, the utter futility of his efforts had become evident as being largely because of these advances. In spite of all the magnificent edifices which he had erected so industriously, man saw himself slipping back to the primitive state from which he had begun his rise.

The technology of machines and tools was perhaps the first phenomenon to shock man out of his roseate dream of progress ad infinitum, but the effect of technology upon the spontaneity of the human organism was not studied and remained, therefore, uncontrolled; its influence within our social structure had remained unadjusted. It was realized, then, that the foundations of human society must first be uncovered before any extra-human superstructure (such as machine technology and the technology of cultural conserves) could be fitted to them.

---

1 See the section on the General Theory of Spontaneity and the Cultural Conserve in "Mental Catharsis and the Psycho-drama," by J. L. Moreno, SOCIOMETRY, Vol. III, No. 3.

My first definition of sociometry was, in accordance with its etymology, from the Latin, but the emphasis was laid not only on the second half of the term, i.e., on "metrum", meaning measure, but also on the first half of the term, (i.e., on "socius", meaning companion). Both principles, it seemed to me, had been neglected but the "socius" aspect had been omitted from deeper analysis far more than the "metrum" aspect. The "companion", even as a problem, was unrecognized. What remains of a society to be investigated if the individuals themselves and the relationships between them are considered in a fragmentary or wholesale fashion? Or, to put it in a positive way, the individuals themselves and the interrelations between them, in toto, cannot be omitted from any study of a social situation. Can the foundations of human society be reached and, perhaps, uncovered if we do not begin with that aspect of human interrelations which all types of human society, from the most primitive pattern of the past to the most complex pattern of the future, must have in common—the patterns of relationships which human beings form with one another and which persist underground, regardless of what religious, social, political and technological structure is superimposed upon them and rules on the surface?

The technological devices which aroused man's deepest suspicion were the products of the printing press, the motion picture industry and, later, the radio; in other words, of the so-called "cultural conserves." Man, as an individual creator, was outwitted by the products of his own brain—his books, his films, his radio voice. He saw himself being more and more replaced by them. He began to look upon himself as a negligible, archaic entity. At the same time, these identical devices revolutionized all previous methods of interhuman communication of ideas, feelings, opinions, news, etc., to an unprecedented degree. These new methods of communication began to play havoc with the old, natural methods of communication whose laws and configurations had not been studied. Now that they seemed to be in danger of being obliterated or, at least, distorted in their functions, their significance, began to loom on the horizon of man's awareness.

The analysis of technological and cultural conserves, especially of the book, the film, and the radio, was thus an important, albeit negative, theoretical preparation for the development of sociometry. This analysis stimulated the projection of constructs as diverse as the category of the Moment, spontaneous creative actions, the category of the cultural conserve, a social geometry of ideas and things, and the original state and situation of a "thing"—its status nascendi. The theoretical ground was thus gradually laid for a positive beginning of a sociometry which was concerned with the patterns of social structures which *actually exist* in human society. The core of a social structure is the pattern of relationships of all the individuals within the structure. Around this core, influencing the configurations of these patterns, are arrayed many levels of stimuli—economic, cultural and technological processes, for instance. A human society which functions without one or another of these stimuli is conceivable, but one cannot conceive a society functioning without some consideration for the individuals themselves and the relationships between them. The core of a social structure is, of course, never entirely separable from these various stimuli; hence, the study of their stratification and their gradual integration with the core becomes an essential part of sociometry.

The original version of the larger sociometric experiment was that the data obtained in any particular research must have, as a frame of reference, the total pattern of human society in order that these data may be useful as a basis for the construction or reconstruction, for the partial or total readjustment, of human society. In order to enlist every individual's interest during the phase of reconstruction, the social scientist must, of necessity, acquaint himself, in the research phase, with the individuals themselves and the interrelations between them. Analysis and action, social research, and social construction, are interwoven.

The Sociometric Experiment

It is significant to differentiate between the major experiment in sociometry and the minor experiments. The major experiment was visualized as a world-wide project—a scheme well-nigh Utopian in concept—yet it must be recalled again and again to our attention lest it be crowded out by our more practical daily tasks in sociometry.

We assumed—naively perhaps—that if a war can spread to encircle the globe, it should be equally possible to prepare and propagate a world sociometry. But this vision did not arise wholly out of thin air. Once we had successfully treated an entire community by sociometric methods, it seemed to us at least theoretically possible to treat an infinitely large number of such communities by the same methods—all the communities in fact, of which human society consists.

The ground is still gradually being prepared for the major experiment. Schemes like Marxism, and others, which have attempted world-wide reorganization of human relationships, have been analyzed and the causes of their failure disclosed. Their failure seems to have been due to a lack of knowledge of the structure of human society as it actually existed at the time of the attempt. A partial knowledge was not sufficient; knowledge of the total structure was necessary. We know that, in order to attain this total knowledge, all the individuals in a society must become active agents. Every individual, every minor group, every major group, and every social class must participate. The aim is to gain a total picture of human society; therefore, no social unit, however, powerless, should be omitted from participation in the experiment. In addition, it is assumed that, once individuals are aroused by sociometric procedures to act, to choose and to reject, every domain of human relationships will be stirred up—the economic, the racial, the cultural, the technological, and so on—and that they all will be brought into the picture. The sociometric experiment will end in becoming totalistic not only in expansion and extension but also in intensity, thus marking the beginning of a political sociometry.

It is a fact that the work to date has consisted in minor experiments and studies. Sociometric investigators have turned their attention away from a general experiment towards a more strategic and practical objective—the refining of old methods and the invention of new ones; the study of every type of children's group, adolescent group and age group; the investigation of communities, closed and open, primitive and metropolitan. The investigators have been concerned with every aspect of a community—the economic, the cultural and the technological—for which there was found some degree of aspiration or expression within the community. At times a project was carried to the maximum point of its domain, not only exploring the structure of a community but also applying the findings to the community situations and thus relieving tensions and producing social catharsis. At other times, however, possible upheaval within the political administration of a community and resistance on the part of its citizens hindered thorough sociometric experimentation. Cases have occurred where the investigator had to be content with gathering only partial data (and this by indirection) because of the low sociometric adaptability of the population under observation, resulting in studies which were only halfway sociometric. In these cases, the findings could necessarily cover only a peripheral segment of a community, and the application of these data to the people themselves was not considered. Nevertheless, a critical survey of all the sociometric studies which have been made to date, evaluating the methods used and the results obtained in all cases, whether completely sociometric or only partially so, would be of substantial assistance in the preparation of more dependable sociometric procedures for future use.

The result of these small scale experiments has been twofold. On the one hand, they led to important discoveries in the realm of human relations which were confirmed by every new study, and, on the other hand, they made it possible to put together, like a jig saw puzzle, the pieces of sociometric structure which had been found in various communities and get, with the assistance of these miniature patterns, a bird's-eye view of the sociometric foundation of society at large. The greater the number of valid studies in the years to come, the more accurate and complete will be our psycho-geographical model of the world, as compared with the still sketchy and primitive model which is available to us today.

Some Fundamental Concepts

Two theses spearheaded my original program of research in social science, 1) "The whole of human society develops in accord with definite laws"; 2) "A truly therapeutic procedure cannot have less an objective than the whole of mankind." From the point of view of "system" the two theses led logically to the differentiation between Sociometry and Sociatry.

According to Sociometry, society systems are preference or attraction-repulsion systems. This is claimed to be true not only of human, but also of sub-human societies. It also claimed that human preferential systems cannot be examined adequately by the old methods of fact-finding objectivity as statistical methods and observational methods, but that the methods themselves and the instruments derived from them have to undergo a process of *subjectification* in order to return to the researcher endowed with a more profound objectivity, having gained a grasp of the social processes on the depth level. This new *sociometric objectivity* can well be contrasted with the old *positivistic* objectivity of Comte.

It is due to this striving of sociometric method towards a superior and more complete objectivity that we gave systematic emphasis:

(a) To the study of social structures in statu nascendi (concept of the moment).

(b) To the shift from the gross examination of social aggregates to minute atomistic events, from the macroscopic to the microscopic method of investigation.

(c) To the development of situational sociology (situation and role analysis).

(d) To operational and measurement procedures, and above all,

(e) To a revolution of the relationship between the investigator and his subjects.

They themselves were thus motivated to be and turned into researchers of each other. A community of a thousand people for instance, became animated by sociometric devices to account for their social feelings and possibly to correct them. Sociometry became then, paraphrasing the famous saying of Lincoln: *the sociology of the people, by the people and for the people.* The operation of sociological research became itself socio (mass) centered instead of individual centered.

The status nascendi.[2] The most neglected aspect of social science is the function of the Moment in a social situation or, in other words, the relationship of a social situation to the moment of its emergence. In a philosophy of the Moment there are three factors to be emphasized: the locus, the status nascendi, and the matrix. These represent three views of the same process. There is no "thing" without its locus, no locus without its status nascendi, and no status nascendi without its matrix. The locus of a flower, for instance is in the bed where it is growing. Its status nascendi is that of a growing thing as it springs from the seed. Its matrix is the fertile seed, itself.

Every human act or performance has a primary action pattern—a status nascendi. An example is the performance of eating which begins to develop the role of the eater in every infant soon after birth.[3] The pattern of gestures and movements leading up to the state of satiation is, in this instance, the warming up process. With satiation comes an anti-climax. In the case of a very complex human performance, such as in the creative arts, the status nascendi and the warming-up process take place in the course of the process of creation. From the point of view of productivity, the anticlimax for the artist is reached when his creation is divorced from him and becomes a cultural conserve. The last act in a process—the last creative brush-stroke on a painting, for instance—is to us only as important as every other phase in the process. The common misconception occurs when the last act of production or creation is taken for, or substituted for, the whole process and all the preceding phases in the development are ignored. This last act undergoes a still more significant change when the technological process enters into the situation. The finished painting is removed from its place at the end of the course of creation or production and, by means of various machines, technologically reproduced over and over again, thus becoming a cultural conserve.

---

[2] See "Das Stegreiftheater," by J. L. Moreno (1923).

[3] See "Normal and Abnormal Characteristics of Performance Patterns," by Anita M. Uhl, Joseph Sargent, and J. L. Moreno, SOCIOMETRY, Vol. III, No. 3, pp. 38-57.

In the case of a social situation, such a love relationship, for instance, the status nascendi exists when the lovers meet and begin to warm up to one another. The last phase, the phase before the anti-climax, in a love-relationship (marriage, for example) is all too likely to be a stereotype, and in many social relationships similar stereotyped institutions are the end-products, parallel to the cultural conserve stage in a work of art. More-over, in the contemplation of, say, the marriage relationship between two people, the consideration of all the phases leading up to it is omitted. It is not to be assumed, however, that processes of human relations cease to exist when a cultural conserve or a stereotyped relationship enters the picture. In either case, a new social situation is begun which requires special methods of investigation.

The social sicences have been too much preoccupied with studies of processes after they have become cold. The status nascendi has been neg-lected. Most of the studies of man-woman relationships occur when the anti-climax has been reached—when the flow of feeling between the man and woman has dried up and the love which brought them together is over. The study of finished products, of cultural conserves and of stereotypes has, of course, its place and its meaning in a system of social science. The preoccupation with them is not surprising. It is much easier to study a rela-tionship when it is finished and established and when it has the deceptive appearance of being an end-result. Perhaps this is why sociology has been chiefly concerned with the study of the tangible structures in society. But it is from the social situations in statu nascendi that the more important inspira-tions and decisions come. Their deep impress upon all human interrelations has been demonstrated. The problem has been how to get at these intangi-ble, esoteric phenomena—how to study them. It is, of course, important that they be studied systematically. A human society without these phe-nomena in statu nascendi would present a lifeless appearance. Therefore, social research which does not give its main attention to these phenomena must be sterile. Any plan for the betterment of society, for the improve-ment of human relations, is hopeless without them. Therefore, theories and methods had to be found. It is at this cardinal point that sociometric and psychodramatic studies have stepped into the breach. The results to date are meager, it must be admitted, but the road is now open.

A study of human interrelations proceeding forward from their status nascendi, instead of proceeding backward from their end-product, has great theoretical advantages. A study of this sort is able to do away with the dualistic character ascribed to social processes. There is no true dichotomy between, for instance, underlying and surface structures, or between genetic phenomena and symptoms. Just as every cause is a part of its effect and every effect a part of its cause, every underlying structure partakes of the peripheral and vice versa.[4] This is the case if we begin with the status nascendi of a situation and follow its warming up process through stage after stage. Dual constructions such as cause and effect become, then, illogical.

The "Tele" Concept. The tele concept is not a purely theoretical construction. It has been suggested by sociometric findings. The statistical distribution of attractions and repulsions is affected by some esoteric factor. The normal distribution into which practically all psychological phenomena thus far investigated fit is not followed by attraction and repulsion patterns. The trend towards mutuality of attraction and repulsion many times surpasses chance possibility.[5] The factor responsible for this effect is called "tele". It may explain why there are not as many human societies as there are individuals—a situation which is at least theoretically possible—with all social relations the product of individual imaginations. Tele can be assumed to be responsible for the operation of the multiple foci in any relationship between two persons, or as many persons as compose a given social situation. It is dependent upon both, or all the individuals and is not the subjective, independent product of each person. Out of these operations of the tele factor a product results which has the character of an objective, a supra-individual, system.

Although it is clear that the tele factor operates, nothing is as yet known about its "material" structure. It may have some relation to gene structure and sexual attraction. It may be that the study of *tele psychology* will provide clues to a better understanding of occult phenomena, as clairvoyance and telepathy.

The Social Atom. As the individual projects his emotions into the groups around him, and as the members of these groups in turn project their emotions toward him, a pattern of attractions and repulsions, as projected from both sides, can be discerned on the threshold between individual and group. This pattern is called his "social atom". It is not identical with the formal position an individual occupies in the group (his position in the

---

4 On the sociometric analysis of home groups, for instance, we find that *some* relationships on the formal level are identical with those on the underlying level and vice versa.

5 See "Statistics of Social Configurations," SOCIOMETRY, Volume I, part I, pp. 342-378.

family, for instance). It evolves as an inter-personal structure from the birth-level onward. The size of the social atom of any particular individual cannot accurately be discerned unless the whole community or group in which he lives is sociometrically studied. Sociometric casework of a single individual may be tolerated in practice, but we must be aware that some positive or negative tele may exist in reference to him which cannot be calculated unless all the individuals around him are tested in conjunction with him. The social atom is the first tangible structure empirically discernible in the formation of a human society. It is its smallest unit. Sociometric studies demonstrate clearly that it develops different patterns of varying[6] degree of cohesion, normal and abnormal patterns. Thus, an individual can be diagnosed from the point of view of how his social atom is patterned. A community can be diagnosed from the point of view of what types of social atoms are in the minority. A study of this sort may suggest the optimum pattern for a well-balanced community in which this or that pattern predominates.

The discovery of social atom patternings is an excellent illustration of how sociometric ideas develop and change in accord with the findings. The first construction of sociometric concepts, like the social atom, for instance, was intuitive, suggested by slight, empirical material. "Social atom" was first a purely descriptive term for a social configuration which was evident in every inter-personal relation system of a community, but we did not then know what dynamic meaning it had in its formation. Only later did we suspect that it might be a basic social unit.

In an early phase of sociometry, at a time when we were studying group structures from the outside, as participant observers (watching children at play, or sitting in a spontaneity theatre and watching the formation of pairs on the basis of various roles, noting how certain persons assumed a leader position in respect to certain others and how some were able and others unable to begin or end an action), we were able to determine with some precision the outer structure of the group.[7] But the deeper structure of the group remained undisclosed and, with it, the social atom. Accordingly, the first charting of inter-personal relation systems showed blank areas. When sociometric tests were applied to a formal group in a public school,[8] the find-

---

[6] See "Psychodramatic Shock Thereapy" by J. L. Moreno, SOCIOMETRY, Vol. II No. 1, p. 29.

[7] See "Who Shall Survive?" by J. L. Moreno, pp. 169-191; also the section on Experiment in "Das Stegreiftheater," by J. L. Moreno mentioned in Note 4.

[8] See "Application of the Group Method to Classification," by J. L. Moreno, 1932, pp. 98-103.

ings permitted an analysis of inner structures, percentages of attractions and repulsions, the number of isolates, pairs, triangles, chains, etc. but the social atom could not yet be discerned—not even on the descriptive level—because the tests were limited to the classrooms. The relationships of the pupils to the families, to the neighborhoods and to other situations in which they were involved were not part of the study. It was not until a still further advanced phase was reached, when a whole community was approached sociometrically, that the social atom became discernible.

Now that we are unable to study social atoms both descriptively and in their dynamic differentiations, the earlier structural analysis of a community as being made up of pairs, isolates, etc., looks rather artificial, although, within its limit, it is still valid. From the point of view of the total community structure, a true pair, for instance, cannot exist independent of relationships with other persons. Our previous procedure of structure analysis may, in the course of time, be superseded by the use of more dynamic patternings of the social atom as a more penetrating guide to the depth structure of a community.

The great theoretical advances which have been made as the result of sociometric become more pointed if we consider them in the light of the contributions of two sociological pioneers, von Wiese[9] and Cooley.[10] From the theoretical distinction between von Wiese's patterns of association and disassociation in human relations to the modern sociometric concepts is a long way. Sociometric concepts had to be constructed anew, as inspired by the dynamics of actual situations. Cooley's concept of primary groups comes close to the realities of social structure. But, although social atoms are certainly *primary structures*, they are not "face to face" or primary groups. To be sure, an individual knows "face to face" a certain number of people composing his social atom—they may belong to his family, home or work group —but he may be ignorant or unconscious of the existence of many individuals who feel strongly about him and there may be some individuals about whom he feels strongly but who are, in turn, either ignorant or unconscious of this fact. In other words, there are primary social configurations, social atoms, psycho-social networks, and others, which are not primary groups.

Another aspect of the social atom which may stand in need of revision is its relation to the findings which have come to us from spontaneity test-

---

9 See "System of Sociology," by Becker-Wiese, 1931.
10 See "Social Organization," by Charles H. Cooley, 1909.

ing of the individuals comprising it. Originally, we constructed two tests, the sociometric test and the spontaneity test. The sociometric test produced findings which suggested the setting up of the concept "social atom", viewed as an attraction-repulsion pattern. The spontaneity test, aided by psycho-dramatic procedures, produced findings which suggested the construction of an additional concept, the "cultural atom", which was viewed as a pattern of role relations. Now, in reality, there is but one atom. From the point of view of the actual situation, the distinction between social and cultural atom is artificial. It is pertinent for construction purposes but it loses its significance within a living community. We must visualize the atom as a configuration of interpersonal relationships in which the attractions and repulsions existing between its constituent members are integrated with the many role relations which operate between them. Every individual in a social atom has a range of roles, and it is these roles which give to each attraction or repulsion its deeper and more differentiated meaning.

Psycho-Social Networks. If we continue to investigate the larger and more inclusive sociometric structures which can be discerned on the psycho-geographical map of any typical community,[11] we can discover many intermediate stages between the social atom and the psycho-social network. We can see, for example, the coalescing of three or four social atoms, the central individuals of which are mutually attracted, forming a triangle or a square. At other places on the map we may see half a dozen social atoms which exist in close geographical proximity to a dozen other social atoms, but with no visible relations between any of their constituent individuals. Elsewhere on the map we may encounter a group of social atoms whose central individuals show a negative tele to the central individuals of another group of social atoms, in the same geographical area. Very little is known about these and more complex structures, beyond their descriptive pattern. Local investigation may disclose that, in the first illustration above, the central individuals are of the same kinship. In the second illustration, they may belong to different social strata—the one group having a higher cultural and economic status, the other a lower. The third illustration may represent individuals of competitive situations. Further exploration is re-

---

11 Individuals cluster together and form psycho-social networks of varying configurations and the communities in which they live are held together by specific emotional currents which can today be mapped with the same precision as the physical geography of that region. In contrast to ethnological concepts such as class, race, etc., patterns of social atoms, psycho-social networks, and many other similar structures actually exist as dynamic parts of human society.

quired which cannot be made by even the most inspired speculation. *The communities must first be mapped as wholes; then a study can be begun.*

The psycho-social networks are not readily visible on a psycho-geographical map. We become interested in the possibility of their existence when we noted that *rumor distributed itself irregularly, reaching one section of a community more easily than another.* We saw individuals who were unacquainted with one another and belonging either to different parts of a community or to different communities, doing or saying things so similar and so simultaneously as to seem to indicate some mysterious correspondence —the "grapevines" of folk sociology. *It seemed logical to assume that individuals, however far apart they appeared to be geographically or on the social scale but who are associated with one another through the devious links and counterlinks of mutual tele, would produce a smooth channel for the transmission of news, opinions, etc. We lifted from the original map all the individuals who were interconnected in the fashion described, regardless of the specific groups to which they belonged, and then transferred them to a new map. Thus, we saw the entire community broken up into several so-called "psycho-social networks."* We saw them partly overlapping one another; we saw that individuals as a rule belonged to more than one network; we saw that only a group proportion of the individuals who belonged to the same network knew each other personally—the large majority were tied to one another by a hidden chain of tele-links. We saw that only a small proportion of the social atoms of a community belonged to any one network; others belonged to different networks or remained unrelated and scattered between the networks, doubly isolated—isolated as individuals, and left out of the networks.

Once the networks in a community were described and mapped, it was easy to demonstrate their dynamic existence by a simple experiment. In a closed community which was under investigation, we were aware that rumors passed continually back and forth from mouth to mouth. *The object of the experiment was to demonstrate that these rumors followed the paths of the networks which we had mapped.* The experimenter entered Group I and approached an individual, M, who, according to the map, belonged to Network A. M was a key individual, that is, he was linked up with 22 other individuals, some of whom belonged to his Group I, and others to Group II, III, IV, and V. *M was chosen to be the person with whom to start the spread of a rumor,* which concerned a leading personality in the community's administration.* We had found that, in networks comprising

---

* This rumor was "planted." See for *spontaneous* spread of rumors, *Who Shall Survive,* p. 256-66.

more than 100 individuals, only very few participated in any one other net-work. It seemed, therefore, that *the chances were that the rumor would spread with ease and speed through M's own network, Network A, and then would need a longer time to filter through to the other networks. We as-sumed that it would take its longest time to reach Network E, into which there was no overlapping from Network A. It was gratifying to see our assumptions verified with great accuracy.* Checks from time to time showed that the rumor was, indeed, following the paths we had expected it to follow.

From the material which had been available, it can be deduced that there are many specific patternings of psycho-social networks. This field is little explored, but some future study may be able to show that com-munities differ in accord with the types of networks which prevail within them. It will probably become apparent that the size of the various net-works differs greatly. Some, we know already, are limited to a particular locality; others operate throughout several communities; still others may cross the whole country, from coast to coast. Microscopic studies of net-works will also show that the tele-links between the connected individuals are held together by ideal images (such as Christ) or sacred symbols (such as the Cross and the Swastika). The different characteristics of its psycho-social networks will indicate the growth or decay of a community.[12]

It is obvious that the relationship between the networks and the modern technological apparatus for the distribution of ideas, opinions, and news—the printing press, the motion picture and the radio—is of prime importance. The distorting effect which the printed page has upon individual spon-taneity and the mouth to mouth transmission of ideas was, indeed, my first approach to the sociometric concept of the network and the realization that this superimposition of a mechanical-social network upon a psycho-social network produces a situation which takes society unawares and removes it more and more beyond the human control.[13] The development of the film, the radio, and modern propaganda has accelerated this process of which we are largely unconscious, to an unprecedented degree.

In an age like ours, the most important message, if transmitted by mouth, can be kept from dissemination by the first man to hear it if he does not choose to pass it on, while the most harmful and least cultured expres-sion, if uttered at the psychological moment over a prominent radio network,

---

12 See Loomis "stayer-" and "mover-" networks in "Measurement of the Dissolu-tion of In-Groups in the Integration of a Rural Resettlement Project," by C. P. Loomis and D. M. Davidson, Jr., SOCIOMETRY, Vol. II, No. 2.

13 See "Die Gottheit als Autor" (The Godhead as Author), by J. L. Moreno, Ber-lin, 1918.

can reach, affect, and disturb almost the whole world. It would be of interest to study what the technological networks, the printing press, and the
radio, for instance, actually do to the psycho-social networks of which human
society consists. There is, however, one important beneficial effect which
our modern radio systems have upon the psycho-social networks. At one
stroke they can bring thousands of independent psycho-social networks in
different parts of the country into a confluence which could not have been
produced by a mouth to mouth transfer of news or opinion, except after a
long period of time. So, in order to reach and exterminate his potential as
well as his actual enemies with the highest possible efficiency, he gave orders
that not only the friends of Trotsky but also the friends of these friends,
and the friends of these friends of the friends of Trotsky be "purged", even
if the suspicion of any friendly relationship was very slight.

PRINCIPLE OF SOCIO-GENETIC EVOLUTION

Whenever repeated sociometric tests have been administered at intervals to the same (or nearly the same) population, the regularity with
which certain specific patterns of interpersonal relations have occurred has
arrested the attention of investigators. The material demonstrating this regularity has been the result of two research projects. One project studied the
formation and evolution of a community[14] and the other studied the formation and evolution of groups from birth level up to the age of fourteen.[15]

Most of the sociometric studies of communities made to date were of
communities which were already established. It was almost impossible to
trace the principle of socio-genetic evolution in these communities as their
past history and their beginnings are unknown. An investigator who attempts to demonstrate the operation of this principle must be present when
the community is in the process of formation, in statu nascendi and he must
follow up its development, step by step. The follow-up must consist of
the application of sociometric tests; the successive maps of the community
will disclose its genesis. An opportunity to make a study of this sort has,
up to now, been given to an investigator only twice.

---

[14] See description of a resettlement project at Mitterndorf, Austria, 1815 to 1918
in "Who Shall Survive?" by J. L. Moreno, pp. 17 and 18, and "Sociometric Planning
of a New Community," by Shepard Wolman, SOCIOMETRY, Vol I, part I, pp. 220-
254. See also discussion by C. C. Taylor of C. P. Loomis' paper on "Informal Groupings in a Spanish-American Village," in this issue.

[15] See description of a sociometric project in a public school with a re-test after a
period of two years; "Who Shall Survive?" by J. L. Moreno, 1934, pp. 23-28.

Sociometric projects, arbitrarily studying groups of children at one or another age level, cannot bring the workings of a socio-genetic evolution into relief. It is interesting to note the relationship between politics and sociometry. There is hardly anything which is more important to a man than his position in the group, or how people feel about him. The ebb and flow of attractions and repulsions within his social atom may be responsible for tensions within him, since he cannot be entirely unaware of how much sympathy or hatred is directed toward him. This is more significant still for the position he has in the psycho-social networks in which he is either active or passive. He may make a guess at what is brewing for or against him—as an individual or as the member of a group, but he cannot know for certain. Political leaders are keenly aware of the "grapevine" phenomenon; they are "practical" sociometrists. In a political campaign, for example, they pick the key individuals in a community and operate through them. Their psycho-geographical maps are, of course, entirely intuitive. If, however, they had real psychogeographical maps of the communities at their disposal, they could make their selection of key individuals with greater precision and prepare their campaigns with better chances of success.

The network theory is able to interpret political phenomena difficult to understand otherwise. One illustration is the purges attributed to Stalin. Why were extensive mass murders committed when relatively few men had actually been found guilty of treason? It would seem unnecessary to punish more than a few, but the cold politician, Stalin, knew that, besides the few men who had been direct associates of Trotsky, there were literally thousands more, potentially equally dangerous, who could be just as threatening to his regime. He knew that, to each of the, say, twelve guilty men, a number of sympathizers must be linked, and to each of these sympathizers, in turn, others were linked, and to this larger circle many others were interlinked, either directly or indirectly, who might become infected with the same political ideas. In other words, he visualized a myriad of psycho-social networks spread over all Soviet Russia in which these actual or potential enemies acted in roles which might be dangerous to him. Unfortunately, he had only a rough, instinctive picture of the networks; he did not know the actual men and their actual positions in their respective communities. The investigator, in order to reach valid material, must approach groups which present a cross section of all the age levels from birth to adolescence. Only then will he be able to compare the most infantile group structure (group structure in statu nascendi) with each successive step in structure formation, from month to month and from year to year. It is upon many more studies of this sort that a competent discussion of the form and existence of socio-genetic evolution can be based.

LAW OF SOCIAL GRAVITATION

The sociometric formula of social gravitation states:

People 1 (P1) and People (P2) move towards each other—between a locality X and a locality Y—in direct proportion to the amount of attraction given (a1) or received (a2), in inverse proportion to the amount of repulsion given (r1) or received (r2), the physical distance (d) between the two localities being constant, the facilities of communication between X and Y being equal.

THE SOCIODYNAMIC LAW

The sociodynamic law is divided into a first and a second part. The first part states that the income of emotional choices per capita is unevenly divided among the members of the group regardless of its size or kind; comparatively few get a lion's share of the total output of emotional choices, out of proportion with their needs and their ability to consummate them; the largest form an average income of choice group within their means to consummate them and a considerable number remain unchosen or neglected. The scores when plotted form a J curve, about two-thirds of the population receiving scores below chance and a relatively few obtaining high scores. Though an equal number would have been expected on the basis of chance the proportion of isolates was generally greater than the proportion of stars.

The second part states that if the opportunities of being chosen are increased by increasing the size of the group and the number of choices per capita, the volume of choices continue to go to those at the top end of the range (the "stars") in direct proportion to the size of the group and to the number of choices permitted per capita, furthering the gap between the small star group, the average group and the neglected group. The excess "profit" gained by the already overchosen members must be ascribed to a chain and network effect which operates in cases of non-acquaintance (with the chosen individual) in addition to the score based on acquaintance (with the chosen individual). The direct factor is proximity choice, the indirect factor, a symbolic choice. An individual, A, may score high in his face to face group, but because of his "role" (he may be a baseball player, an actor, or a senator) his ultimate score may turn out to be a multiple of the initial score (role corresponds here to what is usually meant by status; status is too much of an abstraction, but role implies a living and concrete function).

THE DIALECTIC CHARACTER OF SOCIOMETRY

The dialectic attitude of the sociometric investigator is brought about on one hand by the natural resistance of the community to a scheme which carries the social process to a maximum degree of realization (for which it is as yet unprepared and uneducated and, on the other hand, by the resistance of people who favor other earlier methods and ideologies in the manipulation of population problems. When sociometry began to arouse public attention several years ago, the number of procedures which were ready for application was few as compared with the number of social problems which were to be faced in any community study. Economic, technological and political problems of all sorts pressing for an immediate solution could neither experiment with untried procedures nor wait until they were ready. I recommended, therefore, that supplementary techniques should be used around the true sociometric core, even if they did not fulfill the requirements of genuine sociometric procedures. To the category of supplementary techniques belong, among others, public opinion studies, studies of attitudes and socio-economic measurements.

When I introduced terms like "sociometry", "sociometric techniques" and "sociometric scale", I anticipated that such terms would be applied to types of social measurement which are in some degree sociometric (near-sociometric)[16] in addition to methods developed by me and my closer associates. I also anticipated that, partly because of the influence of sociometry, and partly as a result of the natural development of social science, methods and concepts in sociology, psychology, and psychiatry would become more flexible and realistic and thus approach the point of view which has been fostered by sociometry. An illustration is the development from Bogardus[17] who studies attitudes towards people as a race or as a class and gets an answer which cannot be but a symbolic one and the scale based upon similar data a symbolic scale of attitude to studies like that of Ford,[18] who asks questions which deal with personal contacts. This time the answers must be more concrete—they must be based upon "Experiences"—but they

---

[16] "Near-sociometric" can mean procedures which fall short of the full meaning of the term "sociometric" either in its "socius" aspect or in its "metrum" aspect (see page 18 of this paper). Bogardus and Thurstone provide examples which fall short in the "socius" aspect and the metrum aspect, while case-work studies are typically short in the "metrum" aspect.

[17] Bogardus, E. S., "Social Distance and Its Origin," 1925.

[18] Ford, Robert N., "Scaling White-Negro Experiences by the Method of Equal-Appearing Intervals," SOCIOMETRY, Vol. III, a number.

are still a far cry from the specific individual with whom the contact took place although it is within the field of the status nascendi of a relationship. An attempt is made, at least, to shape a questionnaire in such a fashion that it more nearly covers the actual inter-individual structures which exist.

Another illustration is the development from the older public opinion questionnaire, which expected uniform responses from a rigid, set question, to the more recent refinements in pre-testing questionnaires—adjusting the questions to the group which is to be studied.[19] The latter procedure is also far removed, however, from the sociometric approach which would disclose to the investigator the key individuals in the group, the psycho-social networks through which opinion moves, and whether the opinions which are collected represent the opinions of the key individuals only or the opinions of the groups under their influence. Consequently, what these investigators measure may not be what they intend it to be, an opinion of the public, but the private opinions of a small number of people. It can be expected that sociometric methods which include the interpersonal relation systems in their tests will gradually replace methods which investigate social situations in a more or less indirect and symbolistic fashion.

The other field in which sociometry can demonstrate its value is that of social planning. There are many concepts and hypotheses in the conduct of human affairs which stand in the way of the application to their fullest extent of sociometric ideas. The philosophy of anarchism, for instance, may criticize the various schemes of present-day governments, however liberal, as authoritarian regimes, but in a society which is sociometrically planned, a special niche for anarchists is not necessary because sociometry is based upon the principle of spontaneity and gives expression to even the most extreme individualism. The philosophy of communism, particularly of Marxism, may maintain that the rule of one social class which represents the mass of the producers is necessary in order that a maximum of justice, perhaps arbitrary, may prevail, but in a sociometrically planned society the genuine contribution of collectivism could be brought to its fullest expression without any necessity of resorting to arbitrary measures. The economic factor, and with it the production and distribution of goods, cannot be artificially divorced from the total system of interpersonal relations. Within the scope of sociometric investigation a first clue to the solution

---

19 Blankenship, A. B., "Pre-Testing a Questionnaire for a Public Opinion Poll," SOCIOMETRY, Vol. III, No. 3.

of this knotty problem has been found in the relationship between the socio-dynamic effect[20] and the distribution of wealth. The philosophy of totalitarianism proposes a regime in which a master race, self chosen, is to rule all other peoples, the master race itself being governed by a leader at the top with a number of auxiliary leaders carrying out his orders. But the central problems of this ideology, the leader and the race question, can be handled within a sociometric scheme without violence and certainly with a far greater precision and with a minimum of friction. Within a totalitarian society, the group of leaders who have inaugurated the regime, whether self-chosen or elected, may go stale. This may become the Achilles' heel of the totalitarian society, relying as it does upon a distorted distribution of all the total available spontaneity which places, if possible, all the spontaneity in the leaders (maximum spontaneity at the top) and no spontaneity in the peoples (minimum spontaneity at the bottom). This crucial problem, the proper equilibrium between leaders and followers, can be dealt with by means of sociometric planning without having to resort to a totalitarian regime. It has been demonstrated[21] within a community which is administered along sociometric lines that the set of individuals who are in key positions today can easily be ascertained by sociometric tests. In the course of routine re-testing at regular intervals it becomes dramatically apparent that these key individuals wane in influence and others come up to take their places (in statu nascendi). This raises the question as to whether leadership artificially maintained may not become a "conserve" and therefore a stultifying instead of a spontaneous and inspiring agent. In addition, the problem of race is managed as an inherent part of the sociometric scheme. By means of concepts like race cleavage and the racial saturation point, populations which differ ethnologically can be distributed within a given geographic area without having to resort to forced and hit-or-miss migration.

Sociometry can well be considered the cornerstone of a still undeveloped science of democracy. The so-called democratic process if not truly democratic as long as the large spheres of invisible processes disclosed by sociometric procedures are not integrated with and made a part of the political scheme of democracy.[22] Sociometry can assist the United States,

---

20 See "Statistics of Social Configurations," SOCIOMETRY, Vol. I, part 2, pp. 342-34.

21 See discussion of leaders and leadership, "Who Shall Survive?" by J. L. Moreno, pp. 163, 164.

22 See "Human Nature and Conduct," by John Dewey, Henry Holt & Co., New

with its population consisting of practically all the races on the globe, in becoming an outstanding and permanent example of a society which has no need of extraneous ideas or of forces which are not inherent in its own structure.

York, 1922; and "Cross Cultural Survey," by George P. Murdock, *American Sociological Review,* June, 1940.

III.

POLITICAL SOCIOMETRY

SOCIOMETRY AND MARXISM*

It is now a century since the communist manifesto was proclaimed by Karl Marx and Friedrich Engels. It is three decades since the Russian revolution and the dictatorship of the proletariat was established under the leadership of Lenin and Trotzky. The eyes of all mankind were and still are directed towards these events with a hope, unparalleled since the emergence of Christianity, and with a question mark. What is the total effect and change produced by this Magna Charta of revolutionary social science? Which are its positive returns and negative drawbacks?

Marx made a distinction between the private property of the means of production and the private property of consumers goods. The surplus earnings, called by him "surplus value", because the means of production are owned by a special class, the capitalist class, are collected by a few[1], the owners, instead of by the many, the workers. He raised the question as to who should govern the means of production in order to assure society from uneven and unjust distribution of income. Thus far Marx was correct. But the conclusions he drew from it have not stood up in the crucial test of reality.

His first conclusion was that it is impossible to establish a "classless" society at once. For the transition period the means of production should be taken over and governed by the majority, the proletariat, and a government of the workers, "the dictatorship of the proletariat" should be established. He expected that this "secondary" state would gradually vanish and a totally socialistic society result. Marx was wrong in this conclusion.

A few months after the Russian revolution of 1917 I predicted that "the revolution cannot succeed without a specific sociometric outlook. The substitution of the rule of one class for the other, as for instance the replacement of the rule of the bourgeoisie by the rule of the proletariat is secondary. The essential task is that the second, newly created state, the dictatorship of the proletariat, installed by the suppressed people as an organ of revolution, truly and really vanishes. This state cannot eliminate itself unless a complete inner restructuring of all parts of society has taken place" (22). Fifteen years later I continued my appraisal of the Russian revolution as follows: The error of Marx was the contention "that the economic and psychological problem of Man cannot be attacked as a unit

* Presidential Address, American Sociometric Association, Christmas Meeting, Commodore Hotel, December 26, 1947. Partly published in *Cahiers Internationaux de Sociologie, 1949*, "Methode Experimentale, Sociometrie et Marxism".

159

at one time, that the psychological problem must wait, that so to speak two different revolutions are necessary, that the economic revolution has to precede the psychological and creative revolution of human society. It was a theoretical practical obsession with strategic procedure, the splitting of a unit into two different issues." "The change of economic structure in Russia since the revolution of 1917 does not appear to be accompanied by the expected changes in the psychology of human interrelations. The psychological changes lag far behind the economic changes, the communistic society is still in its first phase, the state has not yet withered away. The Communistic society in its highest state may be a myth, or to apply to it one of his own phrases, 'an opium for the people' to be set aside afterwards as unattainable and Utopian, as soon as the economic program of the first phase, the dictatorship of the proletariat, is achieved." (13). Well, the proletarian state has not vanished, it does not intend to vanish, it has become so strongly entrenched that there is no instrument available by which it could be eliminated. The dictatorship of the proletariat has become just a dictatorship. A new proletarian revolution would be required to eliminate it, a revolution just as violent, if not more, as the revolution which swept away the government of the Czar thirty years ago.

My thesis is that the split in the original matrix of socialist revolutionary theory is the primary cause for the ultimate failure of the revolution. It provides us with a key for understanding the puzzling developments and abrupt changes in policy which have taken place in Soviet Russia during the thirty years of its existence. It is certain that the founder of socialism did not lack the *vision* but the *knowledge* for formulating a complete theory of revolution, or at least a more complete one, one which would have taken care of all the dimensions of society. He prepared a "partial" blueprint, and left the rest in the dark, to circumstance. It is perhaps fair to say that Marx put into the blueprint only what he *knew* and left out what he did not know. He knew that he discovered in what can be called the *capitalist syndrome* an important phenomenon and he started the revolution with the part he knew. He did not know the rest of the social structure and he did not know of instruments by means of which he could explore it. That is why he broke the pattern of revolution into several steps and postponed action on them, indefinitely, until more would be known about their execution.

The second conclusion of Marx was that the "surplus" value is found particularly in capitalistic societies. This was correct within certain limits:

it is correct only if the capitalistic-economic phenomena are studied in isolation, apart from the rest and without considering their dependence upon
the total social structure. Sociometric studies have shown that the surplus
value is a special case of an universally operating tendency, the *sociodynamic
effect*. "The distorted profit picture in economic relations is a reflection of
the distorted tele picture on the interpersonal and intergroup level. The social
revolution of the class struggle is therefore a displacement from the microscopic to the macroscopic level. Marx was operating on the gross macro-
sociological level of events. Being unaware of the social microscopy of
modern sociometry he committed a grave error of insight. The sociodynamic
effect does not cease to be effective in a socialistic society, it assumes only
different forms. It would be interesting to envision what effect this knowledge would have had upon his theory and method of social revolution. It
appears at least that the place of revolutionary action should have been re-
oriented towards the smallest units of human relations, the social atoms, the
primary receptacles of "preferentiation", in order to become truly and permanently effective." (18). There the revolution might spontaneously have
taken a more realistic form. Besides being economic it would have been at
the same time psychological, sociological, axiological and creative, in other
words, it might have taken the form of a sociometric procedure.

Marx was halfway right in his second conclusion. The dictatorship of
the proletariat cured society from the capitalist syndrome, reduced the risk
of mass unemployment, put a brake on the prosperity-depression cycle typical
for capitalistic societies. But the question is whether the revolution was
indispensable and not too high a price for a comparatively meager outcome.
The revolution was a major operation and had many unforeseeable and
unfortunate effects upon the body politic. Less violent measures like
state capitalism, labor-capital contracts and other forms of paternalistic
governments appear able to provide temporary brakes against mass unemployment and the recurrent cycle of inflation and deflation. Both Marx
and Lenin might have hesitated to stir up the masses to revolution, had
they known in advance that it would end in a stalemate, barring instead of
promoting—what after all was their objective—a truly human, classless
and stateless socialistic world democracy. The question is therefore: How
can we avoid the errors which Marx has made on the theoretical and on
the practical level of revolutionary action?

We can avoid the theoretical error by replacing the theory of socialism
with the theory of sociometry, and the practical error by replacing the global
hit or miss socioeconomic proletarian revolution with "small" sociometric

revolutions. This new view can be applied to a) the theory of social revolution; b) the instruments of revolution.

Theory of Social Revolution. Marx assumed that by means of a careful, materialistic analysis of human relations he had arrived at a full comprehension of what is wrong with human society, that it must be changed economically and that the change cannot take place by persuasion but by social revolution. His theory of practice was constructed in behalf of something to be prepared, something to be done, ending in one or several acts of mass violence. His attention was bent upon the dynamic change which he expected was bound to take place in the course of the violent upheaval of the masses and not upon the equally important aspect of its dynamic *failure.* He was not interested in the value of *defeat* of the socio-revolutionary experiment: he was not sufficiently interested to find out that the instrument itself, the socio-revolutionary program was *wrong.* All he was interested in comprehending—in the face of defeat (See "The Class Struggles in France") —was what was wrong with the situation to which the revolutionary idea was to be applied. *He did not permit himself to doubt the value and veracity of the social revolution itself.* The sociometrist, however much the idea to change the world may burn in him, entertains a different point of view. What may be of little significance to the practical revolutionary Marxist is of the greatest importance to him—the sociometrist is interested in the social revolution as a "social experiment". It is to an extent immaterial to him whether it succeeds or fails. Because of our low grade of social knowledge, he is interested in it primarily as an exploratory experiment and not as a social crusade—in what one learns from it and not only whether society improves through it. What would we gain if by sheer luck and blind chance a violent revolution would so criminally and completely succeed, that human society would either be permanently crippled or permanently elevated? There is no guarantee that blind chance might not turn up again and reverse the effect. Perhaps it is better to know the truth although it may never be realized. It may be worthier for mankind to perish with seeing eyes than to live forever in ignorance of its deterioration.

There are similarities and differences between sociometric and socialistic types of change. Some of the similarities are: 1) both are in favor of direct action; 2) both are revolutionary, that is demanding a radical change of the existing social order; 3) both are against symptomatic and temporary measures; 4) both claim that a scientific knowledge of the dynamics of social relations is indispensable for a theory of social revolution; 5) both claim that all social ills, economic, psychological, axiological and cultural are interdependent; 6) both insist that the people act in their own behalf and that they are called to universal social action.

Some of the differences are: 1) a scientific knowledge of economics is important but insufficient for a true change of the social order; in addition to economics the dynamic structure of the socius, of inter-individual and inter-group relations has to be known and taken into account in the construction of a theory of social revolution; 2) socialism is the revolution of one class, the economic proletariat; sociometric revolution is a revolution of all classes, of total mankind, of all people, all individuals and all groups without exception, legal or illegal, formal or informal, small or large, of all nations and states, sovereign and unrecognized. The sociometric proletariat has its victims in all classes, rich or poor, black or white, among people of high or low intelligence, of superior or inferior spontaneity; 3) Marxism tries to fortify the class consciousness of the proletariat, to bring the masses to a realization of its power and of the actually existing economic conditions; political sociometry in contrast tries to develop in the masses a high degree of "sociometric consciousness", that is, knowledge of the structure of social groups in all parts of the globe, especially of the groups in which they hold immediate membership and in respect to all criteria around which groups may be formed (the economic factor is only one vital criterion); it tries to encourage the masses to insist on change of the legal, social, political and cultural order as indicated by its underlying dynamic structure. It insists that economic revolutions are shortsighted, ignorant of the dynamics of the actual structure of human society and that sooner or later the new social order which they create will either relapse to the previous condition which they tried to change or regress into social anarchy.

The idea fix prevails in many minds that before the next step in social revolution can be enacted, every country has to pass through the phase of the dictatorship of the proletariat; that the Russian Soviet type of revolution has to be established everywhere first before a new step can be undertaken. This is usually linked to the idea that the course of social revolutions from feudal to capitalist society, and from capitalist to soviet society is a necessary, irreversible development which could not have been stopped or directed towards an alternate course. But sociometrically there is no such thing as "class", capitalist class, middle class, and worker class. The concept of class is pre-sociometric mythology. What a sociometric study of such large masses of people as class might reveal is a real portion —a complex of microscopic islands of interpersonal and intergroup structures here and there, and a huge biased political organization tying the pieces together.

The greatest advance which sociometry has made as compared with Marxism are: a) its methods by which it can explore causes of social ills; its methods of *social microscopy,* an approach which the French sociologist, Georges Gurvitch, has emphasized independently; b) its linkage to the people in action. The first advance has been made in a spirit similar to the one developed by somatic medicine in the nineteenth century. In somatic medicine the cause of many mysterious ailments was finally found in germs, invisible creatures, in micro-organisms. The cure of many macroscopic manifestations and endemic diseases such as diphtheria, cholera, syphillis, etc., succeeded because of the new knowledge. The sociological medicine of the future, sociatry, will derive similar benefits from microscopically-oriented sociometric research, which tries to isolate the "social" micro-organisms in the social structure, facilitated by sociograms, sociomatrices, and interaction and movement diagrams. Remedies against social syndromes as the capitalistic syndrome, will be found along lines Marx never dreamed of, less violent and more permanent in their effects. Microsociology is, however, still in its infancy. I cannot agree with many of my friends that sociometry has "come of age". It is far from it. Such easy optimism comes from the frequent practice to dilute and reduce sociometric tests to questionnaires and to reduce the status of the participants to be halfway between guinea pigs and people who choose and decide their destiny. It is here also where Marxism has been at fault. As protector of the interest of the masses, it has failed to protect the little isolated individuals, the little informal groups, and last but not least to mobilize the enormous underground networks between one group and the other. There are numerous forms of canalization between distant points in social space. They will be gradually discovered not in the laboratory but through experiments in life itself and as small sociometric revolutions spread all over the globe. The sociometric consciousness and maturity of the people will grow in proportion with the size of the experiments, the number and vitality of the criteria involved and the visible benefit derived from them.

The outcry of unfair exploitation, especially of economic exploitation of the majority of the people, the masses of industrial and rural workers, by a small minority of capitalists has been the well nigh irresistible core of all socialistic revolutions. Little or no attention has been given to the cruelest exploitation of all time practiced not only in capitalistic and communistic societies but by all historically known forms of government. It is the exploitation of the creators of ideas and the inventors of instruments. In their exploitation of this minority communistic and capitalistic societies are silently united into a single front. It is a proverbially and organically productive but powerless minority. In the manifesto of all socialist parties, landowners and industrial barons have frequently been called thieves and burglars, exploiters and consumers of the labour of the working class. As a matter of fact, they both, the consumers and the working class are exploiters and beneficiaries of the ideas, processes and instruments born of the helpless geniuses of all time. The creators, if any, are truly the most exploited minority in the world. They never had a political party, they do not start a revolution of their own to change the world order, they are changing it regardless of what kind of government exists at the time. They are comparatively few in number, they do not form a class, they do not belong to capital or to the proletariat or they may belong to either. They do not belong exclusively to one ethnic group or another, to one sex or another. The universality of their emergence seems to contradict the known laws of heredity, they are the most truly international people, the true *avant guarde* of a world society. It should be clear from this that no world order can be structured from which these forgotten pariahs of all world revolutions are left out. Indeed, it has to start with them as its foundation. A society of the world has to be like a wide open space in which every kind of people can settle and every kind of idea can find productivity. It should be of the greatest flexibility for the freest distribution of people and for the freest ascendance of values. It should be so designed that not a single individual —and not a single group—variety can be left out, that all men have an opportunity to produce a social order which can be called "a creatocracy."

Techniques of Revolution. The term revolution is here used in reference to methods and instruments which attempt to produce changes of a major character in a given social order. The failure of the academic social sciences to develop instruments for change of their own, elemental methods of action which are able to operate "on the spot", has had disastrous consequences in the political arena of our time. Socialism and communism—and with them many of their half breeds like fascism and nazism—have been superior and quicker to seize this opportunity. It is widely understood that mass meetings, political organizations of workers, labor unions, seizing the power and control of the armed and judiciary forces, of press and radio, and other acts of overthrowing governmental authority, are instruments of revolution.

Communists and fascists have a large repertory of dramatic, physical, spectacular, and super-Macchiavellian techniques of all sort. Being without action techniques, the fraternity of social scientists has been taken by surprise.

Living in the midst of wars and revolutions for nearly half a century they had to look passively on and permit generals and politicians to change the world. They tried to argue when elemental measures were required. Intelligent reasoning and polite conference manners were ineffective against party slogans, invectives, laughter, shouting, vulgar jokes and swearing, lies and distortion of facts. They tried to fight action and surprise methods with lyrics and editorials. Before they had learned their lesson it was too late. When they awakened from the state of panic and paralyzed fear the game was taken out of their hands and the initial phase of the battle was lost. In other words, the *avant guarde* of academic social science did not have social instruments of attack and counter attack available in a period of emergency. At last we sociometrists stepped in to the breach and developed "psychological and social shock methods" which may well become scientific instruments of social action, preventives or antidotes against the mass hypnotism and persuasion of purely political systems.

Sociometry has developed, among others, two instruments of change: a) the population test; and b) the sociodrama. The population test is an instrument operating in situ; it brings the population to a collective self expression and to the transaction of its plans in respect to all fundamental activities in which it is, or is about to be involved. It is a flexible procedure which calls for immediate action and for the immediate application of all the choices and decisions made. The population may consist of residents of a village, manager and workers of a factory, etc. The sociodrama is an instrument by means of which social truth, truth about social structure and conflicts can be explored and social change transacted by means of dramatic methods. It may operate like a town meeting with the difference that only the individuals involved in a social issue are present and that decisions are made and actions are taken which are of basic importance to their own community. The productions and solutions in a sociodrama grow out of the group. The choice of the social issue and the decision of its implementation come from the group and not from a particular leader.

Sociodramatic workers have the task to organize preventive, didactic and therapeutic meetings in the community in which they live and work; to organize, upon call, such meetings in problem areas everywhere; to enter communities confronted with emergent or chronic social issues, to enter mass meetings of strikes, race riots, rallies of political parties, and so forth, and try to handle and clarify the situation on the spot. The sociodramatic agent moves into the group accompanied by a staff of auxiliary egos, if necessary with the same determination, boldness or ferocity as a fuehrer or union leader. The meeting may move into an action as shocking and enthusiastic as those of a political nature, with the difference that the politicians try to submit the masses to their political schemes, whereas the sociodramatist is trying to bring the masses to a maximum of group realization, group expression, and group analysis. The methods have opposite aims, the development of the meetings, therefore, takes a different form. The political drama starts from within the politician and his clique, it is pre-arranged and carefully calculated to arouse hostility or bias against a foe. The sociodrama however, starts from within the audience present, it is calculated to be educational, clarifying and energizing to all members.

Sociometric revolutions do not promise violent and rapid results. They dig deep and their success depends upon a new learning process applied to small groups. Similar to an infant, mankind will mature only step by step and to the degree to which sociometric consciousness will refashion our social institutions, the structural readiness of mankind for a world society will ripen. Many wars and social upheavals will torture its sick body. In this transition the doctor may be more important than the engineer.

In 1848 the masses of the proletariat in the industries and armies were of prime importance for production of goods as well as for making wars. In 1948 the situation has at least potentially changed. Another few decades and factories may be robot-ridden and run by one engineer or a single atom physicist.

As human society is ailing we can expect a psychiatric empire to emerge gradually and spread over the globe. Politicians and diplomats will move into second status. Social scientists, psychiatrists, sociatrists and sociometrically oriented socialists will move into first. The mentor in the White House, a future President of the United States may well be a psychiatrist before another century has passed. Is not the whole cosmos beginning more and more to look like a huge mental institution with God as its physician in charge?

Sociometric Theses

1. Human society has a structure of its own which is *not* identical with the social order or the form of government currently in power. Its structure is influenced but never entirely determined by the instrument in charge of its affairs, for instance the state. The state may "vanish" but the underlying sociodynamic structure of society persists in one form or another. It is into the structure of the socius therefore, that a revolutionary effort has to put its teeth if a lasting and true cure of social ills is to be effected.

2. Sociometry has developed two types of instruments, instruments for diagnosing social structures and instruments for changing them. The sociometric test, psychodrama, sociodrama and axiodrama among others can be used for diagnosis as well as for social revolution.

3. The oldest and most numerous proletariat of human society is the sociometric proletariat. It consists of all the people who suffer from one form of misery or other, psychological misery, social misery, economic misery, political misery, racial misery, religious misery. There are numerous individuals and groups whose volume of attractions, or role expansion, of spontaneity and productivity is far beneath their needs and their ability to consummate them. The world is full of isolated, rejected, rejecting, unreciprocated and neglected individuals and groups.

4. The sociometric proletariat cannot be "saved" by economic revolutions. It existed in primitive and precapitalistic society, it exists in democratic societies, and in socialist Russia.

5. Sociometry is the sociology of the people, by the people and for the people. It teaches that human society cannot be changed by indirect, mechanical manipulation or by the arbiter of force. Whatever the type of government and social institutions coerced upon the people, whether they are cooperative communities, communistic, democratic, autocratic or anarchistic types of government, sooner or later they lose their hold upon the people. The people discard them, if they do not root in the productive will of the people and if they are not created with the full participation of every individual member.

6. In order to change the social world social experiments have to be so designed that they can produce change; in order to produce change the people themselves have to be included in its operation. You cannot change the world ex-post-facto, you must do it now and here, with and through the people. Marx had not the slightest intention of developing an experimental method for the social sciences but he has been the only pre-sociometric sociologist who came close to solving the problem. It is true that the social revolutions which he instigated ended in failure—in their major aims—but this does not contradict the fact that his revolutionary theory was the nearest to an experimental method in the social sciences before the advent of the sociometric method in our own time. How could governments and responsible statesmen ever take the work of social scientists seriously, considering the triviality of their findings and the aimlessness of their experimental designs. They took Marx, Engels, and Lenin seriously because they tried to change the world.

7. The dilemma of Marxism can be summed up in one phrase: its ignorance of the dynamic social structure of human society. It ascribes the deep resistance to change and revolution to the property owners, the capitalistic class. It is not aware that *this deep resistance comes directly from the social structure* and if the true cause for it simmers in the mind of some of the followers of Marx, they do not make an adequate effort to take it into account.

8. Sociometric investigations suggest the existence of residual social structures which are traceable to the following phenomena: a) an embryonic social structure which can already be noticed in subhuman societies; b) every social order, after it has had its reign, does not disappear entirely but leaves its mark upon the social structures which it has shaped. The cumulative effects of these "hangovers" plus the above-described embryonic development produce a total impact which explains the resistance against change.

9. The social experimenter cannot know all the factors entering the situation nor all the changes in these factors which may take place between the time he considers the experiment up to the time he executes it, and he cannot know of new factors which may enter the situation in the course of the experiment itself. The sociometric experimenters escape this dilemma, they are the experimenter and the experimental subject in one. Even if they do not know of all the factors entering their situation it is inherent in their feelings, their actions and inter-actions and it must come out in their experimental designs and revolutionary transactions. It may be at times imperfect and unprecise but it is an experiment in vivo, consciously and systematically carried out by the whole group.

10. *Social nature has a sociometric character, that is why sociometry works.* The solution is to replace the experimental method of Bacon and Mill which was constructed to meet the requirements of physics, by an experimental method which is able to cross-examine the reality of social change. The idea of setting up a control group in the realm of social action is pregnant with artificiality and abnormality and bound to distort the results or make them trivial. Spontaneous control groups are possible, but never outside, only within a sociometric atmosphere. The replacement is accomplished by a process of reversal. Mankind itself, in a literal and concrete sense of the word becomes the experimenter and the former autocratic experimenter becomes one of its two billion co-thinking participants.

SOCIOMETRY AND THE INDUSTRIAL REVOLUTION

At a recent meeting of the American Sociometric Association Dr. Charles Loomis drew on the blackboard a diagram trying to illustrate the problem which the rural sociologist of two generations ago had to face. Cooley and others recognized the importance of the primary face-to-face group, but many things happened beneath the surface of the groups which were not visible to the naked eye. They looked for a "handle", a social microscope but they didn't find one. In small rural communities the important processes and functions of living were tied together in the primary group; love and marriage, home and family life, work, leisure, and cultural interests operated in close proximity. But when upon the impact of the industrial revolution the work opportunities were removed from the rural village to a more or less distant industrial center a gradual dislocation of the natural relationships functions and roles took place. Then the need of the "handle" became more acute.

The following statement from "Who Shall Survive" is particularly applicable to modern industrial environments: "The local district or neighborhood is only *physically* one unit. This (sociometric) analysis shows that it is broken up, not, however, into small units, but into parts which have their corresponding parts in other districts and neighborhoods. The local districts are, so to speak, transversed by psychological currents which bind large groups of individuals into units together, *irrespective,* of neighborhood, district, or borough distinctions."

Marx in his analysis of the industrial revolution describing the transition from feudal capitalism to monopoly capitalism stressed correctly the economic and psychological consequences of the use of machines, the separation of the craftsman from his own product. He recognized clearly the dislocations in the work process and the capitalistic consequences in form of surplus value, but *he did not recognize that parallel with the dislocations produced in the economic process profound dislocations took place in the social structure itself.* It is obvious that already in precapitalistic societies a handle as sociometry was needed. Perhaps it did not emerge because the urgency was not sufficiently great.

The industrial revolution precipitated socialism as a process by means of which to cure the capitalistic syndrome; a century later sociometry tries to cure the dislocations in the social structure itself; it is like a repair device for the pathologies inflicted on the community by the industrial revolution. Socialistic theory tried to take care of the pathology inflicted upon the economic structure of society in the course of the industrial revolution, but it was blind to the pathology of the social structure which was aggravated by the industrial revolution. As is well known the Russian revolution of 1917 and the dictatorship of the proletariat in its various stages has tried from time to time to introduce socialist methods of economy into its system, but it has left the dislocated pathology of the social structure untouched. In other words *the social structure of Soviet Russia is just as much in need of sociometric reconstruction as the social structure in democratic United States.* The simultaneous applications of sociometric methods in the United States as well as in Soviet Russia may bring about a rapprochement between the two types of governments. The revolutions of the socialistic-marxistic type are outmoded; they failed to meet with the sociodynamics of the world situation. The next social revolution will be of the "sociometric" type. The next industrial revolution will be of the "zoomatic" type.*

The Second Industrial Revolution

In the pre-industrial period the locus of work and the locus of residence were one of the same or in close proximity, especially in the rural communities. In the industrial period workers had to move to places where the plants were located. The primary work situation was now broken up into numerous industrial centers wherever there was energy available for industrial use. The original unity was gone and has given way to diversification. It may very well be that the second industrial revolution will unify all forms of energy and the previous dislocation of power will disappear. With this, society will return to a state of affairs similar to the one in the preindustrial period. The locus of residence, of work, of leisure, and cultural activities will be again one, centralized and unified. It will be a back-to-the-primary-locus movement. Cohesion and productivity of the small group will be a first desideratum. Sociometric methods may then become very useful because they may provide the social organizer with a handle. Perhaps if he had had a handle like sociometry before the industrial revolution set in the catastrophic social revolutions following could have been prevented or could have at least taken place with less violence. The time may come when the opportunity to use atomic energy will be as easily

---

*For a discussion of "zoomatics", see "The Future of Man's World" by J. L. Moreno, *Psychodrama Monograph*, No. 21, Beacon House, 1945; also contained in *Group Psychotherapy*, A Symposium edited by J. L. Moreno, Beacon House, 1945.

available as the opportunity to light a match today. Destroying the world
or large parts of it by an act of individual violence will be as easy as
putting fire to a building today. The power to destroy the world or to
create it further will be put squarely in the hand of every individual. What
only a world war or a world revolution can accomplish today, the ruin
following them, every little man will be able to do single handed. To
destroy the world will be as easy as lighting a cigarette, as pushing a
button, starting an automobile or turning on an electric light. The law
makers of the future will be busier then ever and more laws will be
manufactured than the human imagination can foresee. But the world
police of the future may be just as ineffective in stopping "atom energy—
bandits", the manufacturing and smuggling of various devices of destruc-
tion, the scheming of a world-hold-up as they are today in controlling
white slavery and the smuggling of drugs. We won't be able to restrain
the use of atomic energy as we have not been able to restrain the use of
fire, electricity, or gas. It will either be universally free, common property,
or it won't be. The control of group violence is the most urgent problem
of our day, in the future the control of individual violence will again become the most important world issue. Cain will return.

SOCIOMETRY OF COOPERATION

Marx defines the surplus value as follows: "The surplus value produced by a given capital is equal to the surplus value produced by each
workman multiplied by the number of workmen simultaneously employed."
If, in this definition given by Marx on page 353, chapter 13 of *Das Kapital*
(all further quotations come from the same opus) we substitute surplus
value by sociodynamic effect or tele value, workmen by individuals, capital
by population, arrive at the following formula. The sociodynamic effect
produced by a given population is equal to the tele value (unit of sociodynamic effect) of each individual multiplied by the number of individuals
(interacting simultaneously and revolving around the same criterion).

Marx assumed that "the individual differences in productivity" can
be neglected. He postulated that these individual differences compensate
one another and "vanish whenever a certain minimum number of workers
are employed together". These individual differences, as sociometry has
pointed out, do not vanish but come out as the sociodynamic effect. This
error of Marx is due to his bias for collectivity, for a collectivity un-

critically conceived. A sociometrically oriented theory of collectivity takes care of this error. It can be well compared to the error which Newton made in his theory of gravitation and which Einstein corrected in his theory of relativity. Sociometry has taken these individual differences seriously, but instead of leaving them on the psychological it has translated them on the sociological plane, and has shown that their cumulative effect has profound and far reaching consequences. Marx comes close to an insight into sociodynamic effects upon economic relationships when he states: "A dozen persons working together will, in their collective working day of 144 hours, produce far more than twelve isolated men, each working 12 hours or than one man who works 12 days in succession." (Page 358) Sociometrically speaking, a dozen persons taking part in a group held together by a specific criterion will produce a large number of attractions, repulsions and neutralities resulting in a complex network of relations, as made visible in a sociogram. If the dozen persons would live apart, twelve units of one each by himself, the sociodynamic effect would be zero. This would correspond to the situation of the dozen workers, each working apart from one another, each the manufacturer and the owner of his own product. Here the surplus value would be zero. If the dozen persons would be divided in six units of two, in four units of three, in three units of four or in two units of six persons, the social structures produced in every case would be simpler and therefore the effects of the interaction less mysterious. The larger the number of workers held together by a capitalistic enterprise, the larger are the possibilities for surplus value gains. Similarly, the larger the number of individuals comprising the community, the more intricate and far reaching are the sociodynamic effects. The mystery is in both cases due to a tele process towards which each contributes his share. But no one "owns" the tele, just as no one owns atomic energy.

Marx was to such extent intoxicated by economic objectives that he was blinded to the fact that this economic surplus value is merely a special case of "sociodynamic law". Marx points out clearly (page 365) that "the captialist does not buy the laboring power of one man but that of 100 and enters into *separate* contracts (italics ours) with 100 unconnected men instead of with one." "He does not pay for the *combined* labor power of the 100. Being independent of each other, the laborers are *isolated* persons who enter into relations with the capitalist but *not with one another*." (Italics ours.) The surplus productivity comes from the "with one another." We sociometrists have isolated the factor which produces sociodynamic effects resulting from the "with one another" and have called it "tele." The capitalist consummates the tele between him and the workers (his profit) but neglects entirely the tele between the workers themselves and its effect upon them. The capitalist takes systematic advantage of the tele factor which is operating between the individual workers and which is responsible for the surplus value of their cooperative productivity. The surplus value is a function of tele. The cooperation-producing factor, the tele, produces the surplus value. It is through the introduction of cooperative strategies that the capitalist makes money, not only through the work of each individual workman alone. The work of the individual workman within the capitalistic system is actually the sum of the work of each individual *plus* the intangible surplus resulting from the cumulative effect of the inter-actions of all workers.

Marx says in another place (page 365): "Hence, the productive power developed by the labourer *when working in co-operation,* (italics ours) is the productive power of capital. This power is developed gratuitous-ly." . . . "Because this power costs capital nothing, and because, on the other hand, the labourer himself does not develop it before his labour be-longs to capital, *it appears as a power with which capital is endowed by Nature—.*" (Italics ours)

The question remains: "What is the dynamic process underlying this mysterious power" with which capital is endowed by Nature?" Coopera-tive dynamism remains in the capitalist form of production unconscious of the sociodynamic effect, but doesn't it also remain unconscious in the socialist mode of production? It does. If we examine a simple process of social interaction which can be observed in all types of societies and in all social grouping, whether capitalistic or non-capitalistic we can see the following things happening—take an individual A who is chosen by n individuals in reference to a specific criterion, for instance, sexuality. He is a center of attraction, each of the n individuals is eager to spend time with him. Each of the n individuals may themselves be centers of attraction, however of a smaller number of individuals. Because of the chain re-actions an individual A may become the center of attractions not only of n individuals who choose him, but also of a considerable number of individuals who choose them and in turn, perhaps, of the n 1 individuals who choose the latter, etc. It can therefore be said about the social power of A with which he is endowed by Nature that it is developed gratuitously, similar to what Marx says about financial capital, that he has a mysterious power for which he cannot account himself but which he enjoys because of the chain reactions and because of the unconscious cooperations of a large number of individuals in the group. He may take advantage of this power in political elections, public opinion matters, job hunting or sexual activities.

Summing up one can say that every spontaneous interaction of individuals in the course of forming a social group reveals the operations of a universal, dynamic factor which I have called tele. A special case of it is the surplus value which becomes manifest in the mode of capitalist production. The capitalistic form of production has only extended, systematized and dramatized a condition peculiar to all group relations.

The capitalist syndrome itself is merely a symptom of a far more fundamental and universal process of a sociodynamic law whose workings are still little known, a challenge for the sociometrist and microsociologist of the future.

TESTS OF ANARCHISTIC, UTOPIAN, DEMOCRATIC AND SOCIALISTIC FORMS OF GOVERNMENT (1947)

The experimental testing of laissez faire, authoritarian and democratic behavior in groups was pressed upon me by theoretical considerations first formulated in *Who Shall Survive?*[1] Reason 1): Sociometric studies showed a greater variety of and a greater productivity for social structure than was theoretically anticipated by sociologists. Reason 2): We may have too rigid a concept of "human nature"; just as its spontaneity appears to be greater than anticipated and open for training on an individual level, this may also be true on the social plane. Before we permit political leaders to take us into adventures on a mass scale, into wars, social revolutions, autocratic systems of government and so forth, we should test the potentialities of such systems of government on a small scale by means of sociometric and sociodramatic techniques, we should let our research imagination go and construct experimental situations for types of government which have failed or succeeded in the past but also for every possible type of government which we could ever anticipate to occur in the future.

I had arrived at a general formulation[2] of this problem: "The

---

[1] See *Who Shall Survive?*, p. 96.
[2] *Who Shall Survive?* p. 96.

sociometric approach of group organization is free from preconception of
the contrast between individualism and collectives or corporate bodies. It
takes the attitude that beyond this contrast there is a common plane, as
no individual is entirely unrelated to some other individuals and no individual is entirely absorbed by a collective. The position of each individual within his kind, however apparently isolated, is one thing and
cooperative acts of such individuals at certain times is another." The contrast between the authoritarian group structure imposed upon the pupils
of the Brooklyn Public School 181 and the inhabitants of the Hudson community was found to be in vivid contrast to the group structure revealed by
sociometric techniques. By themselves these findings appeared to indicate that
autocratic practices were productively as well as therapeutically contra-
indicated, but they did *not* seem to indicate clearly the advantages of
democratic practices. "Democratic" is a vague term and requires operational definition every time it is used in an experiment. The sociometric
approach, by its very momentum, does not take sides, it is *neutral,* it has
an open mind for all types of social structure. Therefore I set up a number of experiments in order to explore the organizational and therapeutic
benefits resulting from the various forms of group organization. (The results of these experiments can be found in the "Sociometric Review," partly
reprinted in this book on page 76-91.)

As John C. McKinney put it: "The study of human interrelations
in *statu nascendi* is the particular, and important, contribution of sociometry. Relationships in their dynamic demonstration are functional,
and thus a study of them is more predictive than is a study of a cultural
conserve. Accuracy of prediction is the essence of science, and it is
reasonable to assume that a study of the social act as it *emerges* in behavior will lend greater validity to predictions of patterns of behavior
and relationships."[3] But social experiments in *statu nascendi* face a
great theoretical and practical problem which I recognized then and whose
importance has been more than borne out by recent developments in
social science; it is *how to set up such experiments free from bias in favor
of one type of government (or system of values) or another.* If the experimenter has a marxistic or a fascistic bias he may set the experiments
up in such a manner that the results will be in favor of his social
hypothesis. If, on the other hand, the investigator has a democratic bias

---

[3] See John C. McKinney, "A Comparison of the Social Psychology of G. H.
Mead and J. L. Moreno", SOCIOMETRY, Vol. X, No. 4, 1947.

he may, consciously or unconsciously, set up the experiments in such a manner as to influence the experimental leaders and the experimentees so that the results show the advantages of democratic society. If he has a cooperative bias he may set up the experiments in such a manner and influence the experimental leaders and the experimentees, so that the results show the advantages of cooperative societies. An illustration of autocratic bias is the Nazi indoctrination of German youth, in their social clubs, or the communistic indoctrination in village soviets. An illustration of democratic bias closer to home and of greater interest to the experimental sociologist is Kurt Lewin's experiment with authoritarian and democratic configurations.[4] His conclusions in favor of democratic structure are suspicious of bias because: a) the experimental setting up was theoretically ill prepared; b) the democratic leaders in the experiment may have been better prepared for democratic indoctrination than the autocratic leaders for autocratic indoctrination. No report of role-playing and role-training was given. The carrying out of such an experiment in a democratic country would, by itself, favor democratic outcomes and leaders for democratic indoctrination be more readily available. We criticize justly the bias of scientists in Soviet Russia who try to coordinate every scientific hypothesis with marxistic theory. We should not fall into the same error here and bring every scientific hypothesis into tune with democratic theory of life. It is for this reason that Lewin's extension of my own experiments are of little value. Indeed, they represent a regression because of the false impression they have made in many places as being a scientifically controlled experiment and carried out on "sociometric" foundations. Unfortunately, they are not. Lewin did not appreciate fully the potentialities of the sociometric matrix versus the official society, whether of democratic or autocratic orientation. The sociometric matrix suggests within the democratic range and beyond it a number of social structures which rarely come to the surface of actuality and which should be tested in each specific case.

---

[4] See also "SOCIOMETRY *and the Experimental Method in Social Science*". p. 29 of this publication.

IV.

MILITARY SOCIOMETRY

ADVANTAGES OF THE SOCIOMETRIC APPROACH TO PROBLEMS OF NATIONAL DEFENSE

These notes were stimulated by an invitation from the Social Science Research Council, Sub-Committee on Methods of Prediction, under the chairmanship of Dr. Samuel A. Stouffer, to write a critique of "The Prediction of Personal Adjustment," by Paul Horst and associates,[1] designed to be of use to the authorities of our National Defense. At the time of this invitation,[2] I prepared, in the form of a memorandum, some remarks on the applicability of sociometric, situation-and-spontaneity tests to military problems.

The relation of concepts like "Stegreif", "impromptu", and "spontaneity" to the concept of "Blitz" is obvious. In military situations of modern times, a premium is placed upon emotional stability, speed of performance and—above all— split-second judgment in action. An individual may be in possession of the knowledge and skills for specific tasks, yet be unable to fulfill the requirements of the immediate situations. The factors beyond skill and knowledge which determine behavior require tests of a new sort. It is at this point that sociometric and spontaneity tests have shown the way—particularly in testing individuals in standard life-situations.

METHODS

A new trend in the testing of behavior has been introduced by sociometric and spontaneity procedures for the study of group and individual behavior, respectively. Since the trend is gaining ground in many other laboratories, it may be pertinent at this time to recall some of the main principles involved.

"The problem was to construct the test in such a manner that it is itself a motive, an incentive, a purpose, primarily for the *subject,* instead of for the tester. If the test-procedure is identical with a life goal of the subject, he can never feel himself to have been victimized or abused. . . . Yet the same series of acts performed of the subject's own volition may be a 'test' in the mind of the tester. We have developed two tests in which the subject is in action for his own ends. One is the sociometric test.

---

[1] "The Prediction of Personal Adjustment," by Paul Horst, with collaboration of Paul Wallin and Louis Guttman, assisted by Frieda Brim Wallin, John A. Clausen, Robert Reed and Erich Rosenthal; Bulletin No. 48, Social Science Research Council, New York, 1941. xii 447 pp.

[2] May 21, 1941.

From the point of view of the subject, this is not a test at all: it is merely an opportunity for him to become active in matters concerning his life-situation. The second test meeting this demand is the spontaneity test. Here, in a standard life-situation, the subject improvises to his own satisfaction, but to the tester it releases a source of information in respect to the character, intelligence, conduct and psychological position of the subject. . . . Through the sociometric and spontaneity tests, the artificial setting of the. . . . Binet intelligence tests is substituted for by the natural life-setting."

"The director sets up the various experimental or test situations . . . situations and roles which they (the subjects) themselves which to produce and which they may have within themselves in some degree or development. . . . The material gained from such tests can be used for diagnostic interpretation."

The situational tests took place before a group of observers averaging 15-20 individuals. Like members of a jury, each of them was able to arrive at an evaluation of the performance.

"A series of situations as they may occur in community life, home life, domestic life, business, etc. . . . is constructed. . . . The situations are either chosen by him (the subject) or suggested to him by the instructor. . . . The students are told to throw themselves into the situations, to live them through, and to enact every detail needed in them as if it were in earnest. The emphasis is placed upon how true to life a certain procedure is.

"One student takes careful record of each performance. A copy of it goes to every student. . . . After each performance, an analysis and discussion of it opens up in which the students as well as the director take part.

"The criticism ranges from consideration of the emotions displayed in the situations, to the mannerisms, the knowledge of the material nature of the situations, the relationships to the persons acting opposite, and the characteristics of carriage, speech and facial expression.

"Many traits which indicate personality difficulties are disclosed: anxieties, stage fright, stuttering, fantasies, unreasonable attitudes, and so on."

To the material obtained from these tests in standardized life-situations was added materials gained from the initial interview, case-study, and the individual reactions to the sympathy, hostility, fear or any other emotion hurled at the subject by the persons placed counter to him in the situation. A test procedure lasted for two or three sessions, the duration of a session ranging from one half hour to an hour. The recording was usually stenographic, but at times speech recording and motion-picture devices were used.

The operational aspect of the test procedure was thus moved into a place of first prominence, and the observational aspect relegated to second place. Sociometric procedures, as applied to group situations, have been described elsewhere. The same general principle prevails with sociometric testing as with spontaneity testing.

PSYCHOMETRIC VS. SOCIOMETRIC APPROACH

Methods of Prediction. The prediction of personal and interpersonal adjustment is made upon the basis of various tools and methods. One method is the psychometric approach, a method which is excellent but one-sided. It is the more one-sided the more the other persons in the situation affect the personal picture. Predictions must, therefore, of necessity be hampered and narrowed by a large number of contingencies, and the more so the more complex the problem is. Another method is the sociometric approach. This approach is important not only in order to make the predictions more accurate, but also to make them plausible and acceptable to those for whom they are made—as well as for those who make them.

Prediction tables can be based upon psychometric methods and sociometric findings separately or combined, and by the integration of the respective findings. As long as prediction tables based upon the psychometric approach are made exclusively to increase our knowledge of individual behavior in general, one can look more tolerably at their statements and conclusions. But when the intention is to use them on actual individuals in real-life situations such as, for instance, choosing for a man his working associates or his vocation, or trying to adjust his interpersonal problems, the consequences are extremely serious. It then becomes of strategic importance to know which steps to take first—that is, which tools to use first —which steps to take second and third, and which final steps to take in order that prediction tables may work in congruence with adjustment tables, and not independently of one another.

Main Tasks in Personal and Interpersonal Adjustment. There are at present two main tasks in all personal adjustment: first, to match one man to another man or to a social group, and second, to match a man to a vocation or a job. According to statistical prediction tables, constructed on a psychometric basis, there may be an extremely high expectancy that John will make a good work-associate for James, or that John will fit into a certain group of workers. To take the extreme case, John and James are to be thrown together strictly on the basis of psychometric prediction tables made with a sample group without John and James ever having met and without the predictors ever having interviewed either of them. A similar procedure might be applied to John's assignment to a vocation or a work-group, although John may never have met any of the men with whom he is to work, and neither he nor they have ever met the predictors.

It does not seem to me that statistical prediction based on psychometrics is as yet sufficiently worked out to be accurate or—in the last analysis—*attuned to certain fundamental ethical demands postulated by the individuals of our culture who expect to take an immediate part in the decisions which are made about their lives.* The sociometric approach is based on their decisions and in addition lends itself better than the psychometric approach to the working-out of prediction tables. Sociometric prediction tables should be able to predict with greater accuracy the potentialities of interpersonal cooperation.

Psychometric vs. Sociometric Case Study. Individual case-study—as a psychometric approach—is an excellent procedure as far as it goes, but it does not go far enough. The individual is still an object—an object of study. Case-study techniques, whether using the oral interview or the formal questionnaire, fail to get the full cooperation of the subject. They fail to make the object of the case study *an enthusiastically and critically participating subject,* as is the case with sociometric techniques.

Sociometric Procedure. It is possible to approach the whole problem of prediction from the opposite end of the prediction-adjustment axis and to begin the work at the level of the real situation of the concrete individual, preparing as the first step adjustment tables and then moving more and more away from the real situations, and gradually developing prediction tables. Into the preparation of these can be integrated any of the research methods outside of sociometry. Prediction tables based in this manner upon the combined sociometric and psychometric approaches will have their feet on the solid ground of intimate knowledge of the actual needs of the individuals and, at the same time, will give this information to the independent technician in such a way that he can draw practical conclusions from it.

Critique of Psychometric Tests; the Advantages of Spontaneity and Sociometric Testing. A basis for psychometric prediction can be found in the following procedures: probationary performance, proficiency tests, and personal and social characteristics associated with success or failure. I believe that the use of probationary performance as a check on behavior in activity—a method both extremely unwieldly and costly in application—should be substituted for by a series of spontaneity tests in standardized life situations for each applicant. On the basis of experiments it has been found that these spontaneity tests provide a highly accurate short-cut to the prediction of behavior in activity—however specialized. Proficiency tests are, of course, indispensable, but they can easily be coordinated with the spontaneity tests suggested above. This procedure has many advantages. For instance, a person may disclose an increased or a decreased skill in a performance when he is working all by himself, when he is working with agreeable partners, or when he is working with associates who are distasteful to him. The personal and social characteristics of the individual can be arrived at by sociometric and spontaneity tests and a sounder basis for prediction thus be achieved than if psychometric methods are used alone.

Application of Sociometric Procedures to Problems of National Defense. The responsibility which the scientist assumes when his suggestions are to be applied to concrete individual situations is so great that it is worth while to challenge the whole view of many psychologists who seem to believe that one can move individuals into jobs or into new communities without their full participation and consent. The defense situation may be particularly tempting for one holding such a view. All of us have been brought up to think that a good soldier is an individual who doesn't think at all but merely obeys orders which come from some authority above him. Blind obedience to orders will go on only as long as the suggestions made by the superior prove logical in the end and successful in combat. But when defeat and failure set in, protest and rebellion spread to the surface from the grapevines.

Sociometric methods, although they are based on the individual's most personal situations, lend themselves just as easily as any of the psychometric methods to the strictest discipline within defense units. It must be made clear that it is the information which comes direct from the individuals—not the decisions which come as a result of the information. These latter are made exclusively by the sociometric technicians or the military authorities in charge. The individuals within a sociometric system of social organization have no influence upon the decisions made by the authorities—merely because he expresses his most objective and most sincere feelings about his job or his associates—than has a soldier who reports to his superior officer what he sees through his field glasses. But the tendency should be to include as many of the key individuals and subleaders in the policy making decisions as possible. The decisions may be made by the leaders responsible for specific tasks, however, if they are not sociometrically adequate subsequent tests will reveal any discrepancies incurred. The soldier tells the truth to the best of his ability. His statements are used by his superior officer according to the latter's best judgment. The officer would be negligent if he did not take full advantage of the information received from every possible individual to whom some responsibility had been assigned. Again, it is like the situation when the soldier has suffered an injury and reports to the medical officer where his pains are, and the latter uses this information—in addition to other media—in coming to a diagnosis. In sociometric work, the authority of final choice and decision rests with the technician and the commander. Both should be sociometrically oriented. The individual is used as the most sensitive instrument we know today for sizing up his own sensations and reactions to his environment. The experts of prediction and the experts of adjustment must come to a common course of action. We should consider, in the present emergency, the commonsense, direct sociometric approach in preference to any exercise of power over individuals, based upon sample groups which have been studied and analyzed independent of the actualities of the individuals and groups themselves.

The sociometric devices which should prove to be particularly helpful for the needs of the national defense program now in development are the sociometric test and the spontaneity test in standardized life situations. Both tests are applicable to the main objectives for which expectancy and prediction are desirable: the assignment of an individual to a vocation and the assignment of an individual to other individuals with whom he is to work, live and function in any defense situation. Although neither of these procedures is an interview technique, they both nevertheless reveal to the investigator what any interview would disclose and, in addition, bring forth other personal and social characteristics which are ordinarily hidden from the observer. They are both systematized shortcut approaches to the individuals in action.

A program which is to assign individuals to communities or to vocations must determine the first step to be undertaken. The first step cannot, in my opinion, be a statistical prediction table—not, at least, in the year 1941 with the sciences of psychology, social psychology and sociology in their present stage of development. The first step cannot—again, in my humble opinion—be prediction tables based upon case work study, nor can the first step be based upon the "observation" of activity and probationary performance by participant observers or spectators. The statistical psychometric prediction table operates in a highly-organized vacuum, but, nevertheless, in a vacuum. The case work methods function with single, independent individuals, but what is needed today is an approach to masses of people and their behavior; statistical prediction considers the mass as an abstraction.

The first step to be taken must be with the consent and the cooperation of the individuals concerned. It must be made by them as if it were their own project—their own design for living. There is no other way imaginable which can enlist the spontaneity, the critical intelligence and the enthusiasm of grown up, thinking people.

There is a systematic approach available today which, under the label of "sociometry" has developed methods which are at the very least able to make a frontal attack—an attack which seems, even to the subjects, to be plausible—upon some of the most crucial problems with which our defense program is faced today, for we are taking men out of the groups and communities in which they have been living and we are banding them afresh into new groups and communities designed for but one purpose: the organization of defense. Here I purposely emphasize this one point, the first step—for I believe that all other steps following the first can make use of many of the researches and methods which lie outside the sociometric domain. If we have the first step right, the prediction tables will follow. If we have the first step wrong, the prediction tables are useless and sterile.

THE SITUATION TEST IN AMERICAN-BRITISH MILITARY PSYCHOLOGY VS. GERMAN MILITARY PSYCHOLOGY
(1949)

This is a discussion of Helen H. Jennings' "Military Use of Sociometric and Situation Tests in Great Britain, France, Germany and the United States", and H. Ansbacher's "Passing and Lasting Aspects of German Military Psychology" (SOCIOMETRY, Vol. XII, 1949).

Did German military psychology originate all the fruitful new ideas which became operative during World War II? Ansbacher says emphatically: Yes. "The present discussion led to some comparisons between German-European and American-English psychology." ". . . European psychology through its emphasis on intuition did originate almost all the fruitful new ideas, both in the areas of theory and of diagnosis." As one of the "chief merits of German military psychology were . . . the development and large-scale application of a selection method for officer candidates which to date represents in principle the best and probably the only practical psycho-

logical method of leadership selection." ". . . German military procedure
of leadership selection has been taken over by Western countries in toto."
. . . "It is the group situation tests which have attracted the greatest attention." ". . . The English had studied the literature of German military
psychology and thus their selection camps were indeed similar in all details
to those described by Simoneit. From the British Army the method was
taken over by the Australian Army. . . . The Canadian Army as well
adopted situation tests for the selection of officer. . . . The American Army
used the method only in its Office of Strategic Services." . . . "From military
psychology the idea has spread to general applied psychology. In England
situation tests have been used by one coal company for the selection of
supervisors, and from Australia an application for the selection of production
managers for a shoe factory is reported."

Jennings says emphatically: No, just the contrary. German military
psychology did not show a full grasp of situational testing as it was developed by American and British psychologists. "As we study the situation
tests used by the military psychologists in Germany under the Nazi regime,
we note that not one of them allows the individual scope and variety in
solutions, nor gives him a chance for personality expression *per se,* nor,
last not least, provides a vehicle for him to show how he would go about
developing well integrated team relationships." . . . "The man is tested as
if he were a group symbol for a part in the Army organization and for
stereotyped settings in that organization. The term 'real' situation is misleading for such a series of tests because who can know what the situation
will be in reality?"

At first sight it seems as if Ansbacher is too anxious to prove his point;
he himself says: "This may appear as a one-sided judgment; but no other
point of view is available to the author." Jennings, on the other hand,
appears too much impressed with the role of American and British democratic soil as affecting psychological testing, with the spirit "of the British
and American military groups, perhaps steming from the relative advantages
of their psychological climate."

I will try to clarify the controversy by asking myself several questions:
1) Did the German military psychologists *originate* the new methods of
selection?; 2) Did the British-American military psychologists *originate*
the new ideas?; 3) How did they originate?; 4) Did they spread from
military to general and applied psychology?; 5) Who applied these methods
first on a large scale?; 6) Are the European and especially the German
methods in psychology more "intuitive" and are the British-American

methods more "quantitative"? I will quote here a number of authoritative sources in order to clarify to whom they, the origins of the new ideas, may be ascribed.

Let us quote first Doctor J. R. Rees,[1] Brigadier and Chief Consultant Psychiatrist for the British Army during the last war. "We Europeans are fascinated as we look at many of the developments in the United States in the study of groups, their structure and dynamics." . . . "The wisdom of the ordinary man was demonstrated when, in the British Army, Moreno's method of "sociometric choice" was used to allow soldiers to select from their own comrades those who should be sent as candidates for officer rank. The careful methods of the Officer Selection Boards showed quite clearly that the choice by the men themselves of those who would be suitable and acceptable officers was considerably better than the selection made by the officers. This is encouraging to those of us who believe in democracy." Doctor Rees, who was in the position to know how the brainwaves have traveled and who was since 1941 (and many years before the war) one of the main carriers of inspiration from one side of the Atlantic to the other, apparently thinks that the new ideas originated largely in North America. He infers that the British workers had a good share in their development but he does not mention the Germans.

Second, let us study an American report, the Report of Special Commission of Civilian Psychiatrists, Drs. Leo H. Bartemeier, Lawrence S. Kubie, Karl A. Menninger, John Romano and John C. Whitehorn, covering Psychiatric Policy and Practice in the U. S. Army Medical Corps, European Theater, April 20 to July 8, 1945. The Commission was sent out under the auspices of the O. S. R. D. and the New Development Division, War Department Special Staff, at the request of the Neuropsychiatry Consultants Division, Office of the Surgeon General.[2] ". . . The organized pattern of the unit and its emotional bonds constitute the dominant constructive and integrative force for the individual soldier in his fighting function. This group life *is* his inner life. When an individual member of such a combat group has his emotional bonds of group integration seriously disrupted, than he, *as a person,* is thereby disorganized. The disruption of group unity is, in the main, a primary causal factor, not a secondary effect, of personality disorganization. "We find that American psychiatrists and other physicians

---

[1] Dr. J. R. Rees, "Mental Health and World Citizenship", *Survey Graphic*, April 1948, New York 3, New York.

[2] Title of the Report is: "Combat Exhaustion", *Journal of Nervous and Mental Disease,* Volume 104, No. 4, October, 1946.

have considerable difficulty in grasping the significance of the group as the core of personality organization for the soldier in his fighting function." . . . "Major Bion, in one of the British hospitals, organized small groups and set them certain specific tasks to accomplish without assigning a leader in order to bring out patterns of interpersonal stresses and relationships." . . . "At Northfield, Major Foulkes organized small groups for the spontaneous dramatization of significant experiences both from early life and from the military scene." . . . "The Commission did not have the good fortune to participate in group sessons in American installations, such as those in which it participated in British hospitals. In spite of this it may be fair to conclude from discussions with others that the use of group techniques in American hospitals emphasized the instructional aspect of the method, whereas the British (somewhat influenced by Moreno, Burrow and Lewin) showed a greater enthusiasm for the spontaneous, emotional and socializing uses of the method."

Let us turn now to a report of British authorities in "Some Approaches to Group Problems in the British Army",[3] by J. D. Sutherland and G. A. Fitzpatrick (this report had been passed by the British War Office Public Relation Department). "In the course of the war, the psychiatrists in the British Army were confronted with a number of problems which were appreciated by them to belong to the institution of the army as a whole or to groups within it and which accordingly could best be treated by methods dealing with the dynamics of the group in its total setting." . . . "This independent development has features in common with certain trends in America where the term 'sociatric' (Moreno) has been introduced to describe measures of this kind for group problems." . . . "Bion suggested that use might be made of the knowledge which any group possesses of its own resources and, to mobilize this knowledge effectively, the men in good units might be awarded the privilege of nominating candidates to appear before the W. O. S. Boards. Trist (who had entered the Army after the start of the W. O. S. Boards) pointed out that this was in fact a real sociometric procedure and he suggested that sociometric methods should be employed." . . . "The method (leaderless group test) consists in presenting to the group a problem of some kind, verbal or practical, and leaving the group entirely free to work out its own solution."

In the official report *Assessment of Men* published by the OSS Assessment Staff (among them were Henry A. Murray, Donald W. McKinnon,

---

[3] *Group Psychotherapy, A Symposium*, Beacon House, New York, 1945, p. 205.

Urie Bronfenbrenner) we read: "These methods were first used on a large scale by Simoneit." . . . "Our particular debt is to the band of imaginative and progressive psychiatrists and psychologists who devised and conducted the War Office Selection Board (WOSB) program for testing officer candidates for the British Army. From them we gained the valuable idea of having staff and candidates live together in the country during the testing period, and the conception of leaderless group situations." The book contains a brillant, varied presentation, situation tests, sociometric procedures and psychodramatic methods as they were used by that agency.

According to Gibb "These situations are not tests of any particular qualities, they are situations in which the candidates are left to act spontaneously." . . . "The use of leaderless groups does not provide all the answers, of course; and it may raise as many problems about candidates as it gives answers. Like the very similar methods of the Sociometric Institute, this is not an easy one to use." (*Journal of Abnormal and Social Psychology,* 42:267-284, July, 1947, p. 277) Neither the British nor the American report mentioned German Army psychological procedure, which does not exclude, of course, that the writers may have been acquainted with the German literature dealing with the subject, but *is emphatically pointed out by them that the methods are American and British ideas* and not of German origin, although some versions were used by them on a large scale in military circles only. They state that the sociometric and group therapy methods are of American origin and that the leaderless group tests are very similar, if not identical to the role playing methods developed by the Sociometric Institute.

Ansbacher's chief claim that German psychology has developed the methods first and that they were adopted by American and English psychology could be substantiated only by comparing individual contributions from workers in Germany between 1923 to 1934, and show their originality and superiority from British and American workers. The question is therefore how these procedures came into being. *Ideas and methods are not originated by armies or governments, cultures or psychological climates, but by individual pioneers and the intellectual chain reactions between them.* We should be careful not to exercise the least bias in favor of one or another country, especially as they have been at war, because it is known that scientific originality does not necessarily go hand in hand with favorable or unfavorable circumstances. The "soil" for their proper application and continued development is another matter. Originators and carriers of ideas may thus leave their own countries if the circumstances continue to be ad-

verse and may migrate to places where the chances for their development
are more favorable. Talent has, in the sciences as well as in the arts, no
geographic or ethnic barrier.

Let us therefore quote from or refer to original publications which appeared before and after Simoneit's *Wehrpsychologie* in 1933.

J. L. Moreno, *Das Stegreiftheater* (1923, summarized by the author,
p. 7):

The problem is "to explore the laws governing an (unrehearsed)
situation or plot in which two or more persons interact in a common task—
as to speed, positions in space and cooperation." As to leadership selection,
see the same opus, p. 51. "The individual who emerges as a leader in a
situation (plot) or in a certain phase within it has also the leadership in
the position taking in space." One is able to observe the emergence of
"the initial leader, the change in leadership and the leader at the end of the
situation." (Translated from the German original which reads: "Führer,
Wechsel in der Führung, Beender" see p. 88.)

J. L. Moreno, *Application of the Group Method to Classification* (1931,
1932):

"This is the problem which occupied us eleven years ago when we first
attempted in Vienna to put it on an experimental basis; we reduced the
task then to its simplest form: a number of persons were placed opposite
one another in a situation whose pattern was unknown to them before the
moment of start and in roles and states which were equally unknown to
them. The writer's first suggestion to them during the initial phase of experimentation was to let loose, unconcerned about involuntary remarks and
gestures, faithfully relying upon the spontaneous aptitudes to act and react
on the spur of the moment. The objective was simply to produce together
in the course of improvised action patterns of a society in miniature."
(p. 27) . . . "The intelligence tests have been made after the standard of
formal interview. But to answer set questions and to meet reality are two
different things. We need, in addition to what we have, a method of testing
which is patterned after a life situation." (p. 13) . . . "To measure . . .
adequately, a *situational test* is necessary." (p. 14, italics here.) . . . "Our
approach has been that of direct experiment; man in action; man thrown
into action, the moment not part of history but history part of the moment
—sub species momenti." . . . "Several persons of the group, with whom
the subject who is to be tested prefers to mix, are placed with him into a
number of swiftly alternating situations." (p. 20 and 21) This monograph,
in which I introduced the term *Situational Test* now generally used, and its

experimental concept in its basic characteristics, has pioneered many later formulations by other workers. It became known also in politically prominent circles within the German government, for instance, to Dr. Bumke, then President of the German Supreme Court—see letter from the German Department of Justice, p. 87.

J. L. Moreno, *Who Shall Survive?* (1934):

"The leader assumes consciously a direct and active role, but he is not the leader of traditional type. He has undergone a change. It is not more or less blind enthusiasm with which he infects his followers and in which he develops the project, but it is an enthusiasm articulated into the group. It is based upon the spontaneous motives each individual has in respect to each other member of the group and in respect to their common aim; second, upon the organization of the group, as the guidance of groups ought to be based upon the knowledge of their organization. The leader thus gains in objective strength through considering the spontaneous forces within the group and does not impair the subjective strength of his own spontaneity." (p. 353.) . . . "Their minds have to be directed not towards an emotional experience and conflict in the past but towards a task in the *present* and the emotional attachment to be developed in respect to it. It is this present which is in need of analytical reflection." (p. 352.) . . . "Through training of individuals for conduct in possibly arising situations, in a variety of roles and functions they may have to assume towards a variety of persons in the possible roles they may assume, the subject learns to meet life situations more adequately." (p. 326.) It is reasonable, therefore, to consider these three books combined as the first in literature to present group situation tests as formally set up procedures.

Among the leaders who have stimulated theoretically or practically the development of selection methods are—aside from my first work in these areas in Europe and later in this country with my earliest collaborator Helen Jennings—Trigant Burrow, M. Simoneit, Henry A. Murray, Kurt Lewin, Leonard Cottrell, W. R. Bion, J. Rickman, E. L. Trist, T. F. Rodger, G. R. Hargreaves, T. F. Main, A. T. M. Wilson, S. H. Foulkes, H. Bridger, Theodore Newcomb, Urie Bronfenbrenner, D. W. MacKinnon, S. Stouffer, C. P. Loomis, G. Gurvitch, P. Maucorps. The list is, of course, incomplete. It is given here merely to indicate some of the actual workers and developers of these methods between whom in the course of the years rapid intellectual exchange has taken place. If I do not mention some German names it is not because they may not have existed but only because I am ignorant of their contribution. Group situation tests and sociometric methods have been applied on a large scale first to *civilian* organizations, in the United States, in closed communities as refugee camps, prisons, reformatories, open communities as rural settlements, resettlements, schools and industries. Twelve volumes of SOCIOMETRY are a continuous and impressive record of this. It appears that the German Army psychologists have applied these methods on a large scale to military situations earlier than others. But the methods, in their adjustment to military situations, suffered distortion and restriction. The rapid integration of these methods in a limited sense within the German Army as compared with the slower process in the armies of the democracies may have been due to the privilege of authoritarian regime to keep certain methods out entirely by decree, and to permit others to be included into their framework, again by decree.

DISCUSSION AND CONCLUDING REMARKS

The relation between "imaginary" and "real" in situation tests[4] is not sufficiently clarified by Ansbacher. Wherever the test is given to a group of men, whether in a laboratory or in an open field, however realistically the test may be organized, and even if the men are made to believe that the situations are the real thing, it is still a "test", it is never the real thing, which can be only the life situation itself, the battle field, perhaps a half an hour later. Once the life situation is on hand, for instance, the battle field, situational techniques can be applied by the men themselves, on the spot. The tester has disappeared and all the motivations for the testing, the men are now alone facing the enemy. Situation tests are replaced by situation practices. There are many terms used in the description of group situational tests which are equivocal, or nearly so, and which are used in literature in a redundant fashion. Terms like psychodrama, sociodrama, life practice, action practice, role playing, role practice, and so forth overlap in one area or another.

It is important that we separate those operations commonly used by all situation testers from the differences in terms and semantic descriptions which often confuse the reader and make him think that the writers describe different operations. To the uniformed reader an experiment may sound

---

[4] The meaning of the word "test" was radically changed when used with individuals who warmed up deliberately and directly into action. In intelligence tests we test something which is already there, ready to be measured. In situation tests the situation to be measured is not given. In order for it to be tested and measured the subject has first to warm up, to produce, to act out, or better, to interact with other subjects before measurement and evaluation can take place.

different on paper although it is the same thing in action. There is not only a common nucleus of operations in all situation tests; there is also a common nucleus of interpretation in them, notwithstanding that several ideological schools have invaded the group situational test field besides sociometry like Gestalt theory, psychoanalysis and behaviorism.

The claim that Europeans and Germans in particular are intuitive and subjective, whereas the British and Americans are more interested in measurement, in quantitative and statistical methods, appears a myth, as one analyzes the development of scientific methods in the several countries.

I am not a historian but I remember from my University days three psychological leaders of the last hundred years, Galton, Fechner and Freud. The Englishman Galton was as great in intuitive ideas as in the development of measurement methods. The German Fechner, almost poetic in his scientific reveries, was prepossessed with measurement projects. Freud is often called an intuitive thinker but his intuitions were based on accurate observations which have proven to be more valuable than thousands of so called scientific laboratory experiments which are now forgotten. I believe that if he had thought that experimental procedures would have helped the advance of psychoanalytic concepts he would have had the talent to devise them. But for what he wanted to attain, the psychoanalytic situation was the most productive device he could contrive. A few years ago I became acquainted with the work of two Americans, whose powers are intuitive and observational with little effort to engage themselves in directly quantifying and verifying their hypotheses—Charles Saunders Pierce and George Herbert Mead.

The country in which the new methods found their most productive soil was apparently the United States of America, more than the British countries, France and Germany, if one considers the number of original experiments published.[5]

Some selection methods, of course, were used in many military organizations as in the German, French, British, and United States armies, before the emergence of the new selection methods, whether situational or sociometric. They had some degree of efficiency but their efficiency depended largely upon judgment of the military personnel, especially of the officers. They were comparatively intuitive and arbitrary. Modern situational testing, when it first began to be applied to military institutions before and

---

[5] For an excellent survey and bibliography up to 1945 see Joseph I. Meiers, "Origins and Development of Group Psychotherapy',' *Psychodrama Monographs*, No. 17, Beacon House, 1945.

during the recent war, merely improved and overhauled the existing, authoritarian methods of selection of leadership. Something similar happened in the formation of military groupings, the old nominational techniques being used in military schools were gradually overhauled by sociometric concepts and procedures. I can well imagine that some military men, unversed in the development of scientific procedures, may think that nothing was really changed thereby.

The fact of two parallel movements towards similar goals in Germany and the United States has a natural explanation in the fact that the Stegreiftheater movement was started in Vienna in 1921 and that *Das Stegreiftheater* was published in Potsdam in 1923, thus stimulating the brainwaves within the German speaking countries. Sociometrically speaking such a spread of ideas is easily understood, and it may be in full accord with Simoneit's statement that so far as he knows he has not been influenced by it nor even heard of it.

Summing up, the turning point in the group testing movement came when my idea crystalized to *"play"* *situations out* "as well as" observing and analyzing them. When such situation playing or testing was limited to a specific aspect of it, for instance, to the roles in which the individuals operated, it became "role playing" or role testing. The idea was that if you can "play a role", for instance the role of God, and develop that role and stop its playing at will, you will begin to learn how not to be possessed by that role. If it were limited to spontaneity it became "spontaneity playing or spontaneity testing", the idea being that if you can mobilize spontaneity adequately in an imaginary situation and more and more in a near-life like situation that you will gradually learn how to make it available at all times, especially in the unrehearsed moments of living.

On the other hand when situation playing was greatly *extended* to a large complex of situations it transcended (but included) situation testing and playing, role playing and testing, spontaneity playing and testing and it *became a psychodrama, a sociodrama or an axiodrama*. Because of their universal significance these methods have been gradually applied in the United States between 1925-50 to education, group work, community organization, psychological testing, psychotherapy, sociological research, cooperatives, business, industry and military schools. From the United States they traveled to France and to all the English-speaking countries where they were further developed.

The reader is, of course, aware that group situation tests and sociometric tests have the same theoretical foundation; that, because of the theoretical linkage one cannot do the one without the other for long. It can be predicted that the German military psychologists, indeed, that military departments in all countries, will follow the American, British and French military schools[6] which are already using both methods jointly. Perhaps the strongest argument against the originality claimed in behalf of German military psychology is the fact that their vision has been incomplete and has tried out situation tests without following through with sociometric procedures *per se*.

---

[6] See "Sociometry in France and the United States", SOCIOMETRY, Volume 12, no. 1-3, 1949.

V.

SOCIOMETRY AND MICROSOCIOLOGY

ORIGINS AND FOUNDATIONS OF INTERPERSONAL THEORY, SOCIOMETRY AND MICROSOCIOLOGY
(1949)

Note: I apologize for the autobiographic character of this paper, but being exposed to the dynamic comments and criticism of such distinguished scientists as Gurvitch, Sorokin, von Wiese and Zazzo made a more direct response necessary (see, SOCIOMETRY, Vol. XII, 1949).

A man may draw his inspiration from a conceptual heaven or hell. Freud once implied (Flectere si nequeo superos, Acheronta movebo," motto to "The Interpretation of Dreams") that he had to go to Hades in order to find some significant connections and interpretations for the world above. My calling was just the opposite, I had to go to heaven to get advice for the world below. I had no alternative, the world in which I found myself when I came to my senses and to my first intellectual formulations about things, was torn to pieces, spiritually and physically. Nietzsche, Marx, and Freud, each in a different area, have brought to effect and to a calamitous end the thought waves which Spinoza had initiated; the Deus sive Natura had further deteriorated to the Lucifer sive Natura. All old values were destroyed for whatever good or bad reasons, new values were not created to replace them. The historical situation compelled me, therefore, to go the whole way of reconstruction in a more radical and extensive way perhaps than anyone else before me in our Western World. Marx saw the position of man as that of a member of society, the struggle within it as his ultimate destiny. Freud saw the position of man as the one of a traveler between birth and death, the cosmos beyond was shattered.

I moved man back into the universe.

Man is more than a psychological, social or biological being. Reducing man's responsibility to the psychological, social or biological department of living makes him an outcast. Either he is co-responsible for the whole universe or his responsibility means nothing. The life and future of the universe is important, indeed the only thing which matters—more important than the life and death of man as an individual, as a particular civilization or as a species. I postulated therefore that *a theory of God* comes first. It must be attained first and is indispensable in order to make the life of any particle of the universe significant, whether it is a man, or a protozoon. Science and experimental method, if it be worthy of its claim, must be applicable to the theory of God or whatever the name which we give to a theory of the supreme value. I was in the strategic position that the old God values were dead and that agnosticism reigned mankind in the first quarter of the twentieth century. I could therefore construct new God values with a certain amount of disregard for past constructions. Theology became to my mind what it literally means—the science of God himself, of the supreme value (not of God's creation, the biography of saints, or the religions of mankind). It is outside of this paper's domain to give a presentation of the theology which I evolved, but it is at least *autobiographically* significant here that my God-universe pattern became the blueprint, the ontological guide after which I modelled sociometry, the idea of a society in which our deepest selves are realized. It is from my theological analysis and experiments that I drew the inspiration and the certainty to forge ahead in to realms which are entirely secular, materialistic and down to earth. The application of experimental methods to theology prepared me for the task of applying them to human relations. These experiments in theometry helped me to see the loopholes in the current experimental methods in science as proclaimed by Mill. The form which the experimental method in theological science takes differs, of course, from the form it takes in social science which again differ widely from their form in biological or physical science. But there is no "absolute" cleavage between interpersonal, experimental dynamic theology and interpersonal, experimental sociometry. The old impasse between science and theology has ceased to exist except for antiquated theologians and ignorant scientists.

The uninhibited journey of a psychodramatic theometrician throughout the universe could not be continued endlessly. As soon as he settled down to a specific task, his sociometric relation to the nextdoor neighbors, the macroscopic journey became increasingly microscopic to the point where the distance between one neighbor and another appeared to be far greater than the distance between him and the stars.

Georges Gurvitch, carefully examining the foundations of sociometry queries the reasons why certain domains of investigation have not been included by sociometrists, particularly as he formulates it, the "we" in its three degrees of intensity, Mass, Community and Communion. As the critique is particularly addressed towards me I am glad to admit that a great many investigations have yet been outside of my opportunities but at no time have they been outside of my vision. In the work which anticipated and precipitated our concrete sociometric experiments the We problems are at their very essence. But to bring them down to earth cannot be done but piecemeal. We made lists of hundreds of research projects of which unfortunately only a small part has been brought to realization. All my publications between 1914 and 1925 are nothing but a reduplication of the ideas of Community and Communion not only as to their theoretical formulations but as to their realization in practice, bringing them to a reality test in front of a frequently hostile world. A careful reader of my situational dialogues about the author, the orator, and the actor, of my speeches about the moment, the meeting and anonymity, last not least of my autobiography of the king, will recognize that my very religious preoccupations conditioned me rather to exaggerate than to underrate the importance of the We experience as expressed in community and communion. Indeed, one may easily recognize that the same brainwave is still operating in techniques like sociodrama and axiodrama and in my revisions of the experimental method in science. What is my emphatic criticism of the mechanical use of the sociometric test, its distortion into a sociometric questionnaire, my recurrent advocation of sociometric town meetings but a structuring of the sociometric method into a community experience, the most violent systematic expression of We feeling yet crystallized in our time? There is nothing mystic about sociometric meetings or psycho-and sociodramatic sessions but they have to be co-experienced as spectator and actor in order to learn of their full significance. It is exactly the "We" which we cannot put into an article when we write about "us". But we can materialize and see some phases of the We in a sociodrama.

Origin of Interpersonal Theory

At the turn of the century the formula "the individual versus the Universe" appeared to be sufficiently wide for expressing the total situation. The socius was yet unborn. One could have multiplied the "individual" by the number of organisms the universe contained. One could also have given every individual the opportunity of projection, everyone projecting his own private world into the universe, filling the universe with more or less harmless bubbles. The psychoanalysts were at that period not interested, for instance, in what these bubbles *actually did to others* but chiefly in the internal dynamics of the individuals from whom they came. The psychologists of that era were dealing with individuals separate from one another. The sociologists were dealing with undifferentiated masses (in this point at least, Comtists and Marxists were in accord). The biologists, social biologists and evolutionary biologists à la Bergson were equally satisfied with the above formula or at least they did not produce any "open revolt" against it. The revolt came—and it is my thesis that careful historical investigation will bear me out—the revolt came unexpectedly from men inspired by

a *neo*theological, or using a more modern term, by an axiological orientation. In many of the great religions ethical prescriptions were part and parcel of their code of morals but they remained imperative and mystic; they
were never permitted to become objects of scientific investigation. But when
in the beginning of the twentieth century the atheistic and agnostic gospels
started to spread world-wide a *pro*-religious movement which countered
them developed. It did not seem to differ much at first from the romantic
movement of the nineteenth century, for instance, Kierkegaard never divorced himself from Christianity as a framework and was entirely sub-
merged by the imperatives of his private existence, at no time reaching
beyond it. The new movement did not appear to be different except for
one thing. It began to emphasize the *You*, the You as a person, the responsibility towards the You instead of only towards the I. Kierkegaard's fear
of losing the "I" in the "You" was transcended by the movement of the
You towards the I taking place *simultaneously* with the movement of the I
towards the You. Gradually some interpretations were given of the You and
I which created for it a radically new position; the idea of *meeting* between
you and I, and any number of Thou's and I's forming a community; the
idea of the "moment", neither as a function of the past nor of the future,
but as a category in itself; the idea of the "situation" and the challenges
emerging from it; the ideas of spontaneity and creativity as universal
processes of conduct, countering the clichés of the ethical and cultural conserves; and above all the idea of urgency, the urgency of their immediate
application. Although they were deeply saturated with value feelings and
ethical aspirations they had an *un*mystical appearance and a character
which one could call "axio-pragmatic". This countermovement had a theoretical and a practical part. The most popular practical manifestation of the
revolt was Mahatma Ghandi. He is mentioned here because of his spiritual
and anti-materialistic message; theoretically he was a reactionary conservative. Ghandi's India did not need and was not ready for a theoretical revolt.
The focus of the theoretical inspiration was naturally assigned to Central
Europe (as it was in a parallel situation with the nineteenth century revolt
culminating in Marx and Kierkegaard as the two extremes). European culture, especially in its axiological top structure was threatened from all sides.
It is here therefore, where the revolt massed itself. One has to study the
trail blazed by some of the neo-protestants following Kierkegaard as Ferdi-
nand Ebner (1921), some of the neo-Tolstoyan disciples, some of the Russian writers influenced by Dostojewsky as Ssolowjow and Berdjajew, some
of the French neo-catholics like Péguy and Rimbaud, some modern exponents

of chassidism like Martin Buber and my own anonymous writings with the
"Invitation to a Meeting" (1914) as the central core, in order to come face
to face with the original inspirations out of which interpersonal theory and
sociometry grew.

All these groups must be counted in as having pioneered the new idea
as to what constitutes *truly human* relationships and to have prepared the
ground for experimentation. Prior to this the structure of the "I" had the
central position. In the new theory of relationships the structure of the
You's moved into the center. And suddenly, out of this insight the *imperative of the meeting,* of the two-way encounter was born, the "invitation to a
meeting," one meeting with the other in the fullest realities of themselves
and in the fullest responsibility toward the immediate situations. It is thus
that by ethically oriented situational imperatives the groundwork of modern
interpersonal theory was laid. Faced with the dilemma of Marxism the secu-
larly oriented social sciences appeared in themselves impotent in integrating
it into or creating the necessary counter concepts and counter instruments.
The religious masses of mankind, in retreat against the onslaught of atheism
and agnosticism shocked their leaders into a new assessment as to what the
essence of all great religious teaching has been and the result was spontaneity-creativity, sociometry and sociodrama, the gift of a dying religious
world towards the foundations of a new social and axiological order. This
hypothesis of the axiological origin of modern interpersonal theory throws a
new light upon the gradual emergence, approximately a decade later, of
social thinkers in Europe and the United States, who paved the way towards
a science of human relations. They, as for instance G. H. Mead, F. Znaniecki, W. J. Thomas, L. von Wiese, P. Sorokin, G. Gurvitch, could not help
being influenced by the ethical and axiological concepts which dominated
our cultural climate.

It was a lucky chain of circumstances which made me the spearhead
of the new ideas so many years ahead of others and of men much older
than myself. As compared with Buber my insistence upon immediate religious
action and my theorizing of the moment and interpersonal relations versus his
interest in retrospective prophesy, was an asset. On the other hand, my
interest in exact science, my early acquaintance with psychiatry and psychoanalysis (my work at the Psychiatric Institute in Vienna began in 1911),
in addition to my preoccupation with practical axiology gave me an advantage over sociological and psychological colleagues and inspired me to attempt a synthesis, not only for science's sake but also in order to maintain
my own mental equilibrium. Among the simplest accounts of my inter-

personal theory and practice is the following quotation (taken from my "Rede Über die Begegnung"—Speech About the Meeting—published by Gustav Kiepenheuer Verlag in Potsdam, 1923, p. 24-26).

"Between any particular place wherein any particular persons live and this or any other particular place, in opposite or in all possible directions, there are many countries. And each of these countries has numerous districts. And every district has so and so many communities. And every community may have more than hundred or more than thousand persons. And each person, when one meets the other, lays claim, one upon the other.

There are situations for one, there are situations for two, there are situations for more than two. There are situations for all. When a situation is so characterized that its problem is related to one, then it can not be solved but in the one, the afflicted one, in himself, alone. But when a situation is so constructed that its problem is not related to one, but two, then it cannot be resolved but in the two, by the afflicted two's, through them and between them, alone. But when a situation is so constructed that its problem is not in relation to two but to more than two, then it cannot be resolved but by more than the two, by the afflicted ones, through them and between them, alone. But when a situation is so constructed that its problems is not related to more than two but to all, then it cannot be resolved

"Zwischen jedem beliebigen Ort, in dem beliebige Wesen wohnen, und dieser oder jeder beliebigen Stelle, in entgegengesetzter und allen möglichen Richtungen, liegen viele Länder. Und jedes der Länder hat mehrere Bezirke. Und jeder Bezirk soundso viele Gemeinden. Und jede Gemeinde hat mehr als hundert oder mehr als tausend Seelen. Und jede Seele, wenn eine der anderen begegnet, erhebt Anspruch eine auf die andere.

Es gibt Lagen für Einen. Es gibt Lagen für Zwei. Es gibt Lagen für mehr als Zwei. Es gibt Lagen für Alle. Wenn eine Lage so beschaffen ist, dass ihr Thema an Einem haftet, kann es nur in Einem, dem Betroffenen, in ihm selbst gelöst werden. Wenn aber eine Lage so beschaffen ist, dass ihr Thema nicht an Einem, sondern Zweien haftet, kann es nur in Zweien, von den Betroffenen, durch sie hindurch und zwischen ihnen gelöst werden. Wenn aber eine Lage so beschaffen ist dass ihr Thema nicht an Zweien, sondern mehr als Zweien haftet, kann es nur von mehr als Zweien, von den Betroffenen, durch sie hindurch und zwischen ihnen gelöst werden. Wenn aber eine Lage so beschaffen ist, das ihr Thema nicht an mehr als Zweien, sondern Allen haftet, kann es nur von Allen, den Betroffenen, durch sie hindurch

but by all, by all the ones who are afflicted, through them and between them.

There are innumerable communities and every community consists of a number of streets. And every street has a number of houses. And every house has a number of apartments. And in every apartment live a number of persons. So there are innumerable millions of persons upon whom our situation depends and whose situation depends upon us. Thus there are innumerable millions of persons who form the knot which chokes us."*

und zwischen ihnen gelöst werden.

Es gibt unzählige Gemeinden. Und jede Gemeinde besteht aus einer Anzahl Strassen. Und jede Strasse hat eine Menge Häuser. Und jedes Haus mehrere Wohnungen. Und in jeder Wohnung leben etliche Personen. So sind es unzählige Millionen von Wesen, von welchen unsere Lage abhängt und deren Lage von uns abhängt. So sind es unzählige Millionen Wesen, die den Knoten bilden, der uns würgt."

This quotation is lifted from a speech which—like all the dialogues and speeches to which it belongs—is strictly *concrete-situational,* that means it is not merely a general theorizing on what interhuman or interpersonal relations are, like in a sociological treatise; it is actualized and delivered in the now and here, in a specific setting requiring exactly *this* speech, *this* audience, and *this* actor and the form of delivery it has, in role, gestures and phrasing. Outside of this setting, its locus nascendi and primary situation, it loses its axio-pragmatic significance or, as we sociometrists say today, its adequate motivation. Lifted from the actual speech, recorded, transferred and quoted in this paper, twenty-six years later, it is here reduced to an aesthetic-intellectual reference. Situationally speaking, all religious, philosophical and sociological literature is of such a "secondary" nature. From this point of view the New Testament is a "report" of highly graded situations; divorced from them and made available for the "coming generations" it is merely a religious conserve. A far more inferior, immediate situation but lived out here and now is qualitatively superior to the high grade new-testamentarian one. Interpersonal theory and the situational imperative grew therefore, hand in hand. The locus nascendi stimulated also the birth of a new significance of the "moment". The moment is now related to and a part of the

---

* For illustrations of interpersonal and group dynamics in situ, see "Der Königsroman" (1923) and my "Dialogues and Speeches" (1918-1919) to be published in translation by Beacon House in the fall of 1950.

situation. It is no longer a part of "time", like the ever-vanishing present, related to a past and a future, the endpoint of past episodes and the starting point of future episodes, submitted to cause and effect, to psychological and social determinism. The moment operates in a totally different dimension from the past-present-future continuity; it is tangential, not identical with it.

A simple account as to what the moment means within a situational context is given in my "Rede Über den Augenblick"—Speech About the Moment —published by Gustav Kiepenheuer in Potsdam, 1922, p. 27-29.

"This speech has no past, no recurrence, no future, it is not an heritage and it is not an end-product. It is complete in itself. A feeling must be related to the object of its feeling. A thought must be related to the object of the thought. A perception must be related to the object of the perception. A touching must be in contact with the object of the touching. This speech is the object of our thinking. This speech is the object of our thoughts. This speech is the object of our perception. This speech is the object with which our touching is in contact. Have then all feelings which belong to it, to our object, have they all emerged now and here? Have then all thoughts which belong to it, to our object, have they all emerged now and here? Have then all perceptions which belong to it, to our object, have they all emerged now and here? Have all touches which are to be in contact with our object, have they all emerged here and now? Or have we had some feelings which are related to the object, did we have them already outside of the object, uncon-

"Diese Rede hat keine Vergangenheit, keine Wiederkehr, keine Nachkommenschaft, sie ist kein Erbteil und kein Ergebnis. Sie ist vollendet. Ein Gefühl muss beim Gegenstand sein des Gefühls. Ein Gedanke muss beim Gegenstand sein des Gedankens. Eine Wahrnehmung muss beim Gegenstand sein der Wahrnehmung. Eine Berührung muss beim Gegenstand sein der Berührung. Diese Rede ist der Gegenstand unserer Gefühle. Diese Rede ist der Gegenstand unserer Gedanken. Diese Rede ist der Gegenstand unserer Wahrnehmung. Die Rede ist der Gegenstand unserer Berührung. Sind nun alle Gefühle, die zu ihr, unserem Gegenstand gehören, jetzt entstanden? Sind nun alle Gedanken, die zu ihr, underem Gegenstand gehören, jetzt entstanden? Sind nun alle Wahrnehmungen, die zu ihr, unserem Gegenstand gehören, jetzt entstanden? Sind alle Berührungen, die zu ihr, unserem Gegenstand gehören, jetzt enstanden? Oder haben wir manche Gefühle, die auf sie bezogen waren, schon auser ihr, unverbunden mit ihr gehabt, die auf der Zeitstrecke

nected with it? Feelings which have emerged in the passage of time, without it and have vanished without? Or have we had some thoughts which are related to the object, did we have them already outside of it, unconnected with it, which have emerged in the passage of time, outside of it and have vanished outside of it? Or did we have some images which are related to the object, did we have them outside of it, unrelated to it, which have emerged in the passage of time, outside of it and have vanished outside of it? Or did we have some touches with the object outside of it, unconnected with it, which have emerged in the passage of time, outside of it and have vanished outside of it? *We did not have them.* Feelings for it, thoughts of it, perceptions of it, touches with it, which have to emerge and vanish only now and here, have emerged and have vanished now and here.

"What is it, therefore, that I, the producer of this speech, must say about it? *It is not a speech which was prepared in advance of the situation. It had reason to emerge and no part of it is missing.* It did not step in to replace necessary pause and silence. It did not force itself in to replace another speech which may have been more fitting. It is unique, unreplaceable, cannot be improved upon. No word is missing in it, no phrase is

ohne sie entstanden und erloschen sind? Oder haben wir manche Gedanken, die auf sie bezogen waren, schon auser ihr, unverbunden mit ihr gehabt, die auf der Zeitstrecke ohne sie entstanden und erloschen sind? Oder haben wir manche Bilder, die auf sie bezogen waren, schon auser ihr, unverbunden mit ihr gehabt, die auf der Zeitstrecke ohne sie entstanden und erloschen sind? Oder haben wir manche Bilder, die auf sie bezogen waren, schon auser ihr, unverbunden mit ihr gehabt, die auf der Zeitstrecke ohne sie entstanden und erloschen sind? Oder haben wir manche Berührungen mit ihr, auser ihr unverbunden mit ihr gehabt, die auf der Zeitstrecke ohne sie entstanden und erloschen sind? Wir haben sie nicht gehabt: Gefühle für sie Gedanken über sie, Wahrnehmungen von ihr, Berührungen mit ihr, die nur hier zu entstehen und vergehen haben, sind nur hier entstanden underloschen.

Was ist es daher, das gefragt, ich, der Werker dieser Rede, uber sie sagen müste? Es ist nicht eine Rede im Bau, müste ich sagen. Sie hat Grund gehabt zu kommen und kein Teil fehlt an ihr. Sie ist nicht getreten an notwendigem Schweigens statt. Sie hat sich nicht gedrangt an anderer Rede statt. Sie ist einzig, unersetzlich, unverbesserlich. Kein Wort fehlt ihr, kein Satz fehlt ihr, kein Gedanke fehlt ihr. Sie hat den richtigen Anfang, das richtige Ende.

missing in it, no thought is missing in it. It has a correct beginning, the correct ending. One sentence develops out of the other, one word develops out of the other, one thought develops out of the other, in logical sequence. It is adequate. Therefore it can be considered as appropriately produced."

Ein Satz ist aus dem andern entwickelt, ein Wort aus dem andern entwickelt, ein Gedanke aus dem andern entwickelt, in unbarmherziger Folge. Sie genügt. So ist sie als entstanden zu betrachten."

These were my origins. Whenever I turned away from ethical-philosophic to scientific objectives I could draw from my old saving accounts. As one can see from the quotations above they take no sides, they can easily be applied universally, except for manner of speech they could be the position of an operational social scientist or sociometrist of today. It is with this heritage of insight and instruments that I moved into the development of sociometry.

Difference Between Sociometry and Psychology*

I am in agreement with the position taken by Gurvitch that "social groups are a reality sui generis, irreducible to the elements of which they are composed." This is in full accord with the core of my writings.

---

* Note: I am often represented as being partial to psychiatric concepts and as poorly acquainted with sociological and psychological contributions of the past, for instance by F. Znaniecki, G. Gurvitch, and L. von Wiese. However, the instance of my being a psychiatrist by vocation has been falsely interpreted. Before I attended medical school my world view was already formed. I had studied philosophy at the University of Vienna, psychology and semantics under Adolf Stöhr, mathematics under Wirtinger, Gestalt theory under Swoboda, but even these influences were secondary to my private studies of theology and philosophy. The scope of my reading was only in a small portion medical. It encompassed all the departments of science and included considerable sociological literature. Among the sociologists whom I read was Georg Simmel, "Die Philosophie des Geldes", Lazarus, Stein and Bachhofen, Marx and Engels, Proudhon and Sorel, and when I became Editor of a monthly journal, *Daimon,* in February 1918, only one psychiatrist was among the contributing editors, Alfred Adler, two sociologists, Max Scheler and H. Schmidt, the poets Franz Werfel, Franz Kafka, Heinrich Mann, Jakob Wasserman, Ottokar Brsezina, religionists like Francis Jammes and Martin Buber. From the company of these men it does not look as if I would have been overly influenced by psychiatrists in the development of sociometry. It should not be denied that psychoanalysis as a *"negative"* factor had a powerful effect upon my formulations. The same thing, however, can be said about Marxism in my sociological, and about Spinozism in *my theological orientation.*

The relation of sociometry to other social sciences, especially to psychology has been put forth by me in my leading article "Sociometry in Relation to Other Social Sciences" (Volume 1, Number 1 of SOCIOMETRY, p. 206-220, 1937).

"The responses received in the course of sociometric procedure from each individual, however spontaneous and essential they may appear, *are materials only and not yet sociometric facts in themselves. . . .* As long as we (as auxiliary ego) drew from every individual the responses and materials needed, we were inclined—because of our nearness to the individual—to conceive the tele as flowing out of him towards other individuals and objects. This is certainly correct on the individual-psychological level, in the preparatory phase of sociometric exploration. *But as soon as we transferred these responses to the sociometric level and studied them not singly but in their interrelations, important methodological reasons suggested that we conceive this flowing feeling, the tele, as an inter-personal or more accurately and more broadly speaking, "as a sociometric structure."*
I have never deviated from this position.

The Difference Between Sociometry and Sociology

I am in agreement with the position taken by Gurvitch that the sociometric concept of reality should give a pre-eminent place to collective phenomena in human relations and not concentrate its interest on "intermental psychology".

It is significant, in support of Gurvitch's comment of a cleavage between collective and intermental psychology, that interpersonal theory was rapidly and well received by psychiatrists. Since 1929, when I met the late Dr. William A. White, an early friend and sponsor of my ideas, interpersonal theory began to make its way. Although only partly recognized— and partly distorted—by the late Dr. Harry Stack Sullivan tried to make them palatable to a declining psychoanalytic ideology, badly in need of a lifesaver.*

Psychiatrists accepted interpersonal theory (which in the last twenty years has changed the tenor of psychiatric textbooks) but they *resisted* sociometry and group psychotherapy, fearful apparently, of being involved in collective phenomena, which they did not know how to tackle, whereas social psychologists and sociologists welcomed sociometry and contributed to its development. By 1941, influenced by the situations in World War

---

*Loyalties to psychoanalytic theory handicapped Sullivan in accepting my ideas in full, although an increasing withdrawal away from official psychoanalysis and towards group theory can be observed in his writings of recent years.

Two a general acceptance of group psychotherapy began, but one can observe in the literature a marked division between individual-centered group psychotherapies and group-centered ones. The psychiatrically oriented workers are inclined to treat an "individual" within a group setting, the sociologically oriented workers try to treat the "group" as a whole. One can observe the same phenomenon in the relationship to action methods, the psychiatrists showing a preference for psychodrama, the sociologists a preference for sociodrama. (Certain inconsistencies in my presentation, especially in the definition of terms are obviously due to the need to carry on our war of persuasion on at least two fronts, psychology and sociology.) However profound and ideologically determined this cleavage may be, we sociometrists can hardly be accused of not having tried to bridge it. Like Gurvitch many other sociologists have recognized the cleavage but they had no device by which to span it. It is exactly here where sociometry made one of its chief contributions. The study of immediate, interpersonal relations, the I and you, the you and I, was not sufficient for sociological requirements. In order to explore the "social group" a procedure was necessary which was able to go beyond the immediate situation. *It is by the invention of the sociogram, as we can see clearly now, looking backward, that interpersonal theory was transcended.* The forerunner of the sociogram was my interaction and position diagram (See *Das Stegreiftheater*, p. 87-95, with sixteen charts) which was apparently the first device consciously constructed for presenting, exploring and measuring social structures as wholes. Therefore, 1923 may be considered as the year when sociometry made its scientific debut.

The relation of sociometry to sociology has been clarified by me on many occasions, particularly in Volume 1, Number 1 of SOCIOMETRY, 1937. I never changed my position. While I was chiefly concerned with creating foundations which enable us to study collective phenomena in human relations systematically and accurately, I refused to be contented with elaborate reflections and sophisticated reveries about notions of collectivity, however noble, notions of legal, social or cultural Institutions, although I knew that I would have been in the good company of many distinguished sociologists. I decided to play with thoughts as little as possible but *to use my imagination to invent* socio-experimental procedures congruous for the task and see what happens in the course of their application. My iconoclastic and neglectful attitude towards dignified and perennial social concepts, as state, religion, family, law, was due to my conscious refusal to fall in line with the scholarly tradition (and with my own early preoccupation with axiological ventures of that type), but to find a new and more promising experimental approach in sociology, always in the hope that in the course of time sociometric research would justify my strategic suspension and throw some light upon what group, class and mass, law, religion and state really are. There can be no question that a logically coherent and consistent presentation of concepts is essential to any well balanced scientific system, but in an experimental and operational science as sociometry there is a logic inherent in the operations themselves which is able to clarify debatable issues, as for instance, when one definition of a concept at one time seems to contradict its definition at another time. What we actually *do* in the course of sociometric operations, sociometric test or sociodrama, defines and illustrates our terms and concepts, it is able to an extent to make up for some inconsistencies or, at least, to correct perceptions coming from poorly worded definitions.

How do we proceed in sociometric research? First step—collection of data: "The responses received in the course of sociometric procedure from each individual, however spontaneous and essential they may appear, *are, materials only and not yet sociometric facts in themselves.*" Second step—two social inventions are introduced: the sociogram and the psycho-geographical map. A sociogram plots all individuals related to the same criterion and indicates the relations they have to each other. "A psycho-geographical map presents the topographical outlay of a community as well as the psychological and social currents relating each region within it to each other region" (see "Who Shall Survive?" p. 241). "The astronomer has his universe of stars and of the other heavenly bodies visibly spread throughout space. Their geography is given. The sociometrist is in the paradoxical situation that he has to construct and map of his universe before he can explore it. The sociogram is . . . more than merely a method of presentation. It is first of all a method of exploration. It makes possible the exploration of sociometric facts. The proper placement of every individual and all interrelations of individuals can be shown on a sociogram. It is at present the only available scheme which makes *structural* analysis of a community possible." " . . . The sociograms are so devised that one can pick from the *primary* map of a community small parts, redraw them, and study them so to speak under the miscroscope. Another type of . . . secondary sociogram results if we pick from the map of a community large structures because of their functional significance, for instance, psychological networks. The mapping of networks indicates that we may devise on the basis of primary sociograms forms of charting which enable us to explore large geographical areas."

The matrix of a sociogram may consist in its simplest form of choice, rejection, and neutrality structures. It may be further broken up into the emotional and ideological currents crisscrossing these attraction and rejection patterns. The third step—study and discovery of social structures: "Once the full social structure can be seen as a totality it can be studied in minute detail. We thus become able to describe sociometric facts (descriptive sociometry) and to consider the function of specific structures, the effect of some parts upon others (dynamic sociometry)". We are now able to study interhuman phenomena on the sociological plane, on one hand removed from the limitations of the psychological plane, on the other hand not abstracted and distorted into generalized, lifeless mass-symbolic data. We may now try to discover the truly dynamic social structures which rarely become visible to the microscopic eye. "Viewing the detailed structure of a community, we see . . . a nucleus of relations around every individual which is "thicker" around some individuals, "thinner" around others. This nucleus of relations is the smallest *social* structure in a community, a *social atom*. From the point of view of a descriptive sociometry, the social atom is a fact, not a concept, just as in anatomy the blood vessel system, for instance, is first of all a descriptive fact. It attained conceptual significance as soon as the study of development of social atoms suggested that they have an important function in the formation of human society."

"Whereas certain parts of these social atoms seem to remain buried between the individuals participating, certain parts link themselves with parts of other social atoms and these with parts of other social atoms again, forming complex chains of interrelations which are called, in terms of descriptive sociometry, psychological *networks*. The older and wider the network spreads the less significant seems to be the individual contribution toward it. From the point of view of dynamic sociometry these networks have the function of shaping social tradition and public opinion."*

These are illustrations as to how primary social structure have been discovered, first descriptively, stimulating the construction of fruitful hypotheses. These discoveries have been made by means of what I have called structural or microscopic analysis. There are numerous discoveries still to be made. Unfortunately most researchers, using sociometric techniques have paid onesided attention to the choice-preference index* which is now so widely applied and so superficially from "How many dates do you have?", "Who are your friends?", to asking children "Whom do you prefer, your

---

*SOCIOMETRY, Vol. I p. 212-14 (1937).

father or your mother?" (exploring Freud's Oedipus hypothesis) frequently without mentioning the sociometric paternity. Without structural analysis of sociograms vital questions, as for instance leadership phenomena cannot be answered adequately. This onesidedness is unfortunate but understandable. Quantitative analysis of choices and rejections is easy and immediately rewarding. Structural analysis of sociograms and psychogeographical maps are painstaking, time absorbing and this the more so the larger the communities which are studied. They have to be studied at many and different points in time and space in order to learn how a community develops and spreads.* Another onesidedness is the reduction of the sociometric test to a number of questions. Without the spontaneity and the warming up process of the total group to the problem they have in common sociometric tests become worthless. Similarly, a sociometric procedure, without observational, interview and follow up methods on the reality level is crippled, deprived of its meaning. Sociometrists, in order to attain the fullest usefulness of their instruments should combine sociometric tests on the choice and on the reality level with psycho-, socio-, and axiodramatic procedures and should always be ready to make modifications in favor of the community of people to which they are applied.

Sociometry aspires to be a science within its own right. It is the indispensable prologue and preparatory science for all the social sciences. It has several subdivisions like microsociology, microanthropology, microeconomics, microsociatry, microecology and animal sociology. It is not merely a slogan indicating a special type of research, a single method or a number of techniques. Its present stage of development is still embryonic and scattered but there can be no question as to the potentialities of the new science. For the future progress of the social sciences it is of the greatest importance that a science of sociometry is set up and delineated, and its relation to other social sciences defined. Its range and boundaries, its operations and objectives are already more sharply visible than the same references in sociology or anthropology. It does not supplant and it must not overlap with sociology or economics, for instance, but their findings on the overt, macroscopic level may receive a new interpretation from the point of view of sociometric research. An illustration for an anthropology without sociometry is "Social Structure" by George P. Murdock (Macmillan Co., New York, 1949, p. 1-22). Dr. Murdock has made a survey of two hundred and fifty human societies. In their analysis

---

*A notable exception is Charles P. Loomis, see for instance "Sociometrics and the Study of New Rural Communities", SOCIOMETRY, Vol. 2, p. 56-76, 1939.

he distinguishes three types of family organization, the nuclear family, the polygamous family and the extended family. This may be so, but a sociometrically oriented microanthropologist, surveying the same two hundred and fifty societies may have added two distinct contributions to the strictly anthropological findings: a) the existence of "informal" group structures surrounding the official family setting like a social aura; b) the existence of "sub"-family forms of social organizations, forms of association including various individuals and structural relations but which may have never crystalized to become a "type", a legally sanctioned and respectable form of family. He may have suggested the hypothesis of a *universal sociometric matrix* with many varieties of structures underlying all known and potential family associations, an interweaving and crossing of numerous sociatomic and culturalatomic processes, but not necessarily identical with the family of one type or another as a social group. Indeed, the matrix, being full of cross currents, and contradictions may, because of its very essence, never be able to mature to a social institution. It is more strategic to explore living, instead of dead cultures and the study of our own culture should be carried out with the full participation of the people; they should not be treated as if they were half dead. The study of dead cultures themselves would gain considerably by their resurrection within a sociodramatic setting.

The Difference Between Sociometry and Anthropology

I am in full agreement with Gurvitch and von Wiese that the processes associating individuals and forming a social group are not of "an exclusively emotional character." (See Leopold von Wiese, elsewhere in this issue, p. 203.) I have repeatedly taken the position that emotional characteristics are only a part of the total social process, although crucial. May I quote here one of my early discussions of interpersonal relationships (in Das Stegreiftheater, p. 28-29) as follows: "Sie is von allen Begriffen der Psychologie verschieden. Affekt sagt nicht dasselbe aus. Dennnicht nur Angst, Furcht, Zorn, Hass sind Lagen, sondern ebenso Komplexe wie Hoflichkeit, Grobheit, Leichtsinn, Hoheit und Schlauheit oder Zustande wie Beschranktheit und Trunksucht. Auch Bezeichnungen wie Gefuhl oder Zustand entsprechen nicht vollig, Denn mit Lage ist nicht nur ein innerer Vorgang, sondern auch eine Beziehung nach aussen gemeint—zur Lage einer anderen Person." (Translated: "It differs from all concepts in psychology. The term affection does not express it, because not only anxiety, fear, anger, hate can be contained in relationships, but also complexes as politeness, rudeness, levity, haughtiness and shrewdness, or conditions like mental inferiority and drunkenness. Terms like feeling or condition do not cover the content of the relationship either, because with relationship not only an internal process is indicated but also a social, external relationship towards another person.")

A complete sociometric procedure may go down to the bottom of relations and may begin with mobilizing the choices and decisions, the attractions and repulsions, but it should never stop with this. It goes through several steps, up the ladder, exploring the motivations for these choices which may show up to be emotional, intellectual or "axionormative." It goes further and puts the individuals linked in social atoms through spontaneity tests which may show of what emotions an attraction or rejection consists. It goes further into role testing, psychodramatic and sociodramatic productions in the course of which the whole gamut of interhuman dynamics comes to the fore. Of particular importance should be to anthropologists the concept of the "cultural atom" which is an essential part of my role theory. The role theory I have introduced into literature independent from G. H. Mead and, whereas the philosopher Mead never descended from the lofty levels of speculation and observation, I provided role theory with experimental methods and empirical foundations.

The Difference Between Sociometry And Axiology

I am in full agreement with Gurvitch and Zazzo as to the need of integrating the "we" feeling, the concepts of community and communion into the sociometric framework. The rapidly growing use of psychodrama and axiodrama in departments of theology and the wide interest they arouse in religiously oriented cooperatives speaks for itself. I am fully aware, however, that there is a long way from the practical use of a method to its scientific integration.

Sociometry and the Doctrine of Spontaneity

I am in full agreement with Sorokin that the concept of spontaneity (s)-creativity (c) is in need of further elucidation. I never contended that spontaneity and creativity are identical or similar processes. They are indeed different categories, although peculiarly linked. In the case of Man his s may be diametrically opposite to his c; an individual may have a high degree of spontaneity but be entirely uncreative, a spontaneous idiot. Another individual may have a high degree of creativity within a limited area of experience but may be capable of spontaneity only in reference to this area; he may be incapable or little able of spontaneity in other areas. God is an exceptional case because in God all spontaneity has become creativity. He is one case in which spontaneity and creativity are identical. At least, in the world of our experience we may never encounter pure spontaneity or pure cultural conserves, they are functions of one another. A cultural conserve, for instance, a musical or a drama conserve needs some degree of spontaneity and warming up in order to produce an adequate response and performance within a social setting. On the other hand an extemporaneous producer cannot help but relate himself to cultural cliches, even if it means that he tries to deconserve them. Spontaneity and the warming up process have no premiums for extraverts, they are equally pertinent to intraverts. They operate on all levels of human relations, eating, walking, sleeping, sexual intercourse, social communication, creativity and in religious self realization and asceticism.*

Summary

The great problem which the western civilization in the twentieth century faces is that after having driven people out from the protective walls of strong and cohesive religious systems, it is anxious to replace them by strong and cohesive secular systems—with the aid of science. The difficulty is that science, especially social science progresses slowly. Then, scientific hypotheses vary and often contradict one another. The automatic safety of the autocratic systems is not easily replaceable, but what is worse, there is no hope, no guiding star given to mankind by science. What people see is, parallel with the ever-new emergence and accumulation of technological gadgets, the ever-new announcements and accumulations of social research techniques *without any over-all vision as to how these millions of little items may ever fit into a single mosaic.* This is a great but tragic sight, a wide spread of spontaneity and creativity emanating from thousands of fine minds, each trying to help by making their contributions, but because of continuous contradictions they increase the confusion of values. Doubt rises in the hearts of men that they may have escaped from a prison but landed in a jungle of scientific trappings. Faith in science begins to wane in many places because it does not keep the promises it has made. But science is neutral, it is knowledge, it cannot save by itself. The title of George A. Lundberg's recent book "Can Science Save Us?" may have to be reversed into "Can Science Be Saved?" It will be crippled or perish if it cannot create the foundations of a new social order. It can be saved if the responsible domain of social science is further extended to include the im-

---

*I wish I could answer the brilliant and challenging comments of Sorokin more completely in this paper especially as to the relationship of spontaneity to energy, but I refer the reader to my paper "The Doctrine of Spontaneity-Creativity" which will appear in a symposium edited by Pitirim A. Sorokin and to be published in the course of 1950 by the Harvard University Press.

mediate and practical structuring and guidance of present day human society on all its levels from the physical up to the axiological plane. This job may have to begin with "burying the dead", cleaning up our research shelves and laboratories, and concentrating all our efforts upon a few strategically selected points. The weakest spot in the armor of present day society and culture is its ignorance of its own social structure, especially of the small local structures in which people actually spend their lives. The time has come, after twenty-five years of research in "catacombs", as prisons, hospitals, reformatories, schools, that sociometry moves from the closed into the "open" community. It is essential therefore, that we move "fearlessly", armed with powerful and dynamic social inventions into the midst of every town, every region, county and state and dare to shake them out of their dreams of individual psyche existence. Only by means of such practical, direct and immediate demonstrations of the usefulness of the social sciences can the faith in science be regained and cemented. Only by such means can science be saved and put to full use. With the cooperation of "all" the people we should be able to create a social order worthy of the highest aspirations of all times. This, and this alone is the meaning of revolutionary, dynamic sociometry.

REFERENCES, PART I, II AND III

1. Bacon, Francis. *Novum Organum,* 1620.
2. Bain, Read. Man is the measure. SOCIOMETRY, 1942, 5: 421-425.
3. Chapin, F. Stuart. *Experimental Designs in Sociological Research.* Harper & Brothers, 1947.
4. Criswell, Joan H. A sociometric study of race cleavage in the classroom. *Archives of Psychology,* 1939, 33, No. 235.
5. Elliott, Hugh. *Letters of John Stuart Mill,* 1910.
6. Greenwood, Ernest. *Experimental Sociology.* King's Crown Press, 1945.
7. Lewin, K. and Lippitt, R. An experimental approach to the study of autocracy and democracy. SOCIOMETRY, 1938, Vol. 1: 292-300.
8. Littre, A. *Comte et Stuart Mill.* Paris, 1877.
9. Mill, John Stuart. *System of Logic,* 1843.
10. Moreno, J. L. *Das Stregeiftheater.* Berlin, 1923. (Translated into English and published as *The Theatre of Spontaneity.* Beacon House, 1947).
11. Moreno, J. L. *Conference on group method.* National Committee on Prisons and Prison Labor, Meeting of the American Psychiatric Association, Philadelphia, 1932.
12. Moreno, J. L. Psychological organization of groups in the community. *Yearbook of Mental Deficiency,* Boston, 1933.
13. Moreno, J. L. *Who Shall Survive?* Beacon House, 1934.
14. Moreno, J. L. Spontaneity training. *Sociometric Review,* 1936. (Also published as Psychodrama Monograph No. 4.)
15. Moreno, J. L. Psychodramatic shock therapy. SOCIOMETRY, January, 1939, Vol. 2, No. 1: 1-30. (Also published in Psychodrama Monograph No. 5.)
16. Moreno, J. L. Psychodramatic treatment of marriage problems. SOCIOMETRY, January, 1940, Vol. 3, No. 1: 1-23. (Also published in Psychodrama Monograph No. 7, 1945.)
17. Moreno, J. L. General spontaneity theory. *Psychodrama,* 1946, Vol. 1: 85-89.
18. Moreno, J. L. Contributions of Sociometry to Research Methodology in Sociology. *American Sociological Review,* Vol. 12, No. 3, June, 1947.
19. Moreno, J. L. and Jennings, Helen. Advances in sociometric techniques. *Sociometric Review,* February, 1936. (Published also in Sociometry Monograph No. 7, 1947.)
20. Moreno, J. L. and Jennings, H. H. Statistics of social configurations. SOCIOMETRY, Vol. 1, No. 3-4: 343-374, 1938.
21. Moreno, J. L. and Moreno, F. B. Role test and role diagram of children. SOCIOMETRY, August-November, 1945, Vol. 8, No. 3-4: 426-441.
22. Moreno, J. L. Erklärung an Spartakus, *Der Neue Daimon,* January, 1919, Vienna.

SPECIAL REFERENCES

Marx, Karl. Capital, 1867.
A Handbook of Marxism, International Publishers, New York, 1935.